Britain & *the* Olympics

1896–2010

A celebration of British gold

Bob Phillips

Britain and the Olympics, 1896–2010: a celebration of British gold

Copyright © Bob Phillips, 2012

First edition

Published in 2012 by
Carnegie Publishing Ltd
Chatsworth Road,
Lancaster LA1 4SL
www.carnegiepublishing.com

British Library Cataloguing-in-Publication data
A catalogue record for this book is available from the British Library

ISBN 978-1-85936-213-6

Designed, typeset and originated by Carnegie Publishing
Printed and bound in the UK by Information Press, Oxford

Contents

Acknowledgments

O VER THE YEARS there has been a massive amount of hub-bub about the Olympic Games. My bookshelves are filled in serried ranks with the volumes that have been written; the internet links are beyond count. Much of what has appeared in print or electronic form is useful but superficial, often repeating unquestioningly dubious tales that owe more to myth than reality. Much else is obscurely academic. In what I hope to be a fresh approach, my intention in this book is to be informative and perhaps entertaining in describing the lives of Britain's champions and how they came to win their gold medals.

The most significant of the numerous sources to which I have referred are to be found in the Bibliography, but special mention must be made of two of the most valuable, both of which are the work of fellow Britons who are highly regarded in this area of research: the late Ian Buchanan, who was the first sports historian to collect together data on Britain's competitors throughout Olympic history, contained in a book published in 1991; and Stan Greenberg, author of a compact almanac of Games-by-Games results and accounts which has appeared every four years since 1983. Also invaluable is the tireless research done by Bill Mallon, of the USA, and Hilary Evans, of Great Britain, who have unravelled so many of the mysteries regarding Olympic results over the years. My thanks, too, to David Thurlow, a long-time friend and fellow sports enthusiast, for reading the draft text and making some invaluable suggestions. Finally, credit is due to Alistair Hodge, the managing director of Carnegie Publishing, who had the idea for this book in the first place.

Bob Phillips
Pontenx les Forges
France

Baron Pierre Frédy de Coubertin was the French educationist who almost single-handedly brought the Modern Olympic Games movement into being. Committed to the principle of amateurism, he was greatly inspired by the ideals of sportsmanship prevalent in public schools in Victorian Britain and by the example of the 'Olympian Games' in Shropshire devised by Dr William Penny Brookes.
TOPFOTO

Preface

*'L'important dans ces Olympiades c'est moins d'y gagner que d'y prendre part.
L'important dans la vie ce n'est point le triomphe mais le combat. L'essentiel ce
n'est pas d'avoir vaincu mais de s'être bien battu.'*

*'The importance of these Olympic Games is not so much to win as to take part.
The importance in life is not the triumph but the struggle. The essential is not
to have won but to have fought well.'*

IN SLIGHTLY VARYING FORMS these famous sentiments have become enshrined
in Olympic protocol. Taking part, competing well and persevering in adversity have
all become part of the ideal. The words first appeared officially at the Los Angeles Games
of 1932 as a message that was displayed on the stadium scoreboard. Four years later, at
the Berlin Games in August 1936, they were heard at the opening ceremony by means
of a recorded speech by the ageing Baron Pierre Frédy de Coubertin, considered by many
as the founder of the Modern Olympic movement. The Baron's original words had been
uttered when he spoke at a banquet given by the government at the time of the London
Games of 1908, in honour of the International Olympic Committee and the British
Olympic Council.

Yet the event which originally inspired this timeless statement had taken place five
days earlier, as the Baron himself acknowledged. It was a sermon preached by the Right
Reverend Ethelbert Talbot, the Bishop of Central Pennsylvania, at a service at St Paul's
Cathedral to which officials and competitors at the Games had been invited. Attending
the Conference of Anglican bishops being held concurrently in London, and conscious
of arguments that had already taken place between British and American officials at the
Games, the Bishop had said:

We have just been contemplating the great Olympic Games. What does it
mean? It means that young men of robust physical life have come from all
parts of the world. It does mean, I think, as someone has said, that this era of
internationalism as seen in the stadium has an element of danger. Of course, it is

very true that each athlete strives not only for the sake of sport but for the sake of his country. Thus a new rivalry is invented. If England is beaten on the river, or America out-distanced on the running-path – well, what of it? The only safety lies after all in the lesson of the real Olympia, that the Games themselves are better than the race and the prize. St Paul tells us how insignificant is the prize. Our prize is not corruptible but incorruptible, and though only one may wear the laurel wreath all may share the equal joy of the contest. All encouragement, therefore, be given to the exhilarating – I might also say 'soul saving' – interest that comes in active and fair and clean athletic sports.

The Bishop claimed no authority in sporting matters and his well-meant sentiments perhaps rang more true for theologians than for Olympic historians. The Ancient Olympics – 'the real Olympia', as he described them – had actually been highly professional events, which was not at all what Baron de Coubertin favoured, and nor is it obvious what the Bishop meant by 'active' and 'clean' sports, but the Baron was surely enthused by the idea of 'the equal joy of the contest'.

The opening ceremony of the 1896 Olympics. Note the narrowness of the track and its sharp bends in the stadium in Athens, built as a replica of the site of the ancient Games at Olympia.
UNKNOWN PHOTOGRAPHER, 1896

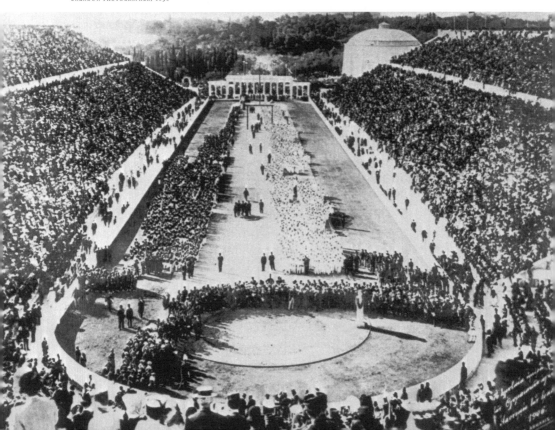

Introduction

'Let us export our oarsmen, our runners, our fencers into other lands. That is
the true free trade of the future; and the day it is introduced into Europe the
cause of peace will have received a new and strong ally. It inspires me to touch
upon the further step I now propose, and in it I shall ask that the help you have
given me hitherto you will extend again, so that together we may attempt to
realise, upon a basis suitable to the conditions of our modern life, the splendour
and beneficent task of reviving the Olympic Games.'

BARON PIERRE FRÉDY DE COUBERTIN, ADDRESSING THE CONGRESS OF THE
UNION DES SOCIÉTÉS FRANÇAISE DES SPORTS ATHLÉTIQUES, PARIS, 23
NOVEMBER 1892

THE OLYMPIC GAMES return to London this year, 2012, having previously taken
place there in 1908 and 1948. This will be the twenty-eighth occasion on which the
Summer Games have been held since they were revived in 1896. The scale has changed
somewhat in the intervening 116 years. At those tentative first Games in Athens there
were 300 or so competitors from a dozen or so countries (although no one thought to
take a precise count at the time). In London 2012 there will be some 10,500 competitors
from 200 or more countries.

If the most confident predictions are fulfilled, Great Britain will win as many as 30
gold medals in 2012, compared with the 3 achieved in 1896. That would bring the total of
recognised British Olympic champions to comfortably beyond 500. The word 'recognised'
is not lightly used because the precise number of British gold-medallists is still a matter
of some debate. For one thing, opinions differ concerning the validity of some events.
Besides, there are unanswered questions about the exact composition of some winning
teams, while some of the successful competitors representing Britain were not, in fact,
of British nationality. Such issues cannot be resolved definitively in the following pages,
but hopefully the discussion of them will be both entertaining and informative. Olympic
research, I can assure all readers, is great fun!

Two previous books, published in 1991 and 1992, have listed British Olympic
gold-medallists in detail, and they are valuable sources which are acknowledged in the

Bibliography. One of them ignored the Winter Games entirely, however, and both books suffered from the same inherent drawback. The champions were listed alphabetically, which is useful for library reference purposes but provides no sense of continuity. It makes for difficult reading when the exploits of, for example, a cycle-riding Jones of 1908 are listed alongside those of a horse-riding Jones of 1968, and a water-polo playing Jones of 1920 precedes a footballing Jones of 1900. My approach has been to contain the most noteworthy names – hundreds of them! – within a chronological text and to link them to common themes where appropriate. The complete list may be found from page 183 of this book.

Baron Pierre Frédy de Coubertin was a visionary educationist and is the man most credited for the modern revival of the Olympic Games, although this came about as something of a side-issue for him. Coubertin had formed the idea, justifiably so, that standards of physical education in French schools were poor and he believed that to an extent this was to blame for the ignominy of defeat by the Prussians in the Franco-Prussian War of 1870. He therefore set out to persuade the French authorities to give more attention to sport in schools. He was influenced strongly in his ideas by the English example, and in particular he revered the headmaster at Rugby School from 1828 to 1842, Thomas Arnold, as 'one of the founders of athletic chivalry'.

The Baron thus visited England in 1883, and again in 1886, and became convinced that 'organised sport can create moral and social strength'. In truth his views were not embraced enthusiastically in France, and this is most likely why he gradually turned his attention towards a wider Olympic concept. In 1890 the Baron was a guest at the 'Olympian Games', which had been conducted from 1850 onwards in the small market town of Much Wenlock, in Shropshire. These Games would become – unlikely as it might seem – one of the ideals by which the Modern Olympic movement was to be formed. The founder of the Much Wenlock 'Olympics' was the surgeon, magistrate and botanist, Dr William Penny Brookes, in his early eighties by the time of Coubertin's visit, who also had an abiding interest in social reform and with whom the Baron continued in correspondence.

Dr Penny Brookes, born in 1809, was a firm believer in education for the masses. He chose 'Olympism' as the theme for study at workers' reading classes which he instituted in Much Wenlock from 1851 onwards, and he promoted physical education at the local 'national' school, reasonably assuming that the pupils would become agricultural labourers or factory workers and would benefit from being bodily fit. He helped form a National Olympian Association, and one of its promotions, at the Crystal Palace grounds in London in 1866, even attracted a youthful Dr W.G. Grace in his slimmer days. Dr Grace entered and won a 440 yards hurdles race, having slipped away from his cricketing duties at the Oval, where he was supposed to be fielding for an England XI versus Surrey after scoring his maiden first-class century, 224 not out, the previous day.

Dr Penny Brookes had close contacts with prominent Greeks interested in promoting the Olympic ideal, and they had held four domestic Games of varying degrees of success from the 1850s onwards. It seems fairly likely that he would have played an initially important role in the 1896 international gathering becoming reality, but he had died the year before it took place. Whatever the circumstances, the Baron, who for all his public spiritedness was an artful political thinker, was to give the doctor no credit for his enterprise in later years.

In fact Dr Penny Brookes was not the only British entrepreneur enthused by the Olympian spirit. Two advocates of the Victorian belief in 'muscular Christianity', Charles Melly (an ancestor of the singer, author, art critic and *bon viveur*, George Melly) and John Hulley, had promoted their own 'Olympic Festivals' in their native Liverpool in the 1860s, ambitiously entitling themselves the 'Athletic Society of Great Britain'. Such pretensions to nationwide authority, together with the enterprise shown by Dr Penny Brookes, had the effect of leading to the formalising of athletics throughout Britain, with the eventual formation of the AAA in 1880 by representatives of Oxford University, who were fearful of seeing the power centre of the sport moving away from them.

In 1892 Baron de Coubertin organised a conference in Paris to mark the fifth anniversary of the founding of the Union des Sociétés Française des Sports Athlétiques, of which he was secretary, and in his speech he proposed the idea of reviving the Ancient Games, but again received little support from the audience. Undeterred, he went to the USA the next year, winning over the influential historian, Professor William Sloane, of Princeton University, who he knew from the professor's visits to Paris to research the life of Napoleon. Then, on his way back to France via London, the Baron met Charles Herbert, the honorary secretary of the Amateur Athletic Association (AAA), then the ruling body for athletics in England, who was equally enthusiastic. Because Great Britain and the USA very largely dominated athletics in the latter part of the nineteenth century, the Baron had acquired important allies. Professor Sloane and Charles Herbert were among the 14 dignitaries who formed the first Olympic committee in 1894.

Organised sport in Britain in the late nineteenth century was institutionally amateur. The enthusiasts who set up ruling bodies and who organised competition and championships in sports such as athletics, lawn tennis, rowing and both Association and Rugby Union football came only from the classes of Victorian society which had time to indulge themselves in the practice and administration of leisure activities. Almost all of these men (no women, of course) were products of the major universities, Oxford and Cambridge, and of the leading public schools such as Eton and Harrow, Cheltenham, Rugby, Shrewsbury, Westminster and Winchester. They were by no means averse to making money from their recreational pursuits. The most famous amateur sportsman of the era, Dr W.G. Grace (1848–1915), for example, having abandoned his ambitions as a hurdler as his waistline expanded, enjoyed a substantial income from playing cricket, well able to afford to abandon his medical duties each summer to the care of a locum. The subtle point was that gentlemen sportsmen such as 'W.G.' could continue to describe themselves as amateurs because they did not need to rely on sport to make their living.

This concept of the 'gentleman amateur' was entirely a creation of the Victorian era. It had absolutely nothing to do with the original Olympic Games in Ancient Greece, which can be dated back to at least 776 BC, and in which the successful contestants at wrestling and foot-racing were unashamed professionals who had gifts lavished upon them by patrons and elders when they returned victorious to their home cities – gifts worth as much as 3,000 times a labourer's daily wage. A German historian, Walter Umminger, writing in 1962, when Modern Olympic contestants were still amateur (or at least supposed to be so), succinctly remarked of those Ancient champions: 'The material advantages showered on Olympic victors when they got home would break a modern amateur's heart. They would even arouse the envy of some 'shamateurs' and state athletes of the kind we know today.'

Perhaps it was in recollection of such largesse that Baron de Coubertin by no means whole-heartedly supported the intransigent stance of the establishment regarding amateurism. He strongly opposed the discriminatory attitude of the ruling body for English rowing which specifically barred from membership anyone of working-class origin, and he was many decades ahead of his time in supporting the idea of paying compensation to those who would lose money from their employment while they were taking part in sports competition. Even so, the Baron readily put his name to the term 'amateur' figuring prominently in the eight fundamental Olympic principles, including the following: 'The aims of the Olympic Movement are to promote the development of those fine physical and moral qualities that come from contests on the friendly fields of amateur sport.' There is no record of his reaction to such later Olympic foibles as the payment of prize money at the Paris Games of 1900 of as much as 3,000 Francs (equivalent to some €7,000 in 2012 values) to the winners of the fencing, polo, swimming, tennis and yachting events.

In effect Coubertin had stage-managed the setting up of the first Athens Games, appointing himself as secretary of his Olympic committee in 1894 and installing a prominent Greek citizen of Paris as chairman. By the next year, when an 'International Athletic Congress' was held in the same city, the honorary members included the Crown Prince of Greece, the Prince of Wales and members of the parliaments of numerous European countries. Even more encouraging for Baron de Coubertin was the news that the Greek authorities – despite the country's economic difficulties – had raised 200,000 drachmas towards the cost of the revival of the Games. The Modern Olympic Games had become a reality. Though concerned, and at times obviously deeply disappointed at the way in which his Olympic ideal would fail to be properly observed to his liking over the years to come, Baron de Coubertin was to remain president of the International Olympic Committee until after the 1924 Games in Paris.

Whatever the setbacks since, the Games in their 116th year of modern existence have become the world's most celebrated sporting event. Olympic champions are lauded, cosseted and heaped with honours for the rest of their lives. The nations which they represent revel in patriotic pride, even misguided chauvinism. Great Britain has contributed significantly to those successes as one of only four countries that have competed at every Games; the others are Australia, France and Greece. Furthermore, in the strictest sense of the term, the British stand unique because no other country has also taken part in all of the odd variations to the Olympic programme – the unofficial 1906

Games, the figure-skating of 1908 and 1920 before the Winter Games were introduced, and the separately held equestrian events of 1956.

Regarding overall success, Great Britain is the fourth highest winner of gold medals after the USA, Germany and the former USSR. These titles have very frequently been decided by margins of hundredths of a second, centimetres or ounces, and so it would be reasonable to suppose that the catalogue of achievements since 1896 is precise and beyond dispute. Yet this is not so – mystery still surrounds some events and even the total of gold medals won by Great Britain is not set in a tablet of stone.

The reasons for this inconsistency are varied and occasionally somewhat bizarre. For example, one of the very first British victories, at those inaugural Games of 1896 in Athens, was actually shared with a German in the lawn-tennis doubles and should perhaps therefore be regarded as only half a gold medal. Four years later, in Paris, the winning helmsman in one of the yachting events had been born of British parents in France and both his crewmen were French. So, understandably, it was the host country that first claimed the honours of victory. The identities of the numerous crew-members of another winning British yacht at those same Games, which chaotically extended over six months, appear to be lost to history. There were also eight wins that year by British professionals in athletics, cycling, lawn tennis and swimming, which have been unjustly excluded over the years by every succeeding chronicler of the results. They are now rightly restored in my reckoning.

Furthermore, opinion remains divided as to whether the so-called 'intercalated' Tenth Anniversary Games in Athens in 1906 were official, and many record books ignore them completely. It is still a matter of debate as to whether two British yachtsmen at the 1920 Games should or should not be regarded as gold-medallists: they were the only entrants in their class and they failed to complete the course in the one race that was held. By contrast, one of the most striking examples of the side-effects of ongoing research into Olympic results is the outcome of the curling competition at the Winter Games of 1924. Only in the year 2006, after a vigorous investigative campaign by the *Glasgow Herald* newspaper, was it finally established that this was a legitimate event, not a 'demonstration', and so the success by a team of Scotsmen, probably including a father and son (though even that is a matter of dispute), was belatedly acknowledged.

The ruling body of the Games, the International Olympic Committee, is of no help in the matter of confirming gold-medal totals because it has resolutely set its face against endorsing any medals tables, and such compilations are therefore left to the media during the Games themselves, eagerly publishing day by day the national 'scores' as if in some premiership league. Even then only gold medals are measured and not gold-medallists, who are very much larger in number because of relay events, team events and team sports. Thus, Great Britain has won 234 gold medals over all Olympics, but there are 482 known British Olympic champions according to my calculations, and perhaps 25 or so more as yet unidentified. Tracing gold-medallists can be somewhat confusing.

Having said that, even then there is a degree of subjective judgment involved. For much of Olympic history it has been the custom to award gold medals only to those taking part in the finals of relay events or team contests, and it has not been until recent years that the rules have been amended to allow others in the teams who were involved in preliminary rounds to receive gold as well. It would be wrong to re-write history and award hypothetical gold medals to every athlete, swimmer, footballer or hockey-player who comes into this category at earlier Games, but where possible such names have been noted for interest in the gold-medallist list in the appendix.

You will find that I have dealt with some Games at greater length than others, and one obvious reason for this is the degree of success by British competitors. From a British perspective it would make no sense to give the same attention to the Games of 1904, where Great Britain won only one gold medal, as to the Games of 1908, where there were 56 British wins. In any case, the latter Games were held in London and therefore have greater historical significance for us in the Olympic year of 2012, as do the so-called London 'Austerity Games' of 1948. The Games of 1912 also receive rather more attention than others because they have not previously been given their full due as the first to be properly organised and the first to undermine Britain's traditionally dominant role in the development of sport.

All this uncertainty regarding the accuracy of results, and the variety of viewpoints as to the importance of each celebration, is part of the charm of the Olympics. No one would seriously suggest that the spare-time tennis player and weight-lifter who won in such a haphazardly amateurish manner for Britain in 1896 can be regarded as the sporting equals of the hyper-dedicated professional champions of the twenty-first century – Sir Steve Redgrave, Sir Chris Hoy, Bradley Wiggins, Kelly Holmes, Rebecca Adlington, Victoria Pendleton prominent among them – but, while records come and records go, gold medals never lose their tarnish.

ONE

The Games of 1896

A royal olive branch rewards an ode to the valour of the Ancient Greeks

*'But that the Tennis Court keeper knowes better than I, for it is a low ebbe of
Linen with thee, when thou kept'st not Racket there.'*

WILLIAM SHAKESPEARE, HENRY IV PART II: ACT II, SCENE II.

AFTER IT WAS ALL OVER, the Baron was extremely satisfied. The inaugural
Modern Olympics of 1896 in Athens had turned out to be a great success, supported
enthusiastically by the public, graced by royal patronage, and most fittingly climaxed by
a joyously acclaimed victory for a Greek runner in the marathon. All this excitement
did more to establish the Games as an on-going project than any amount of genuine
international-class sporting competition could have done. Actually, in the inaugural
Games of 1896 there had been very little of the latter.

The whole affair lasted ten days, taking in competition in athletics, cycling, fencing,
gymnastics, lawn tennis, shooting, swimming, weight-lifting and wrestling, but all of it
conducted in a distinctly casual fashion. In this context it was quite natural that when
an Oxford University undergraduate, George Stuart Robertson, arrived in Athens and
discovered that his preferred leisure-time activity of hammer-throwing was not on the
schedule of events he should be allowed to enter the tennis tournament instead. At Oxford
he had learned of the Olympic revival by chance, catching sight of an advertisement in
the window of a Thomas Cook's travel agency.

As it happens, Robertson's appearance on the tennis court was exceedingly brief,
as he and his impromptu partner lost their opening match. No more successful was a
further venture into the discus competition so dear to Greek hearts. To the chagrin of the
local citizenry, this was not won by their favoured strong-man, who they had considered
unbeatable, but by a visiting American novice. Six decades later Robertson, who was by

now at the age of 84 Sir George Stuart Robertson Q.C., cheerfully recalled, 'I was allowed to play tennis for Great Britain, though I would not have dared to enter for the most modest tournament at home'. Yet he was still to depart from the Games as a prize-winner, albeit for his literary talents.

Having been awarded the Oxford University prize for reciting one of the Acts from Shakespeare's *Henry IV Part II* in comic iambic Greek verse, Robertson found that his mastery of the language would be very much to his benefit at the closing ceremony of those inaugural Modern Olympic Games. He was to write:

> I had composed an ode in Aeolic Greek of the kind that Pindar used to sell
> to champions at Olympic and other Games. The King heard of it, but the
> committee would not allow it to be recited, as they had refused sundry Greeks
> who had sought permission to do so. So he arranged with me that when he gave
> the signal the ode should be delivered. He was so pleased with his victory over
> the committee that he gave me both the olive branch and the laurel branch,
> and a valuable present as well, which was some consolation for my failure in the
> discus.

This nineteenth-century Olympic celebration was a revival of a four-yearly event that had begun as early as 776 BC and had lasted at least until AD 261, and maybe even another 130 years or so after that. No two accounts agree as to exactly how many competitors there were when those pioneering Modern Olympians gathered together in 1896, with estimates ranging from 285 to 311, of whom at least 230 were Greek. There is general agreement that 13 nations were represented: in alphabetical order, Australia, Austria, Bulgaria, Denmark, France, Germany, Great Britain, Greece, Hungary, Italy, Sweden, Switzerland, and the USA. In fact, at these Games the British and American competitors were not entered as official representatives of their respective countries, but as individuals. Even then it could be argued that there should only be 12 countries recognised because Austria and Hungary, each winning gold medals in swimming under separate flags, at that time were united politically as the Austro-Hungarian monarchy.

It would be a fallacy to assume that all of these countries carried out rigorous selection processes before their sportsmen (naturally, no suggestion in those days of women's events) set off on their journey to Athens, which for some of the Britons would involve a six-day sea voyage, and for the Americans considerably longer. Among them were no more than three of the finalists, let alone the winners, at the Amateur Athletic Association (AAA) Championships in London three months later, which were then considered to be an unofficial Championships of the World open to all-comers. The dozen or so Americans competing were mostly from Princeton University, encouraged to undertake the adventure by Baron de Coubertin's American supporter, Professor William Sloane.

As far as prospective British competitors were concerned, almost all of them remained in blithe ignorance until very late in the day that the Games were even taking place. George Stuart Robertson, for one, noted that the authorities at Oxford and Cambridge universities, where so many of Britain's foremost athletes were to be found, were only informed less than a month before the opening ceremony. This seems particularly odd in that the AAA secretary, Charles Herbert, was one of de Coubertin's closest confidants, and could have been expected to spread the Olympic gospel throughout his English domain. However, Herbert was apparently a taciturn individual, which was perhaps not surprising since at the age of 11 he had lost his entire family in an Indian Mutiny massacre. Perhaps he just never got round to voicing his approval loudly enough.

The dedicated readers of *The Times* among the college masters at Oxford and Cambridge might well have noticed previously a report in the issue for Saturday 26 January 1895 that the first meeting of the Games' organising committee had been held in Athens. Then some detail of the timetable and the events was supplied in a letter to the newspaper by the director of the British School in Athens, Cecil Smith, but this did not appear until 29 February 1896, only 36 days before the Games were due to open. Not that this late juncture deterred the travel agent company, Thomas Cook, which in mid-March was still optimistically publicising on the classified advertisements page the 25-day 'Special Conducted Tour' to the Games, at a cost of 30 guineas, including first-class travel and accommodation. By then, of course, Thomas Cook may have been desperately trying to drum up last-minute customers.

The motley British contingent actually fared rather well, and strictly speaking a total of nine medals from ten competitors compares highly favourably with every other Games – Summer and Winter – that has followed, but it has to be said that the opposition was distinctly mediocre in comparison with what the likes of Redgrave, Hoy or Holmes would take on in a rather more competitive era. One of the two British gold-medallists, Launceston Elliot, faced only a single opponent in his weight-lifting event, while the other winner, Jack Boland, having become the tennis singles champion, discovered that the man he had beaten in the first of his four matches, Fritz Traun, of Germany, was now without a partner, and so the two of them joined forces to win the doubles. Traun, who had gone to Athens primarily as a middle-distance runner, was one of the shortest-lived of Olympic champions, committing suicide by shooting himself at the age of 32.

Personifying a cosmopolitan element which would continue to feature in British Olympic successes, Elliot had been born in India, then under British rule, and Boland in the south of Ireland, still then part of the UK. The sporting credentials of the two men contrasted sharply, though both came from privileged backgrounds. Launceston Elliot was one of the country's very best weight-lifters, whereas there is no evidence that Boland was anything more than a sociable tennis player, and there were others far more accomplished than he on the courts who presumably had not got to know anything of the Athens Games. Such men included Harold Mahony, who was the Wimbledon singles champion that same year of 1896, beating Wilfred Baddeley, the winner on three previous occasions. The other outstanding players of the generation, the Doherty brothers, would profit from their Olympic chance four years later.

Launceston Elliot was so christened because it was in the Tasmanian town of Launceston that he was conceived. His father was a magistrate in the Indian civil service; his grandfather had been governor of the island of St Helena; and his great-grandfather was governor of Madras. There were aristocratic connections, as the family was related to the Earl Minto of Hawick, in Scotland, and when they returned to England in 1887 young Elliot, described as 'an exceptionally well-built youth', was able to indulge himself by taking up weight-lifting. Advised by the world-famed strong-man, Eugen Sandow, who is remembered as 'the father of modern body-building', Elliot soon showed an exceptional talent, competing in the British championships for the first time in 1891 at the age of only 16 and going on to win the title within three years.

In Athens Elliot's only opposition was provided by a Danish architecture student, Viggo Jensen, who won their first contest, the two-handed lift, in somewhat contentious circumstances. The two men tied at 111.5 kilogrammes, and Prince George of Greece, as chairman of the judging panel, declared Jensen the winner on the basis of a better style, although it is not apparent quite what qualifications his royal highness had for making such a judgment. The one-handed lift immediately followed, and Elliot's success had a hollow ring to it because Jensen was by then nursing a shoulder injury. By coincidence the two of them had almost identical life-spans – 8 June 1874 to 8 August 1930 for Elliot, 22 June 1874 to 2 November 1930 for Jensen.

The muscle man. Britain's one and only Olympic weight-lifting champion was Launceston Elliot, whose success was achieved at the inaugural Athens Games of 1896. His family was of Scottish aristocratic stock, and he had first competed in the British championships at the age of 16. An enthusiastic sporting all-rounder, he also took part in the 100 metres sprint, rope-climbing and wrestling in Athens and then threw the discus at the 1900 Games.

TAKEN FROM A CONTEMPORARY PRINT

John Pius Boland, familiarly known as 'Jack', was Britain's first Olympic champion, winning the tennis singles and then sharing in the doubles with a German, Fritz Traun, at the Athens Games of 1896. Boland apparently played in everyday leather-soled shoes and used a racquet that he had bought in a local bazaar on the eve of the tournament. Born in Dublin, he was a prominent Irish nationalist politician and received a papal knighthood for his work in education.
COPYRIGHT: INTERNATIONAL OLYMPIC COMMITTEE

Elliot, in the characteristic manner of a gentleman sportsman of the day, was an enthusiastic all-rounder who also competed in athletics, gymnastics and wrestling at the Athens Games with no notable success – by contrast, Jensen was second in a pistol-shooting event – but was to find a niche in British sporting history by throwing the discus at the 1900 Olympics and setting what has been recognised in retrospect as a British record of 31.00 metres. It was said of Elliot in Athens that, 'his handsome figure procured for him an offer of marriage from a highly placed lady admirer', which may be true but is still a

11

good press yarn if it isn't, and in any case he returned home to marry more prosaically the daughter of a Kentish vicar the next year. Subsequently Elliot had some difference of opinion with his family which required him to earn a living and he took up a career as a music-hall entertainer, specialising in balancing a pole on his shoulders from which two cyclists were suspended. He then whirled ever faster on the spot until the intrepid riders were whizzing round him horizontally.

By all accounts the Dublin-born Jack Boland was just as interesting and captivating a man as Elliot. Boland stood well over 6 feet (1.83 metres) tall and was described as follows by one of his five daughters, Bridget Boland, who was a noted playwright and so might have lapsed into some literary licence: 'With an athlete's figure all his days, with eyes of a very light but startling blue, he exuded a kind of intelligent innocence which is a rare combination.' A rather more accomplished cricketer than tennis-player, Boland was educated at private Catholic schools in Ireland and England and then read law at Christ Church College, Oxford, before continuing his studies at Bonn University in Germany.

His father was the founder of the Boland's biscuit-manufacturing company, which allowed Jack the opportunity to pursue at will his various academic and sporting interests, including Greek mythology, and he became friends with a member of the Olympic organising committee who invited him to the Games as a spectator. The story goes that Boland was then persuaded to enter the tennis competition, although it seems logical to suppose that such a thought might already have crossed his mind before he had set off for Athens. A committed supporter of home rule for Ireland, but regarded as moderate in his views, he took up a political career and was the Irish Nationalist Member of Parliament for South Kerry from 1900 to 1918 and general secretary of the Catholic Truth Society for 21 years. He died at the age of 87 on St Patrick's Day, 17 March 1958.

Mention should also be made at this juncture of Teddy Flack, the tennis partner of the triumphant recitalist of odes, George Stuart Robertson. Flack's sporting preference was for athletics and he otherwise occupied himself gainfully at the Games, winning both the 800 metres and the 1500 metres in slow times on the strangely shaped track at the Panathenaic Stadium, constructed with hairpin turns as a replica of the venue for the Ancient Games at Olympia. Flack represented Australia, but he had been born in London, had emigrated with his family at the age of five, and had then returned to further his accountancy career in the offices of Price Waterhouse. As Australia was not to receive any meaningful measure of independence until 1901, Flack could equally readily be claimed as British, but despite having won the Australian one-mile championship of 1893 he was not a runner of great note, even among his fellow-members of London Athletic Club, and he had travelled to Athens primarily to brush up on his enthusiastic knowledge of Greek history.

The laconic style in which these first Games were conducted is also neatly recorded in the diary of an eye-witness, Burton Holmes, who was an eminent American travel-writer of the time. Paying tribute to the superiority of his fellow-countrymen in the various sports, he wrote of Flack's 1500 metres: 'Even this is credited to us, for although won by a splendid fellow from Australia it is put down as an American victory. The Greeks are not strong on antipodal geography, and when we explain that Flack, the winner, is an Australian, not an American, they answer, "Oh, well, that is about the same thing – we congratulate you!" '

Some among the makeshift British team happened to take part for no better reason than that the Games were held on their doorstep, so to speak. Sidney Merlin, for instance, lived in Greece all his life, and although he made no great impression in the rifle-shooting events he would become a gold-medallist at a subsequent Games, as shall be related in due course. Two of the cyclists, Frederick (or Frank) Keeping and Edward Battell (or Battel), were servants at the British Embassy in Athens, whose participation presumably had the full sanction of the ambassador but apparently caused ructions among certain British residents in the city who were aghast at the idea of someone from 'below stairs' representing the flag. Ignoring the social slight, Keeping won a silver medal in a harrowing 12-hour time-trial, covering just 400 yards less than the Austrian winner after more than 195 miles (314 kilometres) on the dust-laden roads. Keeping bequeathed a sporting legacy – as so many other British Olympians were to do – to his son, Michael, who would become a professional footballer with Southampton and Fulham and then coach to Real Madrid from 1948 to 1950.

Baron de Coubertin had proudly taken a place of honour near to King George in the royal box at the stadium every day throughout the Games, and when Prince George – his stint of weight-lifting supervision completed – leapt on to the track to accompany admiringly the Greek winner of the marathon, Spyridon Loues, over the last few metres of the race, the Baron must have been overjoyed to witness such exuberance from so exalted a spectator. The next Games were to be held in the Baron's native Paris, which seemed further cause for celebration, but unfortunately politics and commercialism would soon become an unwelcome Olympic fixture.

TWO

The Games of
1900, 1904 and 1906

Only a brief life remains for one
of Britain's track champions
to enjoy his triumphs

I T T O O K only four years for Baron de Coubertin's Games to get out of hand. In Paris in 1900 there were no fewer than 58,781 competitors in 477 events, many of which – either by default or by design – were open only to the French. Since 1900 many experts have expended much hot air trying to unravel the chaotic results, while at the Games themselves a very great deal of hot air was literally expended by the Count Henry de la Vaulx, who achieved the longest continuous gold-medal performance in Olympic history when he succeeded in flying his hot-air balloon 1,925 kilometres, to land on Russian soil near Kiev after 35 hours and 45 minutes in the air. Sadly for the Count, who had been inspired by Jules Verne, the author who originated the science-fiction genre, this is one of many contests that year carrying the Olympic banner which have subsequently been designated unofficial.

The general confusion at the 1900 Games came about because de Coubertin and his Olympic colleagues unwisely ceded responsibility for the Games to the organisers of the extravagantly titled 'Exposition Universelle Internationale' in Paris (surely if it was 'universelle' there was no need for the 'internationale'?), and the Baron's name appears in the official reports only as one of some 80 members of the unwieldy Games committee. The whole affair was turned into a prolonged charade, containing sports such as motor-racing, croquet, angling, pelota and live pigeon shooting, held at arbitrary dates between May and October, and there were in addition some even less appropriate Olympic pursuits such as canon-firing, life-saving and military drilling.

After all this, a century elapsed before detailed research finally produced a credible list of proper Olympic events, and in the course of this a French professor of physical education and celebrated film-maker, André Drevon, uncovered the achievements of five previously unrecognised British winners, who were all professionals – Edgar Bredin in athletics; Arthur Chase in cycling; Tom Burke and George Kerr in lawn tennis; and Stanley Greasley in swimming. A prime example of the confusion that has reigned regarding the credentials of so-called Olympic competitions during 1900 concerns the yachting, which was held on the river Seine and off-shore at Le Havre. It now seems reasonable to accept the victory of Irish-born Cecil Quentin for Great Britain in the Over 20 Tons Class, but he must have had at least twenty crew-members aiding him as his vessel weighed 96 tons, and the names of these valiant mariners have never been brought to light. Quentin was a member of a Portsmouth sailing club, but none of the local newspapers – even including the *Hampshire Telegraph and Naval Chronicle*, which might be presumed to have a particular interest – made as much as a mention of the achievement. Perhaps we should imagine these twenty or so unrecognised British 'gold-medallists' as being condemned to sail, adrift, for ever as if forgotten survivors of an Olympic *Marie Celeste*.

It should be pointed out that one of the most respected of all Olympic scholars, Bill Mallon, does not wholeheartedly support Professor Drevon's findings. Mallon is a polymath – a highly esteemed orthopaedic surgeon and a former professional golfer who played in the US Open – in whose company the sporting-minded intellectuals of Ancient Greece would have delighted, and he takes a refreshingly candid view of the whole tangled Parisien saga. 'Who knows really?' he was to respond when asked 111 years after the Games had taken place about the status of the professional events. 'I don't really think there can be a definitive answer to this with the rules in use in 1900 and those Games being so unusual.' So there you have it: Bill Mallon has done an immense amount of research into verifying Olympic results, including authorship of 24 books on the subject, and if he remains unsure on this matter then the five Britons should at least have the benefit of the doubt.

Edgar Chichester Bredin, slightly built but exceptionally strong, was one of the most colourful characters of his generation, and this was a generation in the twilight days of the British Empire that produced many men of dash and daring. He had been born in Gibraltar in 1866 and after some success in athletics at Wellington College he went off to Ceylon (now Sri Lanka) in 1887 to set up in business as a tea-planter, where he did no running at all. Within a few weeks of returning to England five years later, he demonstrated astonishing natural ability by placing third in the AAA Championships 440 yards and then running 49⅖ seconds for the slightly shorter 400 metres distance (437.4 yards), in Paris, as it happens, at a time when the world's best performance for the 440 was not very much faster, at 48½ seconds.

Over the next three years Bredin established himself as one of the very best in the world at 440 and 880 yards, winning five AAA titles and equalling the best time on record for the shorter distance. Photographs of him in action show him to be heavily moustachioed and benevolent of expression; rather as if he might be playing the part of Dr Watson in a Sherlock Holmes investigation. By no means a monastically dedicated athlete, he enjoyed a cigarette between the heats and the finals of his events, and he then caused a sensation by turning professional in 1897. For someone of his middle-class background, this was simply unheard of. The 'pedestrians', or paid runners, were notorious

For more than a century Edgar Bredin, winner of three professional athletics events at the 1900 Games, remained an unrecognised gold-medallist. Yet his ability on the track was such that he was awarded the supreme accolade of sport in that era – having his photograph reproduced as one of a set of cigarette-cards so prized by collectors.

AUTHOR COLLECTION

254. E. C. Bredin.

for hob-nobbing with the lower classes of society during their spells of training, usually conducted with some public house as their headquarters, and for 'fixing' races and arranging betting coups which on occasions led to furious spectators rioting and even burning down the grandstand around them.

At the Paris Games Bredin, by now 34 years of age, won the 400, 800 and 1500 metres for professionals, more or less as he pleased, against poor French opposition and did so on the single rain-swept afternoon of Sunday 1 July. He then departed home the same evening to fulfil another engagement the next day in Cardiff. His time of 53⅕ seconds for 400 metres bore no comparison with that of the amateur winner a fortnight later, who was Maxey Long, of the USA, in 49⅘ seconds, although Bredin would surely have run much faster had he needed to. Even so, Long was clearly the better runner of the two as he was to achieve 47⅘ seconds for 440 yards in New York the following September, which would become the first officially recognised world record when these were tabulated from 1912 onwards. The adventurous Bredin joined the mounted police in Canada after retiring from competition and died in that country in 1939.

His amateur compatriots who won athletics gold medals on the grass-and-soil 500-metre circumference track in the Bois de Boulogne have received much more attention over the years, and they deserve the accolade because they were all runners of real class, between them commandeering 12 AAA track titles at distances ranging from 880 yards to ten miles. Over two days in Paris, 15 and 16 July, Alfred Tysoe won the 800 metres, Charles Bennett the 1500 metres, and John Rimmer one of the two steeplechase events, with Bennett second. Then this trio joined with Sidney Robinson, who had placed second and third in the steeplechases, to collect another gold, in the 5000 metres team event. Not only that but in the process Bennett set world records of 4 minutes 6⅕ seconds for 1500 metres and 15 minutes 20 seconds for 5000 metres. Yet before discussing further the merits of these four fine runners, another and much more bizarre story can be told about that 5000 metres team race.

Before the event it must have been glaringly obvious to the officials that the Britons would beat the French with some ease, but it was still deemed obligatory for each country to field five starters, even if no more than four were required to score. Regrettably, although the AAA had contributed £100 to cover expenses, only one other British athlete had bothered to make the short journey to Paris for the track and field events: Patrick Leahy, one of three Irish brothers who were outstanding in the jumping events. Leahy, however, was involved in the triple jump (in those days known as the hop step and jump) that afternoon. So, without any quibbling from the judges, an Australian sprinter, Stanley Rowley, who had a spare day in between winning bronze medals at 60 metres, 100 metres and 200 metres, was recruited. Thus does Rowley remain, to this day, a gold-medallist for a country not of his own choice, in an event whose course he did not even complete, having begun walking after the first lap and then being allowed to withdraw with still 1500 metres to go! This initiative had all been within the rules because Rowley was, strictly speaking, a British citizen, as had been his fellow Australian gold-medallist, Teddy Flack, four years before; in any case, teams of mixed nationality had again been allowed in Paris as they had been in Athens four years earlier.

Alfred Tysoe was a Lancashire agricultural labourer. Having won the Northern Counties' titles at 1000 yards and one mile in 1896, he would undoubtedly have been

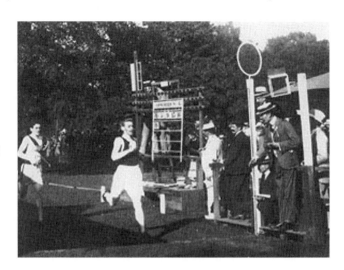

Alfred Tysoe wins the 800 metres at the 1900 Olympics, with John Cregan of the USA second. Tysoe was a highly versatile athlete who was AAA champion at 880 yards, one mile and 10 miles, but he lived a tragically short life. The year after his Olympic success he contracted pleurisy and died at the age of 27.
CONTEMPORARY PHOTOGRAPH OF UNKNOWN PROVENANCE

a very strong contender for the 800 and 1500 metres in Athens that year had the opportunity arisen. He had been recruited to the Salford Harriers club, then one of the foremost in England, and had become AAA champion at the mile and ten miles in 1897 and then at 880 yards in 1899 and again in 1900 nine days before his Olympic success. The Paris 800 metre race was more or less a re-run of the AAA contest because he again beat John Cregan of the USA. Sadly Tysoe did not live long to enjoy his triumphs. He contracted pleurisy and died at his home in Blackpool in October 1901, aged only 27. Part of the inscription on his tombstone, paid for by admirers, reads poignantly, 'Brief life is here our portion, brief sorrow, short-lived care'.

The 1500 metre gold-medallist at Paris in 1900, Charles Bennett, came from Dorset, his occupation that of a railway-engine driver on the Bournemouth–Waterloo line. Then aged 29, he had already won the AAA mile title shortly before going off to Paris, and his range of talents perhaps even exceeded Tysoe's, extending from setting a British record for three-quarters of a mile to winning the national ten miles cross-country championship in both 1899 and 1900. Even so, he never contemplated capitalising on his running skills by turning professional and after one more challenge race against the unfortunate Tysoe (which the latter won), Bennett retired from competition to manage a small hotel in his native county. He was blessed with a much longer life than Tysoe, dying at the age of 77 shortly after the 1948 Olympics in London, where, incidentally, the 1500 metres was to be won in a time 16.2 seconds faster than he had run in 1900. He might well have mused that this represented no great advance in almost half a century, particularly considering improved tracks, much more widespread competition, immensely improved training methods, and sophisticated medical and scientific support.

The other British track winners in 1900 were of only marginally less renown. John Rimmer, for instance, was a Liverpool police officer who oddly has more Olympic gold medals than AAA titles, as his only success at the latter championships had occurred a few days earlier, on the same afternoon as Tysoe's mile, in winning the four miles from Bennett. In Paris, Rimmer took the 4000 metres steeplechase gold, as well as gold in the 5000 metres team race. A team-mate in the latter success was Sydney Robinson, the one son among five children of the village postmaster at Denton, in Northamptonshire, who became a carpenter by trade. To this day only a single other British Olympic champion has come from Northamptonshire – Bill Coales, who had raced against Robinson and was a winner in the same distance-running team event eight years later (although, to be accurate, at three miles, which is 172 metres shorter than 5000 metres). Robinson had enjoyed an earlier personal success in Paris, winning a cross-country race for England against France in 1898 when the visitors had their nine men home before the first Frenchman was able to cross the line.

Other team events and full-blooded team sports contributed handsomely to Britain's gold-medal tally for 1900, and more than 80 individuals, of whom some are still unidentified, could have claimed to have been a part of the action. One of the oddities typical of these early Games was that the British tally included two Frenchmen! This anomaly occurred in yachting, which again has caused much controversy over the years because of the conflicting information concerning the composition of the crews of the 230 yachts which took part (62 of them from outside France), and not least because there was almost 60,000 francs worth of prizes in cash and *objets d'art* on offer to the winners. It was eventually established, for example, that a Briton named Linton Hope, long recognised as a gold-medallist, was in fact the designer of one of the winning craft and had not actually taken part in the Games at all.

Certainly not in dispute was the presence at Meulan, on the river Seine, of William Exshaw, who was the successful helmsman in two races for yachts of 2–3 tons, but the situation is still a complicated one because he was regarded by the hosts as being as much French as English, having been born in the port of Arcachon, in the south-west of France, and then continuing to live in the country as the wealthy manager of his family's brandy-producing business. Exshaw maintained his British links through ownership of an estate in Scotland, and he died at the age of 61 under full sail, so to speak, as his yacht was cruising in the Mediterranean at the time. His crewmen on the Seine had been Frédéric Blanchy, who came from a distinguished Bordeaux family of wine negotiators, and Jacques le Lavasseur, from Marseilles. Lorne Currie, another of the British yachting champions at Meulan, was also French-born, and on board with him was John Gretton, the future Lord Gretton of Stapleford, who was the Member of Parliament for Derbyshire South and is still the only sitting representative of the House of Commons to become an Olympic champion. There was an aristocratic touch, and an international flavour, too, in the British polo victory, which the Honourable John Beresford shared alongside two Americans.

Cricket's sole appearance at the Olympics came in 1900; it was, in all probability, an almost entirely Anglicised affair. The self-appointed British representative was a nomadic touring side, the Devon and Somerset Wanderers, which happened to be in the Paris area for a series of three matches, and the British Olympic historian, the late Ian Buchanan, was probably being kind in describing them 'as distinctly average club cricketers'. Only two of them ever played first-class cricket: Alfred Bowerman twice and Montagu Toller six times for Somerset, and the latter, who was a solicitor by profession, modestly had a highest score of 17 and bowled once, taking one wicket at a cost of 15 runs. Five of the players came from the club in the Somerset village of Castle Cary, near Wincanton, and their Olympic achievement is to be celebrated during the 2012 Games in conjunction with the club's 175th anniversary. Of the Olympic opposition assembled by the host country, only one has a surname that could be French, and the rest were most certainly British expatriates, captained by Philip Tomalin, who had been born in Kensington. The match was played over two days at Vincennes, and Gallic perplexity at this quaint pursuit continues to be reflected by the observation 100 years later by the diligent French chronicler of those Games, Professor Drevon, that Great Britain won by *'261 points à 104'*. For the benefit of those more accustomed to the conventional Wisden fashion of recording scores, the Wanderers made 116 and 145–5, and France replied valiantly but ineffectually with 78 and 26. Montagu Toller had seven of the 'French' batsmen clean bowled in the second innings, but the last of these wickets fell with only five minutes remaining of the match, and had the number eleven 'Frenchman', whose name was J. Braid, managed to survive until the close of play the match would have been drawn and he and his team-mates would also presumably now be considered as gold-medallists.

As befits the inconsistencies of these 1900 Paris Games, the winning medals for cricket were not actually gold at all, but silver and only re-classified in theory as being gold 12 years later, albeit the medals were not replaced, and it may well be that it was not until then that the members of the Wanderers became aware that they had won an Olympic title. Certainly, the marathon champion, who was a local cabinet-maker with the advantage of intimate knowledge of the streets of Paris, remained in ignorance that his race had been an Olympic one until so informed in 1912. The runner in question, Michel Théato, was to figure in another example of the slow unravelling of the history of these 1900 Games because a French athletics statistician, Alain Bouillé, discovered in the late 1990s that Théato had actually been born in Luxemburg, and the medal was re-allocated accordingly – though not to the satisfaction of the International Olympic Committee, who maintain, with some justification, that Théato was competing for France and therefore remains French. No wonder that medals tables compiled by commentators or historians fail to agree!

Water-polo was a sport in which Great Britain was to remain the World leaders for many years to come, winning Olympic gold not only in 1900 but again when it figured on the programme in 1908, 1912 and 1920. This was hardly surprising as the game had been devised in various forms – including one in which the players rode serenely round the pool on wooden horses – in Britain in the late 1870s, and the first national rules had been formulated in 1885. The powerbase of such relentless success had become the expanding industrial conurbation of Manchester, to such an extent that in 1900 the entire British Olympic water-polo sextet was made up of members of the Manchester Osborne Swimming Club, who had won the Amateur Swimming Association championship for the previous five years and provided the nucleus of the England team which the previous year had beaten Scotland 5–1, Ireland 12–0 and Wales 8–1.

Much the same relentless progress was made by the Osborne club in Paris, overwhelming French teams 12–0 and 10–1 in the qualifying rounds and then Belgium (all from the Brussels club) 7–2 in the final. One of the beaten semi-finalists was Yorkshireman Thomas Burgess, who was managing a motor-tyre business in Paris on behalf of the Earl of Shrewsbury and 11 years later was to become only the second man after Captain Matthew Webb to swim the English Channel. Perhaps the most notable of the Osborne players was 21-year-old George Wilkinson, who had not joined the club until shortly before the Games, having been playing in Division III of the Manchester League the year previously. Wilkinson, who was a prolific goal-scorer from his position of left-forward and was renowned for his speciality back-handed flip of the ball, was to enjoy an immensely long career, moving to another club, Hyde Seal, in 1902 and captaining them for 22 years. He was in the Great Britain team again when gold medals were won in 1908 and 1912 and was even a reserve in both 1920 and 1924, by which time he was 46 years of age.

The superintendent of the Osborne Street baths – outside which long queues would form every Tuesday and Thursday evening when water-polo matches were played – was

John Derbyshire, whose son, also named John but nicknamed 'Rob', had been swimming since the age of three. 'Rob' was another member of the Olympic water-polo team, and would complete a remarkable double with a 4×200 metres freestyle relay gold in 1908. The year before that he had become the first Briton to swim 100 yards in less than a minute. An internal dispute caused the break-up of the Osborne team a year after the Olympic success and none of the other players, even including the youthful centre-forward, William Lister, who had made his England debut at 15 in 1897, was to appear again at the Olympics.

Preceding Rob Derbyshire and his fellow gold-medallists of 1908 as the first British Olympic swimming champions were the freestylists, Jack Jarvis and Stanley Greasley, amateur and professional winners respectively in 1900, although both collected cash prizes. In a later edition of the first comprehensive history of swimming in Britain which had been published in 1893 – and co-authored by the future Sir William Henry, founder of what is now the Royal Life Saving Society, who played in the preliminary rounds of the water-polo tournament at the 1900 Olympics – it was delightfully said of Jarvis that his 'records were far in advance of those considered wonderful by the older race of swimmers'.

Football – another sport that was codified, if perhaps not exactly invented, by the British – was to provide Great Britain with regular Olympic honours in the pre-First World War era. In 1900 the gold-medal winning team was drawn entirely from one Essex club, Upton Park FC, which contrary to its name had little connection with what was to become West Ham United. To a man the Upton Park players were members of the professional classes of society, and although no one seems to know how they came to be 'selected' for the Paris Games, it may well be simply a case of someone in the team having gleaned by chance that the tournament was taking place. The club was not the one of the same name which had been among the 15 entrants for the first FA Cup competition in 1871–72 but since disbanded. Instead, it had been formed in 1883 as Belmont FC and assumed the Upton Park name seven years later.

What is more to the point, however, is that there is very little justification for regarding the 1900 'tournament' as official, and it was certainly not thought of as such at the time by the Olympic organisers. Five countries had originally entered, and the only matches arranged were for France to play, in turn, Belgium, Germany, Great Britain and Switzerland, but then the Germans and Swiss withdrew, and merely two fixtures survived. Upton Park met the champions of Paris, Club Français, and won 4–0, and three days later Club Français beat a Belgian students' XI (including an English wing-forward named Eric Thornton) 6–2. Thus, neither the arrangements beforehand nor the actual outcome in any way justified the description 'tournament'. Nevertheless, the IOC later decided to recognise football as having been an official part of the 1900 Games. So here we have another mystifying example of the reinterpretation of Olympic history.

The one player in the Upton Park team who was to make a lasting impression was the right-back, Percy Buckenham, but he did so on the cricket pitch rather than the football field. He was a gangling fast bowler for Essex who took more than 100 wickets in a season in 1906 and again in 1911 and played in four Tests on the 1909–10 tour of South Africa. He served in the army in the First World War and then became cricket coach at

Repton School in Derbyshire, where he contributed significantly to a tradition which has seen no fewer than 130 first-class players produced there since the nineteenth century; one of the first was the great sporting all-rounder, C.B. Fry, who also equalled the world record for the long jump and could well have been a winner at the 1896 Olympics had he attended. Another famous Repton old boy of a later generation who went on to win an Olympic gold medal at 100 metres (he was also the best long jumper in Britain in his time) was Harold Abrahams, in 1924.

The tennis tradition inadvertently set in motion by the Irishman, Jack Boland, in Athens was maintained rather more convincingly by the Doherty brothers, Laurie and Reggie, and by an elegantly garbed 29-year-old Miss Charlotte Cooper, who thus became Britain's first female Olympic champion. All three were in the very front rank of the game and won the four Paris 'amateur' events between them, collecting 2,950 francs in prize money in the process. At Wimbledon Reggie had been the singles champion for the previous three years and would be again in 1900, and the younger Laurie followed him for five successive years from 1902, while together they were to accumulate a record eight doubles' titles. Miss Cooper, who to preserve her decorum wore a full-length white dress buttoned to the wrists which swept the ground as she moved daintily about the court, had won the Wimbledon singles on three occasions, and after marrying a future president of the Lawn Tennis Association, Alfred Sterry, in 1901, added two more successes – the last of them at the age of 37.

At the beginning of the twentieth century lawn tennis was very much a pastime for the leisured classes, and the Doherty brothers had been educated at Westminster public school and then at Cambridge University and were able to spend part of each summer on the Riviera winning regularly at the annual tournaments at Cannes, Nice and Monte Carlo. Yet despite their sporting prowess, which included five undefeated Davis Cup appearances, both soon suffered from poor health and died young – Reggie at 38 and Laurie at 43. The pair of them might yet have been seriously challenged in Paris had they been allowed to play the professional winners from Britain, both of them Irish-born, Tom Burke and George Kerr, who were working as coaches in the city. In the singles Burke, renowned for his passing shots and lobbing, beat Kerr, whose forte was 'a tremendous forehand drive'. The latter made a habit of keeping a flask of whisky by the court (bringing a new meaning to the term, 'a spirited player'), and the two of them combined to win the doubles but were paid rather less than the amateurs for their efforts – 1,300 francs.

Idiosyncratic by modern standards the 1900 Paris Games might have been, but in general terms they were a success. What followed four years later at St Louis has been much less favourably regarded. Politics, and finance, interfered with the staging of the 'Olympics' in 1904, and the event was a pale shadow of what had been intended. Britain won just a single gold. The programme of sports events which lasted from 1 July to 23 November had in fact all become something of a side-show, subsumed in what was termed the 'World's Fair Louisiana Purchase Exhibition'. What an irony that a century after France had sold off its claim to 828,000 square miles of territory to the United States for some $15 million ($219 million in present-day terms), Baron de Coubertin and his

Charlotte ('Chattie') Cooper became the first British woman to win a title in any Olympic sport, winning the women's singles gold in lawn tennis in 1900. Five times Wimbledon champion, she also gained a second gold medal for Britain in the mixed doubles, partnered by Reggie Doherty. The next year she married Alfred Sterry, future president of the LTA, and she lived to the age of 96.

The elegant Doherty brothers, Laurie (*left*) and the elder of the two, Reggie, were the finest doubles players of their era, winning eight times at Wimbledon and remaining undefeated in the Davis Cup. They took the Olympic title in 1900, while Laurie also won the singles and Reggie shared in the mixed doubles. Sadly, they were plagued by ill-health and died young.

PHOTOGRAPHS: TOPFOTO

colleagues should, in effect, 'sell out' their Games. Chicago had been the original chosen venue, but when the St Louis Exhibition organisers said they would go ahead with the sports events at their promotion in opposition – and their stance had gained the support of President Theodore Roosevelt – it was inevitable that de Coubertin would have to agree that they could take over the Games.

23

The opening chapter of what is actually a splendidly detailed official report of the athletics events – some of which were of a very reasonable standard – is headlined 'America Welcomes The World', but in reality few responded to the call. Estimates of the number of competitors vary, but a likely figure is 687, of whom at least 525 were from the USA, and of the rest 52 were from Canada, 17 from Germany and only 3 from Great Britain. The total number of countries, 12, is the lowest in Modern Olympic history, and Americans, not surprisingly, won 80 of the 99 gold medals.

The sole winner for Britain was distinctly reluctant to acknowledge the fact. Tom Kiely certainly deserved his gold medal because he was the most versatile athlete of his era. He won the 'All-Around' competition, which involved, in a single day, and under a driving rainstorm, ten athletics events – 100 yards, shot put, high jump, 880 yards walk, hammer-throw, pole vault, 120 yards hurdles, 56lbs weight throw, long jump, and one-mile race. But he was adamant that his victory should be regarded as one for

Tom Kiely was the only British Olympic champion at the US-dominated Games of 1904, but he would not have thanked you for describing his success in this manner. Born in County Tipperary, he refused the offer of British Olympic officials to pay his expenses to compete in the 'All-Around' athletics competition in St Louis and proclaimed his success as being one for his native Ireland. His gold medal was hard-earned – ten events had to be completed in a single day.
TOPFOTO

Ireland, not Great Britain. He had been born in the village of Ballyneale, in County Tipperary, the son of a farmer, and was 34 at the time of his Olympic achievement. He won 44 Irish titles between 1892 and 1907, and it was said of him that he accumulated 3,000 prizes throughout his athletics career. In fact, he had sold some of these to make his own way to St Louis after refusing the offer of financial aid from the British Olympic authorities. Kiely is one of a number of nationalist-minded Irishmen who represented Britain unwillingly in those early Olympic years, and historians have tended to re-classify them as Irish since, but the fact is that Ireland did not become a separate entity until 1921, and whatever their political convictions such men as Kiely were British at the time of their participation.

That was not quite the sum total of Britain's contribution to the St Louis fiasco, as two of the finest athletes of the early twentieth century, Martin Sheridan and John Flanagan, won the discus and the hammer respectively. Sheridan had been born in Bohola, County Mayo, and Flanagan in Kilbreedy, County Limerick, but both had emigrated to the USA in the late 1890s. The marathon was won for the USA by Birmingham-born Tom Hicks, although by any recognised standard of sporting behaviour he probably should have been disqualified because a photograph clearly shows him in an exhausted state at 23 miles, being supported by two men, either onlookers or aides, while the race officials look on impassively from their accompanying automobile. The official report remarks guilelessly that 'the marathon race, from a medical standpoint, demonstrated that drugs are of much benefit to athletes', explaining that two or more doses of strychnine, each of about one milligram, which worked as a stimulant, were administered to Hicks during the race by his 'handler', Charles Lucas.

It is worth noting that at those blighted 1904 Games there were at least three other Britons with a gold-medal claim (and presumably a drugs-free one), as Alexander Hall and Albert Linton, members of the winning Association football team from Galt, Ontario, were Scottish-born, and one of the Canadian lacrosse players, Billy Brennaugh (or Brennagh), had been born in England. Hall returned to Britain in 1907 and played professionally for Newcastle United, Portsmouth, Dundee and Dunfermline Athletic.

We now arrive at the unusual intermediate Athens Games of 1906. Against de Coubertin's wishes, the Greeks had the idea of holding celebratory 'curtain call' Games every four years from 1898 onwards, although for financial reasons only one of these ever took place, in 1906, and even this remains a footnote of Olympic history, widely regarded – most notably by the International Olympic Committee – as not being official. This is a pity if only because the 1906 'Intercalated' Games were actually better organised than any of those before, while a leading US Olympic historian, David Wallechinsky, goes as far as to conclude categorically that they had 'helped save the Olympic Movement'. Britain's share of 8 of the 78 gold medals that were awarded in 11 sports was exceeded only by France (15) and the USA (12), and again Irish athletes were to the fore as Con Leahy went one better than had his younger brother, Pat, six years before, by winning the high jump, and on the same day Peter O'Connor took the hop step and jump, with Con Leahy second. The British Olympic Association had been formed the previous year,

25

and for the first time the country's representatives at the Games had actually been *selected*, rather than deciding to attend for themselves.

Con Leahy was three days past his thirtieth birthday when he won in Athens, after a tediously drawn-out contest that lasted five hours because the officials insisted on raising the bar only one centimetre or less from 1.37 metres upwards, and Leahy eventually beat his 25 opponents at 1.775. This was very much below his best of 6 feet 4½ inches (1.94 metres), achieved two years before, and with successive AAA titles in 1905, 1906, 1907 and 1908 to his credit Leahy was to become one of the very best high jumpers of his generation, also placing second in the next Olympics in London, 1908. If anything, O'Connor's niche in athletics history is even more secure as he had also long jumped 24 feet 11¾ inches (7.61 metres) in 1901, which remained a world record for 20 years and was not surpassed by a Briton until a future Olympic champion, Lynn Davies, did so in 1962, and not by another Irishman until 1990. In Athens in 1906 O'Connor had been beaten by Myer Prinstein, of the USA, in the long jump three days earlier and only went ahead of his compatriot, Leahy, for the 'triple jump' gold in the last round.

For two other champions of 1906 the connections with the country they chose to represent were tenuous, although their fathers were British. Sidney and Gerald Merlin have been referred to as brothers but were 28 years apart in age and were actually uncle and nephew. Both had been born in the port town of Piraeus, no more than 12 kilometres from the centre of Athens, and the Merlin family were wealthy landowners who still have a street in Athens named after them. Sidney Merlin, who had also competed at the 1896 Games, was the son of the British vice-consul in Athens and was married for a time to the daughter of the Greek prime minister. The two gold medals for the Merlins came in clay-pigeon events, and Gerald Merlin took part with rather less accuracy in another 9 of the 11 shooting competitions in Athens.

By stark contrast to the affluent Merlins, the winner of the one mile freestyle swimming race held in the open sea, Henry Taylor, was a mill-worker in his native Oldham, in Lancashire, orphaned at a young age and brought up by his elder brother. His training was largely carried out in noxious local streams and canals. Despite these humble circumstances, Taylor would become Britain's most prolific Olympic medallist in any sport, winning two more individual golds in 1908, plus another gold, three silvers and a bronze through to 1920, by which time he was 35 years old. He lacked any formal education and was tutored by a team-mate, Jack Jarvis, who was Britain's other outstanding swimmer of this era. Jarvis's two Olympic freestyle titles in 1900 had included the 4000 metres in the river Seine – by a margin of 10½ minutes – and he was second to Taylor in the Athens mile race, albeit more than two minutes behind.

Between them Jarvis and Taylor won 39 national titles during their competitive careers, whereas Britain's sole champion on the athletics track in Athens, Lieutenant Henry Hawtrey of the Royal Engineers (later a Brigadier and aide-de-camp to George V), had not a single other major victory to his career and failed to finish in the heats of the 1500 metres which he also contested in Athens. However, Hawtrey led for most of the distance in the five-mile (8km) race and won the gold medal by a margin of around

50 metres. Two more competitors with odd credentials were Arthur Rushen, who worked as a builder's labourer, and Johnnie Matthews, a carpenter by trade, who were involved in both of the first two Olympic cycling successes for Britain. Riding as a tandem pair, they won their speciality, despite only ever being national champions once in that event, and the same day paced Billy Pett to success in a 20 kilometre track race. Pett had scant opportunity for training as he worked an 11-hour day in the wine cellars at the Harrods' store in London's West End.

The first phase of the Modern Olympic revival ended in 1906. From that date onwards the Games began to leave behind some of the idiosyncracies, eccentricities and anomalies that are such a delight to modern readers. By the time of the 1908 London Games Great Britain had won 37 gold medals at the Games since 1896, but no one as yet was taking Olympic history seriously enough to compile such records or to ponder the sociological implications of a list of champions which ranged from members of Greek high society to an illiterate Lancashire mill-hand. The Ancient Olympic Games had lasted more than a thousand years. The Modern Olympic Games had merely survived its first decade, sometimes precariously, and more trouble was already brewing – if, that is, molten lava can be said to 'brew'.

Ready for a dip … Jack Jarvis was Britain's first double gold-medallist in swimming, winning the 1000 metres and 4000 metres freestyle events at the Paris Games of 1900. The races were contested in the river Seine, and Jarvis's victory margin in the latter was more than 10 minutes. After finishing the 1907 world championships 500 metres, it was reported that 'turning, he watched as an interested spectator the struggle for second place'. He won that race by 46 seconds.

CONTEMPORARY PHOTOGRAPH OF UNCERTAIN PROVENANCE

THREE

The London Games of 1908

Mistakes on all sides, but what does it matter so long as we part friends?

*'The attention of the world at large was far more concentrated on the Games of
1908 than had been the case at any previous celebration.'*

THEODORE COOK, AUTHOR OF THE ORGANISING COMMITTEE'S OFFICIAL
REPORT

EVEN AS the 1906 Games were taking place in Athens, the destiny of its successor
was being decided. Rome was supposed to be the venue for 1908, but on 7 April
1906 – just 15 days before the Athens opening ceremony – a volcanic eruption of Mount
Vesuvius in the south of Italy reached its climax. The Italian government very soon made
the decision that the economic implications of the destruction that followed were such
that they could not afford to stage the next Olympics, and by November of that year
London had been appointed instead.

Accounts of the 1908 Games tend to focus on some of the fiery happenings within
the Olympic stadium: a number of 'incidents' were reported during the Games involving
differences of opinion or varying interpretations of the rules, particularly between the
all-British organising committee and the US contingent. Yet there are only two such
clashes which are cited regularly, and one of these – the disqualification of the Italian
marathon runner, Dorando Pietri – would have been unavoidable in any sporting arena.
As it happens, the man who benefited from Pietri's demise after he had received assistance
in a state of collapse from worried officials a few yards from the finishing-line was an
American, Johnny Hayes, who was awarded the gold instead. In later years Hayes would
falsely claim Irish birth when it suited him.

The one track race which caused major dissension was the 400 metres, which in the
general custom of the day was not run in lanes. The lone Briton in the final, Wyndham
Halswelle, faced three Americans, and the winner was John Carpenter, but by the time he
crossed the finishing-line the worsted tape had been broken by the judges to signify that

Stadium, Franco-British Exhibition, London, 1908

The White City Stadium, at Shepherd's Bush, in north London. This was the main venue for the 1908 Games, and so named because of the brickwork used in its construction. It was the scene of a dramatic 400 metres and marathon, in both of which races the first athlete to finish was disqualified.
MUSEUM OF LONDON

a foul had been committed and that the race was void. Carpenter had clearly obstructed Halswelle, and at an inquiry held that evening attended by at least ten British officials, but not apparently by any US representative, it was decided that the race should be re-run two days later, with the athletes separated into lanes divided by string, but that Carpenter would be disqualified and not allowed to start. The rule regarding 'jostling' had been printed in that day's programme and the starter of the race told the inquiry panel that he had reminded the runners of it before sending them on their way. The other two Americans withdrew from the re-arranged final in support of their colleague, and Halswelle 'ran over' on his own.

The Times thought so little of the importance of the disqualification that its correspondent's allusion to the matter was preceded by lengthy descriptions of the heats of the 110 metres hurdles, the 1500 metres freestyle swimming (taking place in a pool installed on the infield of the stadium), the wrestling bouts (also alongside the running track) and the 200 metres final. Having stated that the obstruction of Halswelle was

29

Wyndham Halswelle won the Olympic 400 metres of 1908 in somewhat unfortunate circumstances. The race was re-run after the American winner was disqualified for 'jostling' and the two other finalists, both also from the USA, withdrew in support, leaving Halswelle to cover the course again in solitude. An officer in the Highland Light Infantry, Halswelle lost his life during the First World War at the age of 32, shot by a German sniper.
TOPFOTO

'deliberate and pre-arranged', the writer then largely absolved Carpenter by adding, rather generously, that such tactics were not regarded as unfair in the USA, concluding: 'It is much to be hoped that both countries will agree to say as little in the future as may be possible about this most unfortunate incident.'

Summing up the Games after the closing day, the same un-named journalist found a neat classical reference to make his point: 'In the immortal language of our old and common friend Euclid (who must have seen many Olympic Games), there have been mistakes on all sides. What else could we expect, and what, after all, does it matter, so long as we part friends? That, fortunately, we may and will do.' The same article revealed that Halswelle, who was of Scottish descent and was serving as a lieutenant in the Highland Light Infantry, had not wanted to run the final on his own, had waited several minutes in the hope that the two remaining Americans might have a change of heart, and had then been prevailed upon by the AAA officials to start. He never raced again after 1908. Promoted to captain at the outbreak of the First World War, Halswelle was shot dead by a German sniper in March 1915.

Tragically there would be no fewer than fifteen other gold-medallists from Britain at the 1908 and 1912 Games who would die as a result of war service, all of whom had competed in either team sports (football, hockey, polo) or in team events in athletics, lawn tennis, rowing and yachting.

There were many more competitors in London than at any previous Games – probably 2,002 men and, most significantly, 37 women – representing 22 countries. Britain won 56 gold medals to the USA's 23, including all of the titles in boxing, lawn tennis, rackets, rowing and yachting, plus the team sports of football, hockey, polo and water-polo. There was an element of sheer weight of numbers in this medal count because as many as 12

Great Britain's football team of 1908, consisting entirely of English players, regained the title won in 1900. The teams they beat were Sweden 12–1, Holland 4–0, and then Denmark 2–0 in the final. The only other country to take part in the competition was France. Most of the British team had the experience of playing as amateurs for professional league sides.
PHOTOGRAPH FROM THE OFFICIAL REPORT OF THE 1908 GAMES

competitors were allowed per country in individual events in nine of the sports, including athletics, and even 30 per country in archery, which gave the host country a widespread advantage. Britain had 839 entrants across the range of sports to the USA's 160.

Even so, only in archery, polo, a yachting event and four of the six tennis categories were British wins a foregone conclusion because no one else entered, and although there were no more than three polo teams this was still a greater number than took part in lacrosse and rugby union, which were played off as straight finals, with Britain losing both, to Canada and to Australasia (Australia and New Zealand combined) respectively. It was perhaps of greater significance that in athletics the USA had 15 winners to Britain's 8, and this was clear evidence that the balance of power had started to shift irresistibly in what was to continue to be for the next century and more the major Olympic sport.

At least British distance-running honours were preserved on the track with wins in the five miles, the three-mile team race and the steeplechase. Both three miles and five miles

31

were odd distances for the AAA organisers to have scheduled because all the other track races were metric and at their own championships the comparable standard events since 1880 had been four miles and ten miles. The Olympic five-mile champion who had won the AAA title at the shorter distance ten days before was Emil Voigt, born in Manchester of a German father, and he emigrated to Australia in 1911, prospering as a pioneering radio-station owner and living to the age of 90. The team of doughty cross-country men called upon for the three miles included a Boer War veteran, Joe Deakin, who eventually set an even more impressive record for longevity as he had started running competitively in 1903 and didn't stop until 1969, three years before his death at the age of 93.

An Irish tradition also prevailed in the field events as Tim Ahearne, from County Limerick, succeeded his fellow-countryman, Peter O'Connor, in winning the hop step and jump in the most decisive fashion, with a new world record of 48 feet 11¼ inches (14.92 metres) in the final round. The man who was to beat that in 1910 and again in 1911 was Tim's brother, Dan, who had emigrated to the USA and for some reason chose to spell his surname without a final 'e'. Also a fine hurdler and long jumper, Tim Ahearne unknowingly started a trend with the manner of his Olympic success which would last 60 years: the world record in the event would also be beaten at the Games of 1924, 1932, 1936, 1952 and 1968. Ireland's continuing success in athletics was largely due to the country having remained predominantly rural and therefore having kept faith with the jumping and throwing events at village fêtes. Ireland even claimed ancient roots for its own Tailtean Games, a recurring sporting festival which dated – some claim – from perhaps as early as the seventh century BC and which were to be revived in 1924 with the Dublin Tailtean Games in the newly independent republic of Ireland. Other Irish-born winners at the 1908 Games were Martin Sheridan (discus), and John Flanagan (hammer), each for the third time for the USA, and Bobby Kerr, of Canada, at 200 metres.

If a British 'Man of the Games' were to have been decided upon, then a logical nomination would have been another star performer at the Shepherd's Bush stadium – but in the swimming pool, not on the track. Henry Taylor, whose eventual tally of eight Olympic medals remains unmatched by any Briton more than 100 years later, had three freestyle wins at 400 metres, 1500 metres and the 4 × 200 metres relay. The times may now seem unimpressive (for instance, Taylor took 22 minutes 48.4 seconds to complete the 1500 metres freestyle, while the 2008 title was won in 14 minutes 40.84 seconds), but he remains one of the foremost of all British Olympians.

Had there been a British 'Athlete of the Games' then George Larner might have been preferred to a sympathetic vote for Wyndham Halswelle. Larner had an apparent natural advantage as a race-walker because he was a policeman by profession, but he had in fact retired from competition after making a very belated debut at the age of 28 and having set nine world records in two years. His duties with the Brighton police force did not allow him sufficient time to train, and it was only after the intervention of his chief constable that he was given leave of absence to make an Olympic comeback. He won both track races, again illogically set at distances of 3500 metres and ten miles, achieving another world record in the latter. Larner retired for good shortly afterwards and became for many

Orphaned at a young age, and training by swimming in local streams and canals in his native Oldham, in Lancashire, Henry Taylor remains one of Britain's most successful Olympians, winning four freestyle gold medals in 1906 and 1908 and eight medals in all. His 880 yards world record lasted from 1906 to 1920, and he also played water-polo for England. Alongside him in this photograph is the British team trainer, Walter Brickett.

TOPFOTO

years a highly respected race-walking judge. The long-striding Larner was regarded as a fine and fair stylist, but track walking would have a chequered existence at the Olympics and was finally dropped from the programme after a blatant display of running by medal winners in 1952.

Of the clean sweep by Britain of the four rowing titles, three went to graduates or undergraduates of Oxford or Cambridge, but the exception would have gladdened the heart of the egalitarian Baron de Coubertin had it been brought to his attention. In the single sculls final Harry Blackstaffe beat the Henley Royal Regatta winner, Alexander McCulloch (also an Oxford product). Blackstaffe was a 40-year-old wholesale butcher who had won at Henley two years before despite the reluctance of the stewards to allow a mere tradesman to compete in their regatta. Amends were made in later years when Blackstaffe was elected a senior life vice-president of the Amateur Rowing Association.

The winning British crew in the eights, drawn entirely from the Leander club, included at number 6 the 41-year-old Guy Nickalls, who remains the oldest ever Olympic rowing gold-medallist. Educated at Eton, where he was known as 'Luni' because of his reckless behaviour, it was said of him by a contemporary rowing writer that 'it must be an inspiration to the rest of the crew to have the broad back of this iron oarsman swinging up and down with an untiring vehemence and slogging at every stroke as if he had no thought whatsoever of the strokes that had to come after'. He later became rowing correspondent for the *Morning Post* newspaper, which was acquired by the *Daily Telegraph* in 1937.

Another police officer to win gold was Albert Oldman, in the heavyweight boxing category, but he had rather an easier 'beat' than the walker. Oldman fought less than a round in each of his only two bouts, winning both by knockouts, to achieve his gold. Ultimately, though, the best known of the five champions would be John William Henry Taylor Douglas, who because of his elongated initials was popularly known as 'Johnny Won't Hit Today', but this tag referred to his subsequent displays as a dour batsman captaining Essex and England rather than to any lack of commitment in the ring. As a boxer he was noted for his aggressiveness and won both his preliminary middleweight bouts at the Games in the Oldman fashion, by knockouts, before scoring a narrow points win over Reginald 'Snowy' Baker, of the combined Australia/New Zealand team, in the final and receiving his gold medal from his father in the latter's capacity as president of the Amateur Boxing Association.

There is an intriguing sequel to this bout. In later life Baker claimed that Douglas Senior had actually been the referee, but this was clearly untrue … and Baker, who was to be described as 'a venal and florid egotist', had no excuse for being in error. The referee was a Frenchman named Eugene Corrie who had settled in England and has a place in boxing history as the first man to control bouts from inside the ring. To give Baker his due, he told local newspapermen on his arrival back in Australia, 'I think the better man won'. This despite the fact that a few days after the Olympic final the pair of them were alleged to have fought a return match bare-fisted at the National Sporting Club in which Baker knocked Douglas out.

One of Douglas's fellow pugilists was featherweight Dick Gunn, who worked at his father's London East End tailoring business and more than a century later still remains, at the age of 37 years and 254 days, the oldest Olympic boxing champion. Gunn had won the first of three successive ABA titles in 1894 and had then retired voluntarily at the request of the organisers because of his 'acknowledged superiority over all comers'. He gave his services to the ABA Council instead and returned to action only in London Olympic year. He was said to have lost but one bout in his career and he gave up fighting again after 1908, living to the age of 90. Fred Grace, the lightweight champion, also had a long career, winning four ABA titles between 1909 and 1920, but Harry Thomas, the bantamweight champion, was only 20 years of age at the time of his Olympic win and a comparative novice with a single ABA crown to his credit. Thomas emigrated to the USA in 1911 and served in the US Navy in the First World War, while his six brothers were with various branches of the British forces.

Lawn tennis had already provided seven titles for Britain at the Games of 1896 and 1900, and six more were added in London with a clean sweep of the men's singles, men's doubles and women's singles both indoors and out. The covered-courts tournament at the Queen's Club in May was much the less impressive of the two, attracting only 18 entries in total, although the men's singles winner, 40-year-old Wentworth Gore, did beat the future outdoor champion, Major Ritchie ('Major' being a given name, not an army rank), in the semi-finals, and also won the doubles. Gore was a capable enough player in his own right, winning at Wimbledon three times and accumulating the astonishing record of playing every tournament there from 1888 to 1927. His doubles partner, Roper Barrett, who was a solicitor by profession, was also of a durable nature, taking part in the Davis Cup from 1900 to 1919, although his more lasting achievements would be as non-playing captain of four successful Great Britain teams in the 1930s. The women's singles indoors suffered from the withdrawal of Dorothea ('Dolly') Lambert Chambers, who had been three times Wimbledon champion, and so Gladys Eastlake-Smith took the title instead and two days afterwards married a Hampshire doctor, Wharram Lamplough, with whom she would win the Wimbledon 'married doubles' in 1913.

Even the author of the official report of the 1908 Games bewailed the absence from the outdoor tennis in July of such prominent British players as Laurie Doherty and Chattie Cooper (now Mrs Sterry), plus Norman Brookes of Australia, and Tony Wilding of New Zealand, but the competition was still a genuinely international affair, with players from nine countries in the men's singles. That title went to Major Ritchie in rather surprising fashion as one of the five Germans taking part, Otto Froitzheim, had shown much the better form in the qualifying rounds but then in the final allowed the 37-year-old Briton to play the wily baseline game at which he excelled. Froitzheim was also out-manoeuvred by British opposition in immensely more trying circumstances six years later as he and his team-mate, Oskar Kreuzer, had been playing a Davis Cup semi-final in Pittsburgh when war was declared, and after the ship in which they returned to Europe was sunk off Gibraltar the pair of them spent the next four years in a British prison camp.

The ladies' champion, Dolly Lambert Chambers, was born and raised in Ealing, where her father was a vicar, and was thus a near neighbour of the 1900 winner, Chattie Cooper, who was eight years her senior. Mrs Lambert Chambers won the Wimbledon singles title seven times in all, of which four were after her marriage, and it was not until 1938 that another woman, the USA's Helen Wills Moody, surpassed that tally. In the Olympic final Mrs Lambert Chambers beat Dora Boothby 6–1, 7–5, and the outcome was repeated in the Wimbledon finals of 1910 and 1911 – on the latter occasion Miss Boothby achieving an unenviable feat that can never be surpassed, losing 6–0, 6–0. When unoccupied by tennis, Dolly had devoted her energies to becoming twice All-England badminton champion and to playing hockey for Middlesex. She said her final goodbye to Wimbledon in 1927 at the age of 48, going on to become a professional coach.

Apart from tennis, there were three other women who won gold medals for Britain in 1908. As one might expect in an age when women still did not have political equality (they were denied the same voting rights as men for another 20 years), and whose participation

'Dolly' Lambert Chambers demonstrates her forehand. There was no foreign opposition for her when she won the women's singles lawn-tennis title at the 1908 Games, but she was also Wimbledon champion on seven occasions from 1903 to 1914 and played there until 1927, by which time she was 48 years old. She was also All-England badminton champion twice and played hockey for Middlesex.

Sybil ('Queenie') Newall was the 1908 women's archery champion at the age of 53. The eldest of seven daughters of the owner of a large country estate in Lancashire, and grand-daughter of a Member of Parliament, she won the gold medal within three years of taking up the sport and continued competing until 1928, by which date she was 74 years old.

in leisure-time activities was severely limited, these 'sporting suffragettes' all shared an uncommon strength of character. Sybil Newall was an archer, Madge Syers a figure-skater, and Frances Rivett-Carnac a yachtswoman. As yet, the number of events being staged for female competitors was severely limited. For instance, women would have to wait until 1928 to be able to participate in athletics events at the Olympics. Nor was there any swimming, though that would soon be put to rights by the next Games. As for cycling, equestrianism, fencing, modern pentathlon or the Winter Games skeleton sled event – in all of which sports British women would also eventually win gold when the chance was given them – the very idea of women indulging in such vigorous pursuits under public gaze in 1908 would have had Queen Victoria turning in her grave.

Sybil Newall, known familiarly as 'Queenie', came from a Lancashire family of landed gentry recognised by the College of Arms back as far as the fourteenth century. She was one of seven sisters, and her maternal grandfather had twice served as the Liberal MP for Rochdale. Her Olympic triumph was achieved after only three years' experience of archery, and at 53 years of age she remains the oldest woman ever to win Olympic gold in any sport. She gained the title after trailing overnight the remarkably versatile Lottie Dod, who was five times a Wimbledon singles winner, British amateur golf champion and founder of the England women's hockey team. Lottie and her elder brother, Willy, who was the men's archery winner at the 1908 Games, possessed exemplary credentials for their Olympic sport: an ancestor, Antony Dod of Edge, Cheshire, had led the victorious English bowmen at the battle of Agincourt in 1415 and been knighted by Henry V for his efforts. Oddly, the best female archer in Britain in the early twentieth century was an unexplained absentee from the Games. The following week Alice Legh beat Queenie Newall by 151 points for the Grand National title and won it 23 times in all between 1881 and 1922. Queenie was nevertheless the champion in 1911 and 1912 and continued shooting until the age of 74.

Florence Syers, nicknamed 'Madge', was the first of Britain's Winter Sports gold-medallists, although there was not to be a separate Winter Olympics until 1924, and the men's and women's figure-skating events were held on 28–29 October as part of a sort of 'Autumn' Olympics, along with football, hockey and lacrosse. Madge was one of 15 children of Edward Jarvis Cave, of fashionable Kensington, in London, who is described in his biographies (ironically, perhaps?) as a 'gentleman of leisure'. She had won the first British pairs' competition in 1899 with Edgar Syers, 19 years her senior, whom she married the next year. Syers became her coach, persuading her to change her programme from the static English manner of skating to the free-flowing continental style. Mrs Syers, or maybe her husband, had mischievously noted that there was no ruling regarding the gender of competitors in the world championships and she created a sensation by placing second in 1902 to Ulrich Salchow, of Sweden, whose influence on the sport is enshrined forever in the name of one of the standard jumps. She also won the open British title in 1903 and 1904, beating her husband on the latter occasion, and took the Olympic gold with ease, placed first by all five judges. She suffered from ill-health, however, and died in 1917 at the age of only 35.

Madge Syers, the figure-skating gold-medallist of 1908, was the first British Olympic champion in a winter sport, although the Winter Games would not be held as a separate event until 1924. Mrs Syers had married her coach, 19 years her senior, and as there was no rule barring her from the hitherto all-male world championships she had created a sensation in 1902 by finishing second, thereby causing the scandalised officials to create a separate event for women, which she then won in 1906 and 1907.

Frances Rivett-Carnac's 55-year-old husband, Charles, came from a wealthy family: such were the riches they had acquired in India that they were remarked upon by Rudyard Kipling in one of his novels, and among the presents at the couple's marriage in 1906 was a sumptuous gold vase from the King of Siam, to whom Rivett-Carnac was financial adviser. He was owner and helmsman of the winning seven-metre yacht, *Heroine*, which had a distinctly easy passage as the only other entrant failed to put in an appearance, and thus, after completing the first of two laps of a course off the Isle of Wight starting from Ryde Pier, Rivett-Carnac and his crew were declared champions and invited to sail triumphantly back into harbour. These were familiar waters to the Rivett-Carnacs because they were members of the host club, and they became the first married couple to win gold for Britain at the Olympics, although the first woman gold-medallist in yachting, and for that matter the first in any sport, had been the Countess Hélène de Pourtalès, of Switzerland, eight years earlier, also in her husband's company (or, to be more accurate, crew).

At football and hockey, Britain led the world in 1908. The footballers won their successive matches 12–1 against Sweden, 4–0 against Holland, and 2–0 against Denmark in the final, and the single goal that was conceded was put through his own net by the England centre-half. The hockey players, even more dominant, ran up successive scores of 10–1, 6–1 and 8–1, but in their case the tournament was contested, for no obvious reason, by separate teams from England (the winners), Ireland, Scotland and Wales, and the only two visitors, France and Germany, were summarily despatched in the first round – the French by that 10–1 margin. France suffered even more painfully at football, losing their opening match against Denmark 17–1 and thus allowing Sophus Nielsen to establish at least one record on the pitch that wasn't British-held by scoring ten goals for Denmark.

Nine of the England footballers had league experience alongside professionals, for clubs such as Everton, Luton Town, Tottenham Hotspur, West Ham United and Wolverhampton Wanderers. The Spurs' player was Vivian Woodward, who would score 19 goals in 27 matches during the 1908–09 season to help his club to second place in Division II and promotion to Division I. He would go on to become one of the outstanding players in the game, winning a second Olympic gold in 1912, and it was later said of him that he 'relied on artistry and accuracy rather than speed and power, held the attack well together and was an able dribbler'. These skills brought him 23 full England caps and 44 amateur caps, and his aggregate of 29 goals against professional opposition remained an England record until 1958. An architect by profession, and later a farmer, he was unusually – maybe uniquely – a director of the Spurs' club in 1908, when he won his first Olympic honour, and later a director of Chelsea.

Another of the 1908 team who would defend the title successfully four years later was Arthur Berry, who learned soccer at Oxford University, winning his 'blue' against Cambridge in 1908 and 1909, and was to play in 32 amateur internationals through to 1913. An elegantly concise description of his style of play was that it was 'a complete art without tinsel or gaudiness', and he appeared in league football for Liverpool, Everton, Fulham and Wrexham, qualified as a barrister, and after serving as adjutant with the Lancashire Fusiliers in the First World War joined the family's law firm in Liverpool.

By the time that the football gold was won, a full 180 days had elapsed since the start of the opening Olympic event, the racquets tournament. In this, incidentally, a former sporting editor of *The Times*, Evan Noel, and a future proprietor of that newspaper, John Jacob Astor, both won gold. And after the football final, there was still another week to the hockey final. No one seemed to have concerned themselves too much with compiling medal totals for the various countries which had been involved over those six months and more, and *The Times* in its final report on Monday 2 November, tucked away on page 17, certainly made no mention of such detail.

Instead, there was a lengthy description of the celebratory dinner for 450 officials and competitors which had been chaired by the president of the British Olympic Association, Lord Desborough of Taplow, at the Holborn Restaurant the previous Saturday evening. The summaries of the speeches by Lord Desborough and the BOA secretary, the Reverend Robert de Courcy Laffan, were peppered with selected laudatory phrases such as 'athletes who had fought amicably ... close comradeship ... perfect physical development of a new humanity ... the spirit of the truest chivalry ... bonds of peace and mutual amity', and the responses of the audience were also carefully noted (repeated cries of 'Hear! Hear!'). The entire company ended the evening convivially by singing *Auld Lang Syne* and *God Save The King*.

It was the perfect patriotic farewell to a splendid occasion, and no doubt the diners all made their way home in excellent spirits. Britain and the Olympic movement seemed at ease with each other ... but it would not be too long before voices started to be raised in dissension.

FOUR

The Games of 1912

More dignified, more discrete, more intimate. Or mere wishful thinking?

IT WOULD not have been an unfamiliar story if had it appeared a century later: the Olympic year of 1912 – with the Games to be held in Stockholm – had only just begun, and almost immediately a savage attack was launched in the respected columns of *The Times* upon the Council of the British Olympic Association. Coming in for severe criticism were the Council's membership, its public accountability, and even the management of the funds remaining in the bank from the London Games of four years before. An article in the edition for Tuesday 16 January proclaimed that the Council 'is torn by internal dissension, which has caused much uneasy apprehension for some time in the minds of the sporting public'. The names of the 42 members of the Council were listed, together with the organisations that they represented, and the writer – unidentified, as was the newspaper custom of the time – concluded, 'It is difficult to realise how such an unwieldy body can have come into existence'. If some readers were perplexed as to why the Council should include, among others, delegates from the Royal Automobile Club, the Motor Yacht Club, the Royal Life Saving Society, and the Royal and Ancient Golf Club of St Andrews, then it was clearly the intention of the writer to sew such seeds of doubt, and he further stated that 'it is known, although the meetings of the Council are not reported in the Press, that many bitter struggles have been waged between the representatives of the more important purely amateur sports and games, who are present in a minority at the Council'.

Within two days the letters column of *The Times* was filled with aggrieved replies from the chairman and secretary of the Olympic Council. Lord Desborough and the Reverend de Courcy Laffan both stoutly defended their positions, as one would expect, but in March the newspaper returned to the assault unabashed, claiming extravagance by the Council: 'There is, of course, an obvious temptation to point out that a great many people are of the opinion that the present "office organisation" is on a superfluously grandiose scale.' The writer added a sting in the tail regarding the Council's executive capacities in relation to the sports to be contested at the forthcoming Games: 'Wherever there is any conflict of authority, any difference, any uncertainty, there is not the smallest evidence (except in the one particular of the civilian riding competitions) that the British Olympic Council is being of any use whatever.'

In that same month of March *The Times* despatched their 'special correspondent' – presumably the same writer, who was in all probability Henry Perry Robinson, a future war correspondent of renown – to Stockholm to check on arrangements for the Games. He sent back two long reports which were almost entirely favourable in their content. 'Nowhere is the smallest suggestion that the work is out of hand; rather, everywhere a general content, almost a joyousness, that things go so well,' he enthused, though adding a warning note for Britain's Olympic administrators: 'The extraordinarily thorough work which is being done in preparing the Swedish athletes, largely under an American trainer, is, though we had heard of it, in the nature of a revelation in comparison with our gay, happy-go-lucky ways.' When the athletics selections were announced by the BOA, the same writer was scornful: 'Many of the British team have had no more vital communication with the advisory board than is necessary to provide a suitable costume in which to run at Stockholm. Clothes may make the man, but they do not make the athlete. Might not some of the scanty funds that have been spent on the making of the clothes have been properly diverted to the making of the athletes?'

A 'Chief Athletics Adviser' to the Amateur Athletic Association had been appointed, but this had happened only six months before the Olympic athletics began, and one wonders what the incumbent Fred Parker, from London Athletic Club, was expected to achieve in such little time remaining to him, during which, it had been promised, 'He will visit all the principal training centres in England and will advise athletes in their preparation'. Certainly Mr Parker could not possibly have done much to improve those jumping and throwing events where prolonged and careful technical preparation was needed, and it did not take him long to realise that he lacked the resources for that. Only a month after setting up his office at the Stamford Bridge stadium in West London, he was enterprisingly interviewed by the London correspondent of the *New York Times*, who gently but firmly chided him for relying on coaching by post – 'a scheme long in disuse in the United States because of its impracticability' – and elicited a surprisingly frank admission from Parker which showed up the severe limitations of the enterprise.

'It's all very well for people to talk about employing efficient and sufficient coaches,' Parker responded peevishly, 'but where is the money coming from to pay them? The Amateur Athletic Association is not rich by any means. In fact, its financial resources are limited and it simply cannot afford to spend a lot of money in this connection. What is wanted is a Government appropriation or some fund raised to put us on the level of other countries.' Parker came from a banking family and was more than 50 years ahead of his time in suggesting such central financing of Olympic teams.

There were not, of course, any athletics events in Stockholm for women, who would have to wait another 16 years for Olympic recognition (though even then Great Britain did not join in), but there would be competition for women in swimming (there were, for instance, 27 entries for the 100 metres freestyle) and in diving and tennis. An indoor tennis tournament had already been held in Stockholm at the beginning of May as a sort of official curtain-raiser to the Games, and the gold medal in the ladies' singles had been won by Mrs Edith Hannam, who came from a well-known sporting family in Bristol, and she had then been partnered by a 39-year-old solicitor, Charles Dixon, to success in the mixed doubles. There would be no British players for the outdoor tournament at the Olympics because it unfortunately clashed with Wimbledon, where Dixon, who had been educated at Haileybury public school and Cambridge University, was to win again in the men's doubles.

Once again, the entire US team was well prepared and highly competitive across the full range of sports, just as it had been at the London Games of 1908 somewhat to the discomfiture of the British, but the host country, Sweden, was also taking the Games very seriously, as the man from *The Times* had revealed. The country's leading athletes had been gathered together in Stockholm since the beginning of April preparing specially for the Games and living communally in comfort in a newly built hospital building that had not yet been commissioned. In addition, Swedish army officers and national servicemen had been given leave of absence from their duties, and many business concerns had also released their employees to train under the guidance of the Swedish-born coach, Ernie Hjertberg, who had been brought over from the USA and had been in residence ever since 1910, travelling the length and breadth of the country to hold training seminars. Hjertberg had previously been coach to the prestigious New York Athletic Club and as a competitor had won the US national title in the steeplechase in 1891 and 1892, and at three miles in 1896.

The Swedish army had provided one of its indoor horse-riding schools for training during the country's severe winter, and the expenses had been paid of leading Swedish-American athletes so that they could temporarily return home to represent the country of their birth at the Games. All of this enterprising activity was readily revealed in great detail in the official report of the Games' organising committee, and it is to be wondered quite how Baron de Coubertin and the International Olympic Committee might have viewed such revelations in the context of the debate about professionalism. But then, of course, the enormously weighty report did not appear until 1913, and there is no evidence that the authorities ever thought of taking any remedial action.

The Baron had spelled out his desires for these 1912 Games at the IOC meeting three years before which had made the choice of Stockholm ahead of Berlin. 'It will be necessary to avoid attempting to copy the Olympic Games of London,' he had pronounced. 'The next Olympics must not have such a character. They must not be so competitive. There was altogether too much in London. The Games must be kept more purely athletic. They must be more dignified, more discreet, more in accordance with classic and artistic requirements, more intimate, and above all less expensive.' These were tough demands to be met, but the Swedes set out with every intention of realising the Baron's dream.

They proposed to the IOC that the Games should last only eight days, instead of London's 187. They also suggested that the programme should be reduced drastically to a shortlist of those sports which 'from their character are accessible to all' – athletics, gymnastics, swimming, wrestling. They set themselves a modest budget of KR 415,000

(£23,000 in 1912 money values). When the programme had at last been thrashed out the first of the Games' events was to be held on 5 May and the last on 22 July, with the main bulk of the programme occupying 25 days instead of the hoped-for 8. The events had also expanded to cover 14 sports rather than just 4. None of this was the fault of the Swedes; nor could they stand accused of extravagance when the final bill came to KR 2,474,769, or roughly six times their original estimate. Did they but know it, but the Swedish organisers of 1912 were merely suffering the same traumas of complex logistical problems and mounting costs that would continue to assail every single Olympic host city for the next 100 years.

In all, 28 countries sent teams to Stockholm, five more than there had been in London. The exact number of competitors is not known: the Stockholm organisers claimed 3,282, but this included 1,035 gymnasts, many of whom were confined to giving displays and did not take part in the official medal-earning events. More recent studies have come up with figures of 2,381, 2,484, 2,543 or 2,547, which vary so little as to scarcely matter. What is more generally agreed upon is that no more than 57 of those participants were women.

By the time that the Stockholm athletics events were completed on 15 July, the USA had proved its superiority convincingly, with 16 gold medals. Finland had won six, Sweden three, Great Britain two, and Canada, Greece and South Africa one each. Of the total gold medals in all sports, the USA had 25, Sweden 24 and Great Britain 10. By twenty-first-century standards, third place in an Olympic medals table would be regarded as a resounding success for the British, ahead of every other European country except the hosts, but it goes without saying that the Games of 1912 were very different to those of, for instance, 2008. Perhaps most notably, representatives of not fewer than 87 countries were to win medals at the 2008 Games, and almost half of these did not even exist independently in 1912.

The two British gold medals in athletics had been obtained by Arnold Jackson at 1500 metres, and by the 4 × 100 metres relay team, and all but one of the victories in the other sports had come in events which had also been won in London – tennis, as already mentioned, plus football, rowing (the single sculls and the eights), shooting (small-bore rifle team) and water-polo.

The 1500 metres gold-medallist Jackson (to whom further reference will be made later in this chapter) was perhaps the archetypal British athlete, whose rudimentary approach to the technical aspects of the sport was rapidly being outdated by the dedicated methods of the Americans and continental Europeans. When he lined up for the final he was, on paper, 50 metres slower than the fastest of the Americans, Abel Kiviat, who was the eldest of seven sons and daughters of a Jewish refugee from Poland. Yet Jackson beat the phalanx of US runners – who numbered 7 of the 14 finalists – with an electrifying finishing burst in the home straight that earned a heartfelt tribute from a leading American official, James E. Sullivan: 'He is the greatest and brainiest runner I have ever seen.' Almost as much of a surprise was the success of the British 4 × 100 metres relay quartet, including the 200 metres bronze-medallist, Willie Applegarth, as three other countries had between them set five world records in the preliminary rounds. However, both the USA and Germany

Britain's successful crew in the eights rowing event of 1912 was drawn entirely from the Leander club for graduates of Oxford and Cambridge universities. Not only that, but Leander beat New College, Oxford, in the final, and of the 18 competitors (including the coxes) all but one had studied at Oxford. The exception was Sidney Swann, who had been at Cambridge and also has the distinction of being the only British Olympic gold-medallist in any sport to have been born in the Isle of Man.

PHOTOGRAPH FROM THE OFFICIAL REPORT OF THE 1912 GAMES

British sprinters have won the Olympic 4 × 100 metres relay on two occasions. The first of these was in 1912 in Stockholm when the victorious team was, from left to right, Willie Applegarth, Vic D'Arcy, David Jacobs and Henry Macintosh. Macintosh was to be one of the victims of First World War, dying in action while serving with the Argyll & Sutherland Highlanders in 1918.

PHOTOGRAPH FROM THE OFFICIAL REPORT OF THE 1912 GAMES

were disqualified, the former in the semi-finals after beating and apparently eliminating Great Britain, and the latter in the final, both for faulty baton changes. In that final, in any case, the British had crossed the line first. Such lapses would become a common failing by all and sundry in this event in many Olympic celebrations to follow, and Britain would not win this relay gold again for 92 years.

Although it was not really remarked upon at the time, Britain's overall athletics showing in Stockholm might actually be considered rather more impressive than the

Britain's Ernie Webb and Canada's George Goulding (in third place here, wearing the familiar maple leaf on his vest) contested the Olympic 10,000 metres track walk of 1912, and it was the latter who took the gold. Yet this would be one of more than 50 wins at the Games over the years for which Britain could claim some credit because Goulding had been born in Yorkshire and had emigrated at the age of 19.
PHOTOGRAPH OF UNCERTAIN PROVENANCE

bald figures of the medals table show, because there were several other British-born successes. For example, the marathon winner, Kennedy McArthur, of South Africa, had been born in County Antrim, Northern Ireland. The 10,000 metres walk winner, George Goulding, of Canada, was originally a Yorkshireman, born in Hull. The shot and hammer champions for the USA were Pat McDonald and Matt McGrath, both of them Irishmen and born respectively in County Clare and County Tipperary. Goulding had emigrated in 1904, having competed in gymnastics and long-distance running, and had taken up race-walking after arriving in Toronto. He had returned to the country of his birth for the 1908 Olympics, where he was fourth in the 3500 metres walk and also ran the marathon, finishing twenty-second.

Following the success of the wholesale butcher, Harry Blackstaffe, four years before, the single sculls rowing title was won again for Britain by an artisan rather than an 'Oxbridge' product. Wally Kinnear was a Scots-born draper who worked for the Debenhams store in London and beat the elegantly named Belgian, Polydore Veirman, by a length, in a pulsating final. The eights title in rowing was also retained – and in swashbuckling fashion. A crew from the Leander club, exclusively for Oxford and Cambridge universities, including Angus Gillan (later Sir J.A. Gillan KBE CMG), who became the first Olympic oarsman to win two gold medals, was first; another from New College, Oxford, second.

The vividly contrasting extremes of Britain's social scale were illustrated on the one hand by these privileged graduates and undergraduates of the rowing team and on the other by an audacious young lady swimmer in the British team who won relay gold and individual bronze. She was Jennie Fletcher, from Leicester, who was one of 11 children in an under-privileged family and could only train after working 12 hours a day, six days of the week, for a textile manufacturer, coached in her severely limited spare time by the famed Olympian, Jack Jarvis. With her team-mates she had posed guilelessly by the pool-side in surprisingly revealing one-piece costumes to provide one of the enduring and iconic images of those Games. Almost a century before 'skin suits' became a controversial

Women had been competing at the Olympic Games since 1900 but only in such sedate sports as archery, lawn tennis and sailing. These daring young swimmers in their surprisingly revealing costumes formed the British team that won the 4 × 100 metres freestyle relay at the 1912 Games – Belle Moore, Jennie Fletcher, Annie Speirs and Irene Steer. The competition itself was relatively undramatic: 'Great Britain showed its superiority from the first moment,' concluded the official report by the Games organisers, 'and the race never became exciting.'

aid to record-breaking, these young ladies had been decked out in silk costumes which were apparently so skimpy that they could be drawn through a wedding-ring, and to preserve some modesty they were required to wear knickers underneath and to don a floor-length bathrobe until the moment they entered the water. Despite this, one can perhaps imagine the sensation caused by the sight of Miss Fletcher and her team-mates – 17-year-old Bella Moore, the Scottish champion from Glasgow; Annie Speirs, of the Liverpool Ladies' club; and Irene Steer, from Cardiff

In the football tournament at Stockholm there was a great deal of experience among the all-English team – experience of varied walks of life as much as experience on the pitch. In addition to Vivian Woodward and Arthur Berry from the victorious England team of 1908, there was Arthur Knight, manager of an insurance office, who was a regular member of Portsmouth's first team, occasionally opened the batting for Hampshire, and would after the war become the first player from a Third Division football club to win a full England cap. By contrast, another team-member, Harry Walden, of Halifax Town, who scored 11 goals, including six against Hungary alone, was a soldier who had enlisted at the age of 14 by concealing his age. He was later to pursue a successful career as a music-hall comedian. The outcome of the Olympic football tournament was exactly the same as four years before – Great Britain gold, Denmark silver, Holland bronze – with Britain winning the final 4–2 but against a Danish side reduced to ten men through injury. That would be the last British gold in Olympic footballing history.

There was no hockey tournament in Stockholm, but in the other team sport in which Britain was dominant, water-polo, there were five of the gold-medallists from 1908 to call upon, thus making them clear favourites. They duly won their three matches, including an 8–0 defeat of Austria, but a warning note was sounded when they were taken to extra time by Belgium before prevailing 7–5. Eight years later, when the Games were held again after the tragic interruption of the First World War, the margin against the same opponents would be even narrower. In shooting, where Britain had won six golds in 1908, the US and Swedish marksmen proved much the more accurate this time, winning 14 of the 18 titles between them. Britain's sole success in 1912 came in a miniature (or small-bore) rifle team event on the 50-metre range which was actually won rather easily, with 762 points to 748 for Sweden and 744 for the USA. One of the Great Britain four was 47-year-old William Pimm who had also won gold in this event four years earlier and would remain Britain's only double Olympic champion in shooting for 76 years.

Despite the narrower programme of events, the Stockholm Games had been a resounding success; there was no doubt about it. They had been well organised, enthusiastically supported by the Swedish public, and almost entirely contested with cheerfulness and goodwill. Of course, there had been issues. There were wrangles over the judging of the fencing and wrestling bouts, one of the latter lasting 11 hours 40 minutes. There were numerous annoying false starts in the sprint races on the athletics track because the organisers had decided in their wisdom that no one would be disqualified for such an offence. Yet even such a tragedy as the death of a Portuguese marathon runner from sunstroke and heart failure could not throw an enduring pall over the proceedings.

Looking back from a century later, it could well be argued that the outcome of the 1912 Games ensured the survival of the Olympic ideal which might otherwise have withered from neglect in those early years. At the time few commentators could have predicted, despite militaristic rumblings across Europe, that the next Games planned for Berlin in 1916 would never take place because of what was to be the horrific global ordeal of the First World War; but the achievement of Stockholm would at least prevent the Olympic ideal being quietly forgotten afterwards. As it happened the first post-war Games was a somewhat stop-gap affair in Antwerp in 1920. Many of the British competitors who fortunately survived war service went on to lead distinguished lives, of which the most prominent was perhaps Philip Baker, who had run in the 1500 metres, placing sixth in the final in Stockholm. He was to compete again in 1920, when he took the silver medal behind his team-mate, Albert Hill, after selflessly setting the pace, and he became a member of parliament, a government minister and a committed campaigner in the cause of disarmament, for which he was to be awarded the Nobel Peace Prize. When, as Lord Noel-Baker, he came to write about his Stockholm Olympic experiences more than 60 years after the Games he was still agog at the memory:

> The Stockholm Games were an enchantment – the word was Coubertin's in the speech with which he brought them to a close. As a competitor, I thought them an enchantment and looking back, six decades, two World Wars and twelve Olympiads later, my memories enchant me still. Partly, no doubt, it was discovering Sweden. Landing in Gothenburg, soon after the dawn of a lovely summer day, travelling by train through woods and lakes and past smiling Scandinavian farms, the charm and the excitement of our adventure grew upon us hour by hour. But it was the Games themselves, the great concourse of the teams from all the continents, the thrill and fascination of the contests, the sheer beauty of the spectacle they offered – it was these that captured our imagination and our hearts. We went to Stockholm as British athletes. We came home Olympians, disciples of the leader, Coubertin, with a new vision which I never lost. The Stockholm Games were everything that Coubertin had desired that they should be. There were no 'incidents'. The endemic chauvinism, which for 20 years had been a festering sore, was temporarily silenced. In the stadium, in the pool, in every sports hall, the Olympic spirit had begun to live.

It was a view that was shared by the Americans. Typical of the press coverage was the opinion of R.M. Collins, the correspondent of the Associated Press news agency, writing as the Games were in progress:

> The Olympian Games certainly are justifying the ideals of their founders. Men of all nationalities are competing here as gentlemen. There have been a few minor disputes, as is bound to be the case in hotly fought sports, but they were the merest ripples on the big ocean of good fellowship and comradeship. If it served no other purpose, this convention is well worth while for healing the wounds the United States and England suffered at London four years ago. The teams and the followers of both nationalities have a feeling that that was a misfortune which should be forgotten, and they are going out of their way to bury it.

It must therefore have been the cause of considerable regret to 20-year-old Philip Baker, then an undergraduate at King's College, Cambridge, that little of his euphoria was reflected in the pages of *The Times* in the weeks that followed the closure of the 1912 Games. Instead, the column inches were filled with recriminations. There were further critiques from the newspaper's athletics correspondent, elaborating on his *cause célèbre* of the incompetence of British officialdom and the casualness of the competitors; and there was a succession of letters from readers taking sides in a debate that evolved into a much broader question of whether or not Britain should compete in the Olympic Games at all.

Bemoaning the fact that the British public did not seem to have much regard for the

Olympics, the correspondent for *The Times* observed, perhaps realistically from his point of view but with more than a hint of chauvinism:

> It is undeniably true that the Olympic Stadium cannot have, and probably never will acquire, the atmosphere of Lord's, of Henley, of Cowes, or Wimbledon, or Queen's Club on the day of the University Sports. Measured by the standard to which we are accustomed, the Olympic Games have seemed to us to be rather second-rate things; and herein our very strength has been our weakness. Other countries have no Lord's or Henley or Wimbledon. To them the Olympic Games stand alone, representing the very best.

One reader who may well have reflected a widespread public opinion – or at least thought that he did – was Hugh Legge, who had been an oarsman of note, though not of Olympic calibre, and his letter published on 8 August, no more than a fortnight after the Games had ended, made provocative points regarding the nature and the range of sports contested at the Games:

> I venture to suggest that there is a large number of folk who would be heartily glad if we avoided the Olympic Games altogether. In the interests of amateur sport it is surely not good that the spirited competitions between friends and neighbours at home should be regarded as technical schools for the production of specialists who are to meet specialists abroad, or should be complicated by the introduction of strange pastimes.

This drew an immediate response from G.R.L. Anderson, writing from his home in Thornhill, Dumfriesshire:

> It is too late to stand upon our dignity and declare we are too grand to play. It is too late to say that we are old-fashioned, respectable people who cannot be expected to compete with foreigners in these questionable sports. We have competed; and if we announce to the world in Mr Legge's words that in the interests of amateur sport we mean to avoid the Olympic Games in the future, we shall convince nobody, least of all ourselves.

Curiously, but maybe as a matter of policy, the letters editor of *The Times* did not add a footnote that would have given much greater weight to these sentiments: that Mr Anderson had actually competed at Stockholm. He was, in fact, the hurdler, Gerard Anderson, who would lose his life in the war little more than two years later, in November 1914, and this gives a special poignancy to the continuation of his letter:

> Whether or not we organise our athletics before the next Olympiad, it is inevitable that British competitors will travel to Berlin in 1916. They cannot be expected to stay at home in deference to views with which they may not agree, or to be satisfied with parochial sports when they have the chance of representing their country. Go they will; no argument can make any difference

49

to the fact. It only remains to settle whether the British contingent is to consist of a keen but inglorious mob, or of a properly selected, properly trained team which will, it is hoped, do credit to the country.

More recognisably modern concepts of Olympic participation were beginning to gain ground in Britain as elsewhere.

Among others who did not for one moment contemplate a British withdrawal from the Olympic movement was one of the most celebrated men in the country, Sir Arthur Conan Doyle, literary creator of Sherlock Holmes, who commendably resisted the temptation to address Britain's Olympic supremo with the time-honoured words, 'Elementary, my dear Lord Desborough'. Sir Arthur was deeply interested in sport, had been commissioned by the *Daily Mail* to cover the marathon at the 1908 Games, and had accepted the presidency of the Field Events Association, set up by the far-sighted coach, F.A.M. Webster, to improve standards in the jumps and throws in Britain. Originally qualified as a general medical practitioner, Sir Arthur had played football for an amateur side in Portsmouth as a goalkeeper until the age of 44 and was a useful cricketer, appearing in ten matches for the MCC, with a highest innings of 43 and having once taken the wicket of the great man, Dr W.G. Grace himself.

Conan Doyle's analysis of the situation was truly 'Holmes-ian' in the simplicity of its deduction: 'Every one is agreed in our possessing the material. There remain only two factors – the money and the management.' He then asked, 'Can we not find among our rich men some one who will make the Games his hobby and be the financial father of the team? How could a man spend his money better?' How indeed! This proposal, and his further recommendation of setting up special training centres before future Games, would, on the face of it, have seemed probably far too radical for Lord Desborough and his colleagues, but the British Olympic Council concluded their considered report less than two months after the 1912 Games in a commendably frank and forthright manner:

> It has now become obvious that the standard required for winning an Olympic gold medal is very much higher than has always been realised, in this country at least. This means that though natural talent, unassisted, may sometimes serve us, as it did in one brilliant instance on the track, yet on the whole it has become necessary to pay far more attention than has hitherto been our custom to the *minutiae* of training in running and, more especially, in field events.

The 'brilliant instance on the track' referred to here had been provided, of course, by the 21-year-old Oxford undergraduate, Arnold Jackson, in unexpectedly and dramatically winning the 1500 metres. He had been an oarsman at Oxford until a year or so before the Games, when his uncle, Clement Jackson, who had been one of the founders of the AAA and was now the university's athletics coach, told him that he would never win his blue for rowing but could be made into a runner instead. Heeding the advice, Jackson precociously gained his place in the Olympic team by winning the Inter-Varsity mile the following March, but he was no committed year-round athlete. In fact, he was scarcely

The USA provided 7 of the 14 finalists for the 1500 metres at the 1912 Games, including the fastest man ever at the distance, Abel Kiviat, but Arnold Jackson astonished them all with his finishing effort to win the gold. According to the official report, 'the finish along the final straight was one of extraordinary severity, each man doing all he knew. Jones, Taber and Kiviat ran abreast of each other in a hard spurt, with Jackson some distance behind them, and Wide about 10 metres in the rear of Kiviat. The last-mentioned runner drew away from Taber and Jones in the last 30 metres and seemed certain of success, when, all of a sudden, Jackson came on, passed the pumped-out U.S.A. men with gigantic strides and broke the worsted 3 metres in front of Kiviat, who suffered a complete surprise.' Kiviat was second, Norman Taber third and John Paul Jones fourth, with Ernst Wide, of Sweden, fifth. Jackson, previously an oarsman at Oxford University, only turned to running the year before the Olympics and claimed never to have done any training – exercising only with walking and golf.

PHOTOGRAPH FROM THE OFFICIAL REPORT OF THE 1912 GAMES

a committed athlete at all. Before the Games he never ran in the AAA Championships; nor did he to do so in the two further years that he competed. Jackson was the very personification of the English gentleman amateur who seemed to achieve everything without any untoward effort. When asked about his training methods he said that he merely played golf and went for the occasional long walk, and there is every reason to believe he was speaking the truth.

Christened Arnold Nugent Strode Jackson, he became the youngest brigadier-general in the army during the First World War and served with Britain's delegation to the peace conference in Paris before going to the USA to live, where he changed his surname to Strode-Jackson. He was another of the numerous letter-writers to *The Times* during August 1912 and made a spirited defence of the team's efforts. 'Let us not forget that under the circumstances our men for the most part ran above any previous form that they showed in England', he said. Jackson and some of his friends among the athletics team found time before their races for appreciation of the contribution by women to the Games, and he still fondly recalled over 40 years later that 'we would assemble at the lawn tennis courts to applaud every stroke of Madameoiselle Broquedis, the French ladies' singles champion, one of the most delectable sights ever to appear on a court'. But even this dashing young Frenchwoman wore a long dress which allowed Jackson and his equally enamoured companions no more than an occasional tantalising glimpse of trim calf or ankle.

The 'Man of the Games' at Stockholm had been a Native American, Jim Thorpe, who had won both the five-event pentathlon and the ten-event decathlon and had been justifiably told by an admiring King Gustav at the medals presentation that he was the greatest athlete in the World (Thorpe apparently replied, 'Thanks, King'). Unfortunately, Thorpe's tenure as champion was cut short prematurely. In January 1913 it was revealed that he had earned money playing baseball four years before and he was duly stripped of his Olympic medals. The rules were crystal clear, and Thorpe could hardly claim ignorance of them. The entry form for Stockholm had contained a detailed declaration regarding amateurism to be endorsed by each individual signatory, as follows: 'An amateur is one who has never (a) competed for a money prize or for monetary considerations or in any way drawn pecuniary gain from the exercise of his sport, (b) competed against a professional, (c) taught in any branch of athletics for payment, (d) sold, pawned, hired out or exhibited for payment any prize won in a competition.'

In 1983, 30 years after his death, by which time most Olympic sports were openly professional, Thorpe was reinstated as gold-medallist by the International Olympic Committee.

FIVE

The Games of the 1920s

His hurdling Lordship beats the Americans, but an era is ending for Britain

A LBERT HILL was one of the lucky ones who survived the trenches of the First World War, serving for three years in France as a signalman with the Royal Flying Corps. Having resumed his running career in peacetime, he equalled the British mile record but was then beaten in the 1920 AAA Championships 880 yards, and only by vociferously arguing his case with the selectors was he permitted to enter both the 800 and 1500 metres at the Antwerp Olympics a month later.

His official birth date gave him an age of 31, but Hill, now working as a railway guard, later admitted to being 'the wrong side of 35', and he thus deserves even greater credit for winning both his events at the Games – a feat that would not be equalled until Peter Snell, of New Zealand, did so in 1964. Hill's times were of no consequence, and he would have lost hypothetical races against Snell by at least 50 yards at the shorter distance and 150 yards at the longer, but Hill's was still an era in which training for athletics was minimal by the standards of 40 years later, consisting of at most three or four sessions of easy running each week, and the Antwerp track on which he ran was little better than a sand-pit.

In his memoirs written 44 years after the Antwerp Games, Hill recalled the spartan circumstances of his Olympic adventure:

> Our quarters were in a school, and we had to sleep on frail camp-beds with hard mattresses, some of which collapsed under the weight of the British tug-of-war men. Most of my leisure time was spent in taking long walks in a park, and our journey to and from the track was in an old lorry with wooden seats which almost shook everyone to pieces.

He didn't say as much, but his Antwerp experiences must at times have seemed little different to his wartime military service.

It was no wonder that these Antwerp Games were a makeshift affair. The city had

Albert Hill, having survived military service in the First World War, was champion at both 800 metres and 1500 metres at the 1920 Olympic Games; the only other man to have matched that feat since is Peter Snell, of New Zealand, in 1964. In this photograph Hill is winning his semi-final on the slow Antwerp track; the others pictured are Paul Esparbès, of France, who was eighth in the final, and Anatole Bolin, of Sweden, and Harry Davel, of South Africa, who did not qualify.
TOPFOTO

been chosen as host by the International Olympic Committee at its congress in June 1914 ahead of Amsterdam, Budapest and Rome, but the world had been in turmoil since then and very little time remained after the end of the war for the Belgian organisers to have everything ready. They were offered the opportunity by the IOC to postpone their candidature for a year, or even until 1924, but insisted that they could cope, and it was not until April of 1919 – 16 months before the scheduled Games opening ceremony – that they were given the go-ahead. The reasons for Antwerp's confidence seemed to be caught up in financial self-interest rather than patriotic pride, and though these 1920 Games remain among the least documented in history, rarely if ever have those responsible for staging an Olympics been so reviled in later years. Dr Roland Renson, professor of sports history at the University of Louvain, is the foremost present-day authority on the subject and he has expressed the condemnatory view that 'it is clear that the proposal to host the Olympic Games in Antwerp formed part of a greater commercial project that the financial and business elite of Antwerp had set up for themselves'.

Whatever this hidden agenda, the Games were conducted in Antwerp in 1920 amicably enough. Great Britain's haul of gold medals from the 18 sports contested was a respectable 14, behind only the USA (41), Sweden (19) and Finland (15). However, it seems inappropriate if not distasteful to attempt to draw comparisons between respective medal hauls in 1920, particularly those between European countries and the USA. For a large proportion of a whole generation of British and European youth had been mown down in the war. And in the meantime the population of the USA had continued to increase – by 15 per cent in the previous ten years to over 106 million. From the mid-1920s America began to close the door on mass immigration, but in 1920 some 13.7 million of its people were foreign-born. The contribution which recent immigration had already made to US Olympic achievements is indicated by the fact that its list of gold-medal winners since 1896 included such names of continental European origin as Bonhag, De Genero, Desch, Dvorak, Gutterson, Kraenzlein, Maurer, Nuesslein, Prinstein, Schardt, Scholz, Schriver and Schule, and names with Celtic roots such as Connolly, Flanagan, Kelly, McCracken, McDonald, McGrath, Ryan and Sheridan. This is hardly to belittle their individual athletic achievements, but one must always remember that the momentous and sometimes tragic events of war and migration provided the abiding context of all of the Games of the 1920s.

One of Britain's medal winners in Antwerp was a sprinter, Harry Edward, born in British Guiana (now Guyana), who took bronze in both the 100 and 200 metres. It would be more than another 60 years before sportsmen and sportswomen of Caribbean parentage began to share significantly in Britain's Olympic success. Apart from Albert Hill in the 800 and 1500 metres, and a surprising victory at 4 × 400 metres, Britain's other athletics champion was the steeplechaser, Percy Hodge, who made a habit of delighting spectators at local meetings by a trick display of clearing barriers while carrying a tray of glasses and a bottle, never spilling a drop, and who remains to this day the only gold-medallist to have been born on Guernsey. Some considerable credit could also be taken by Britain for the Antwerp 400 metres victory of Bevil Rudd, though it was gained for his country of adoption, South Africa. Rudd, who was the man who had beaten Albert Hill in the AAA 880 yards, had been born in Devon, educated at school in South Africa and England and at Oxford University, and had served in the war as a lieutenant in the Argyll and Sutherland Highlanders, later becoming athletics correspondent for the *Daily Telegraph* newspaper.

Britain's directly attributed wins in Antwerp were earned from a now familiar mix of team and individual events, including the tug-of-war by a stalwart band of City of London policemen, despite all those restless nights in the team's makeshift sleeping-quarters so graphically recalled by Albert Hill, and others in boxing, cycling, hockey, lawn tennis, polo, water-polo and yachting. Yet these successes excited an adverse reaction from a most unexpected source. The controversial intervention by Sir Theodore Cook, formerly a senior British Olympic official, brought to the surface some of the tensions or at least ambivalence towards Olympic participation that could occasionally be perceived in Britain. Cook had been a member of the British Olympic Association from 1906, had edited the official report of the 1908 Games, and had been elected to the International Olympic Committee in 1909, but had resigned after only six years. Britain's Olympic competitors were still immersed in the Games in Antwerp when Sir Theodore publicly announced his disaffection. In the first of two long letters to *The Times*, published on 16 August, by which time only one of the 29 athletics finals had been decided, he stated his case: 'This country has made it perfectly clear that the whole movement which resulted in the modern revival by Baron Pierre de Coubertin of the Olympic Games has in its latest phases become entirely alien to English [*sic*] thought and character.'

He justified his belief, not unreasonably, by saying that the public had 'bluntly signified the national disapproval of the Olympic movement in general by utterly refusing to subscribe sufficient money to give our representatives in Belgium any chance of showing their best form'. In fairness, the athletics programme had barely got under way, while only 4 of the 22 sports had been completed, and in three of them Britain had actually done very well, winning gold in cycling, polo and yachting. Presumably, Lord John Wodehouse (later to become the Earl of Kimberly) and his polo team-mates had little need of any public funding, anyway, as he was a distant cousin of the humorous novelist, P.G. Wodehouse, and is said to have been the model for the fictitious 'idle rich' character, Bertie Wooster.

It was a nice irony that Sir Theodore himself was a silver-medal winner at what he dismissively but obscurely described as 'the ritual funerealistic Games'. He had been a sportsman of some repute, having rowed for Oxford in the 1889 Boat Race and founded the university's fencing club two years later, but his Olympic success – and medal – came not for sporting achievement but in a very much more sedentary activity – the literary division of the Olympic arts competitions. As he was the editor of *The Field*, described as 'The Country Gentleman's Magazine', composing an essay on an Olympic theme was second nature to him.

Perhaps not surprisingly, Cook was criticised as being 'entirely and absolutely mistaken' in his opinions by all 40 British athletes, headed by the team captain, Philip Baker, and the vice-captain, Vic D'Arcy, who penned their reply before they had even departed from Antwerp:

> We can only suppose that Sir Theodore Cook shares the views of the numerous but ill-informed critics of the Games who for so many years have spread the belief that the Olympic Games are not carried out in a sporting spirit, that they lead to 'bad blood' among the nations who take part in them, and that they lead also inevitably to professionalism. If these views were correct we would agree that the Games were 'alien to British thought and character'. But we wish as emphatically as we can to deny that they are in any way correct.

Neatly, undemonstratively, the letter had put to rights Sir Theodore's *faux pas*: the team was 'British', not 'English' as he had described it, perhaps without thought, in his letter to *The Times*.

The whole purpose of the Olympic movement had been attacked by a former member of its own inner circle ... and all the athletes in the British team had put their names to a spirited response defending their right to compete. What a story such a controversy would have made leading up to the 2012 Games in London; but this was 1920, and in fact the matter did not generate a vast amount of fuss or publicity. Maybe in the aftermath of war, and with an understandable desire to get back to normality, the people of Britain were sated with drama and dissension. Maybe they just wanted a peaceful life.

The British-ness was personified by numerous others who, like Albert Hill, had served in the First World War. Lord Wodehouse's polo team-mates were the Irish-born Captain Frederick 'Rattle' Barrett, of the 15th Hussars, together with Lieutenant-Colonel Teignmouth 'Tim' Melvill DSO and Major Vivian Lockett, both of the 17th Lancers. The seven-metre yachting class which was raced off Ostende was won by Cyril Wright, who had been in the Royal Navy Volunteer Reserve, and whose crew included his wife, Dorothy, thus emulating in the very same event Mr and Mrs Rivett-Carnac of 12 years before. The successful men's doubles pair in tennis were Noel Turnbull, who had won the Military Cross with the Royal Army Service Corps during the Battle of the Somme, and Max Woosnam, who had fought with the Royal Welch Fusiliers.

Woosnam was one of those remarkable sporting all-rounders in the mould of C.B. Fry produced by Britain in the late nineteenth century and early twentieth century, and justly deserves the entire biography that was written of him more than 80 years after his Olympic triumph. Woosnam was also an outstanding footballer who, while remaining an amateur, captained the England professional team on one occasion and led Manchester City when they finished runners-up in the First Division in 1920–21. Furthermore, he played cricket (captain at Cambridge University), golf, racquets and real tennis at the highest level. He had been asked to join the Great Britain football team in Antwerp, but he decided that tennis was enough for one Games. His nephew, Phil Woosnam, would be a Welsh amateur and professional football international from 1951 onwards and later coach to the US national team.

Another wartime winner of the Military Cross was Stanley Shoveller as a captain in the Rifle Brigade, and he became the first man in Olympic history to be presented with two hockey gold medals, having also been in the all-English winning team of 1908. Shoveller celebrated his 39th birthday while the Antwerp tournament was in progress, but had lost none of the scoring capabilities which were to bring him 76 goals in 35 matches for England from 1902 to his retirement in 1921. The Great Britain team in Antwerp, again exclusively English, hit 17 goals in its three matches against Belgium, Denmark and France, and Shoveller scored eight in one match alone. Seven of his team-mates were also in the army during the war, including Rex Crummack, who was severely gassed while serving as a captain with the South Lancashire Regiment, and an eighth, Harold Cassels, born in China of missionary parents, had left school to enlist as a pilot at the age of 18 and within a few months had become a prisoner-of-war.

Water-polo players tended to be of more mature years, and five of the seven gold-medallists in Antwerp were aged over 30, including the 41-year-old goalkeeper, Charlie Smith, who had also played in the winning teams of 1908 and 1912. Like so many leading players of that era, Smith was a Lancastrian and his career was astonishingly protracted, holding his England place from 1902 to 1926 and making a fourth Olympic appearance in 1924. Even then he was to be soon overtaken by Paul Radmilovic, who won the same three gold medals and whose Olympic experiences would stretch from 1906, when he reached the 100 metres and 400 metres freestyle finals, to 1928, when he was again in the water-polo team at the age of 42. 'Raddy', whose father was Greek and mother Irish, had been the first Welsh-born gold-medallist in 1908, at both water-polo and the 4 × 200 metres freestyle relay, and scored the winning goal in the Antwerp final against the host country. Regrettably, the Belgian supporters showed little of the comradely spirit expected of wartime allies, physically attacking the British team as they clambered out of the pool. Britain had won 3–2. In water-polo, then, the rest of the world was catching up ominously.

Taking into account the composition of winning teams, 51 Britons were awarded gold medals in Antwerp, 11 of whom were products of Cambridge University, including five in hockey, two each in athletics and polo, one in tennis and the heavyweight boxing champion, Ronald Rawson (a rare recipient of the Military Cross and two bars during the war as a captain in the Royal Engineers). Two other hockey-players were from Oxford University. In all, it was a clear sign of the status of sport at the ancient universities that slightly more than a quarter of the Olympic champions were from Oxbridge and slightly less than three-quarters weren't, including the eight tug-of-war constables and another policeman, Harry Mallin, who won the middleweight boxing title. The successful tandem cyclists, Tommy Lance and Harry Ryan, became respectively a Brighton bookmaker and the managing director of the family machine-tool business.

Despite the obvious advantages of having an Olympic boxing champion keeping order on the streets of central London, Harry Mallin's superiors in the Metropolitan Police force were not of a generous frame of mind. Mallin, writing more than 40 years later in the magazine, *World Sports*, about 'How I Won Gold', explained as follows:

> As a working policeman, I had to hurry back to London as I had taken most of my annual leave for the Games and the rest as time off without pay. I went back on the Thursday and the medal presentation was not due until the following Sunday. At Bow Street, where I worked, there was a great welcome for me and I was warmly congratulated by the superintendent. I thought it would be a good opportunity to ask if I could return and collect my prize. He said, 'Certainly, you've got some of your holiday left, haven't you?'.

The British success in tennis in Antwerp was achieved by the doubles partnership of Kathleen ('Kitty') McKane and 43-year-old Winifred McNair, who had famously beaten the French pairing of Suzanne Lenglen and Elisabeth d'Ayen in the semi-finals. Mlle Lenglen, who was the Olympic singles gold-medallist that year, was the finest woman player of her era, winning 31 championship titles, including the Wimbledon singles six times. Kitty McKane acquired four other medals (two silver, two bronze) in all at the Games of 1920 and 1924 and was also Wimbledon singles champion twice and won

Barrow

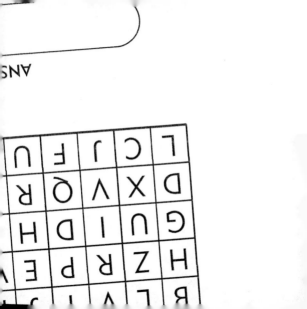

Harry Mallin was the first Olympic boxer to defend his title successfully, at middleweight in 1920 and 1924, and no one else would win a second Olympic gold in the sport until László Papp, of Hungary, did so in 1952. The decision in Mallin's quarter-final bout in Paris in 1924, which the Briton seemed to have won, was not reached until 24 hours later by the Jury of Appeal when his French opponent, Roger Brousse, was eventually disqualified for biting.

PHOTOGRAPHS: TOPFOTO

Kathleen ('Kitty') McKane shared the 1920 women's doubles tennis title with Winifred McNair, and also won silver in the mixed doubles and bronze in the singles that year, followed by another silver and a bronze in 1924. In that latter year she unexpectedly became Wimbledon singles champion after trailing 4–1 to Helen Wills, the Olympic champion from the USA, in the second set. It was the only singles defeat that Wills suffered in nine Wimbledon appearances.

the mixed doubles with her husband, Leslie Godfree, in 1926. She was, additionally, an outstanding badminton player, winning eight All-England titles, while Mrs McNair's other speciality was golf in which she reached the final of the English ladies' championship in 1921.

Oxbridge would continue to bolster Britain's Olympic endeavours, but times were changing, as would be demonstrated at the Games of 1924 and 1928. At these two Games, in Paris and then in Amsterdam, Britain won 12 gold medals, which was two fewer than in 1920 alone, and this decline in fortunes tends to be overlooked in historical perspective because of the dramatic nature of the wins themselves. Two of these in 1924 which were achieved on the athletics track – by Harold Abrahams at 100 metres and Eric Liddell at 400 metres – were to be immortalised almost 60 years later in the award-winning film, *Chariots of Fire*, which for all its liberal interpretation of the facts depicts with accuracy the motivation of the two main characters: Abrahams, the son of a Jewish refugee from Lithuania, who was regarded askance at Cambridge University for employing a professional coach to improve his sprinting skills; Liddell, for his part, was the God-fearing Scottish medical student destined for a missionary's life, turning his speed as an international rugby-football wing-threequarter to use at an unaccustomed track distance.

The story goes that Liddell decided only after his arrival in Paris to run the 400 metres, having just discovered that the 100 metres heats would take place on a Sunday, his devout day of rest. Somewhat more mundanely, however, the truth is that Liddell did know the full details of the Olympic timetable well beforehand, and in preparation for the Games had decided to run the 220 yards and 440 yards, and not the 100 yards, at the AAA Championships the previous month. What is quite extraordinary is that he should have improved by a dozen or so yards to win the 400 metres title. There survives a splendidly graphic description of Liddell's eccentric style written by Guy Butler, the relay gold-medallist of 1920 who finished third on this occasion. Butler later became a respected coach and innovative cine-film maker and was to write in 1938, 'I can still see that wonderful quarter-miler, Eric Liddell, running with his head thrown so far back that he appeared to be gazing up at the sky; his body apparently perfectly erect and his arms pounding the air with seemingly a maximum of wasted effort and a minimum of scientific drive.' This extravagant action was to be reproduced perfectly in *Chariots of Fire* by the actor who played Liddell, Ian Charleson.

Abrahams and Liddell both won their titles from Americans by decisive margins – Liddell by eight-tenths of a second – and no one would do better in the event until Michael Johnson ahead of Britain's Roger Black in 1996. Unfortunately for both the new British champions, this turned out to be the climax, and almost the end, of their athletics careers. Abrahams injured himself seriously during the long jump the next year and was forced to give up competition but continued until his death in 1978 to be deeply involved in the sport as an administrator, historian, statistician, writer and broadcaster. Liddell was Scottish champion again in 1925 and raced occasionally after joining his father's mission in China, but he died of a brain tumour at the age of 43 in a Second World War Japanese concentration camp.

Abrahams' time in winning the 100 metres in 1924 was recorded electrically at 10.52 seconds. By way of comparison, such a time would have left an athlete at least ten metres behind current world-record holder Usain Bolt, while Eric Liddell's time at 400 metres of 47.6 seconds would concede 30 metres or so to Michael Johnson. But circumstances in 1924 were very different. Importantly, the cinder tracks of the day were far less helpful underfoot than the all-weather surfaces that were to be introduced from the 1960s. Besides, there was complete lack of awareness of the benefits of harder training and the

As realistically depicted in the film *Chariots of Fire*, Eric Liddell ran as hard as he could all the way from the outside lane in the 400 metres at the 1924 Games, and nobody could catch him. This photograph shows Liddell's winning effort, with Horatio Fitch, of the USA, finishing second, and another American, Coard Taylor, falling to the ground in his vain effort. Contrary to what the film suggested, however, Liddell had already decided before the Games to run this event instead of the 100 metres.

Harold Abrahams perfected his 'dip' finish as part of the sprint training supervised by his professional coach, Sam Mussabini, and it served him well at the 1924 Olympics, where he won the 100 metres from Jackson Scholz (USA), seen here on the right of this photograph, and Arthur Porritt (New Zealand). Abrahams was later to become one of the dominant figures of British athletics as an administrator, journalist, broadcaster and statistician.

use of weights. There was little knowledge of expert physiological, medical or scientific support. And there was none of the regular world-wide competition which would come to be facilitated by vastly improved travel systems. Above all this, however, the amateurism of the day must be borne in mind, as even Olympic champions were merely enjoying themselves, doing something they were good at in their spare time from studies or work, before they got on with the business of 'real life'.

In Paris in 1924 a third gold medal was won on the track, at 800 metres, by Douglas Lowe, who was an undergraduate at Cambridge University, while the entire winning coxless fours crew was from Eton and Trinity College, Cambridge, and had variously figured in the Boat Race victories of 1923 or 1924. Lowe was to win the same event again in 1928, as we shall see, and another gold-medallist for Britain in 1924 to record successive wins was Harry Mallin, who became the first man successfully to defend a boxing title, although on his way he had to wait 24 hours before his French quarter-final opponent was disqualified for biting, and that completed an undefeated career for Mallin of more than 300 bouts. He returned to the Olympics in 1936 and 1952 as manager of the British boxing team, and in 1937 he achieved the distinction of giving the first ever television sports commentary, featuring two amateur contests at the Alexandra Palace, in north London, where the BBC television service had been established two years earlier. Britain had a second boxing gold at light-heavyweight from the Devon-born Harry Mitchell, and it would be another 32 years before such a double was achieved again.

These 1924 Games also marked the start of a remarkable golden sequence in rowing by Jack Beresford, which would not be equalled by another British oarsman until Steve Redgrave almost 70 years later, and, of course, subsequently surpassed by him. Beresford's father, Julius, who was from Poland and whose original surname had been Wiszniewski, which he had changed at the outbreak of the First World War, had won a silver medal in the 1912 Olympic coxed fours, and Jack began his Olympic saga with second place to Jack Kelly, of the USA (incidentally, father of actress Grace Kelly), in the single sculls of 1920 but only qualified for the 1924 final via a repechage, having lost to another American, Garrett Gilmore, in the heats. These two met again in the final, and Beresford this time won rather easily by 2½ lengths. Further glory was to come for Beresford with victories again in the 1932 and 1936 Games.

Shooting had already produced seven gold medals for Britain at previous Games, but the success of the Running Deer Target team in Paris by a single point over Norway would be the last British win on the range for 44 years. The captain of the quartet was Cyril Mackworth-Praed, who was yet another Olympic champion to have been educated at Eton and Trinity College, Cambridge; later he became a wealthy stockbroker while indulging a passion for African ornithology which earned him election as a Fellow of the Royal Geographical Society. He additionally won two silver medals in individual events in Paris, and at the age of 60 he was to make a long-delayed second Olympic appearance in 1952 in the clay pigeon event.

Two of Mackworth-Praed's team-mates were renowned military men. First there was Philip Neame, later Lieutenant General Sir Philip Neame VC KBE DSO DL, who is the only Olympic champion to date to have been awarded the Victoria Cross. He led an altogether adventurous life, meeting his future wife when she nursed him in hospital in India after he had been mauled by a tiger while big-game hunting. Second, there was Allen Whitty, aged 57 in 1924, who had joined the army at the age of 13 and risen to the rank of regimental sergeant major. Then, after being commissioned and winning the DSO with the Worcestershire Regiment in 1916, he was promoted to lieutenant colonel. By comparison, the third shooter, Herbert Perry, had retired from the Royal Artillery in 1920 with the mere rank of captain, but it was his score of 39 points from the final ten shots of the Olympic competition that clinched the gold.

As in shooting, Britain's solitary swimming gold would be the last for a very long time; the next would not be won until 1956. The Paris champion was a surprising one because Lucy Morton went to the Games only as the number two in the team to the world-record holder, Irene Gilbert, at 200 metres breaststroke, but the latter was not at her best in the final and Miss Morton won by eight-tenths of a second from Agnes Geraghty of the USA, taking the lead in the last 50 metres. It was the only event of the seven in women's swimming and diving that the Americans lost, and for the 26-year-old winner from Blackpool it was the peak of a long career that had begun with her first Northern Counties' title in 1913 at the age of 15. Her father was attendant to the Mayor of Blackpool, and the town baths had been opened especially early that Olympic year of 1924 so that she could train. At a civic reception after her win she was presented with a piano. Married in 1927, she continued to teach swimming in her home town for 40 years afterwards and lived to the age of 82. A month before her death in 1980 the Olympic title at her event was won in a time of 2 minutes 29.54 seconds; in 1924 a rather more sedate 3 minutes 33.2 seconds had sufficed for Lucy Morton's unexpected triumph. In some sports the advances in athletic achievement during the period of the Modern Olympics has been quite prodigious.

The protracted wait for Britain's next shooting and swimming golds after 1924 was no coincidence. The competition in every sport was getting stronger. Others were learning from the British example, and no longer was the Olympics a contest between the USA, the British Empire and a few European countries. Dominance in the team sports had passed on to India in hockey, winners at every Games from 1928 to 1956; to Uruguay in football, champions in 1924 and 1928, and then to various continental European countries; and it passed to Argentina in polo, winners of the tournaments played in 1928 and 1936, after which the sport was dropped from the Olympic schedule. There had been 29 countries taking part in the 1920 Games, and 15 of them had won gold medals. By 1928 there were 46 countries entered and 28 of them won gold.

There was, however, another success for Britain in 1924, although it took 82 years for it to be recognised. The first Winter Olympic Games were held at Chamonix, in France, during ten days in January and February, and a men's team from the Royal Caledonian Curling Club, Perth, in Scotland, overwhelmed Sweden 38–7 and France 46–4. Yet these results were consistently disregarded in subsequent years despite the fact that the official report of the Games contains a detailed description of the curling tournament, several photographs (including one of the British team ready for action, each wearing a flat cap, shirt and tie, tweed jacket, plus-fours tucked just below the knee into thick woollen socks, and stout boots), and no suggestion that this was not a recognised part of the Games. Prompted by an enterprising campaign conducted by the *Glasgow Herald* newspaper, the IOC confirmed on the eve of the 2006 Winter Games that the doughty Scots were, indeed, proper Olympic champions. The 86-year-old son of one of the team had sadly died just a few days before the announcement was made.

The Royal Caledonian Club had been founded in 1838 and was granted its charter by Queen Victoria after she had enjoyed a demonstration of the sport on the polished floor of the ballroom at Scone Palace, once the setting for coronations of Kings of the Scots, and famous for its 'Stone of Scone', also known as the 'Stone of Destiny'. What a delicious irony that the sport which features the propulsion across the ice of granite stones weighing between 36lb and 44lb should have received its royal seal of approval at Scone! A bizarre aspect of the 1924 Olympic tourney was that one of the Scotsmen, Major D.G. Astley, who was actually Irish-born, also obligingly turned out for Sweden and thus won a silver medal and a gold for two different countries. Major Astley and his fellow curlers were not the only British-born gold-medallists at the 1924 Winter Games because one of the rampaging Canadian ice-hockey team was Duncan Munro, who had emigrated with his family as a child from the Moray region of north-east Scotland. His was just as convincing a success as the curlers had been: his team won their qualifying matches 30–0, 22–0, 33–0 and 19–2, and then they beat the USA 6–1 in the final.

At the next Olympic Games in Amsterdam in 1928 the showing by British competitors was by far its most modest since the esoteric Games of 1904: three gold medals won, with the country ranking eleventh in the medal table behind the USA (22), Germany (10), Finland (8), Italy, Sweden and Switzerland (7 each), France and Holland (6 each), Canada and Hungary (4 each). Yet only the USA had more silver-medallists than Britain's ten, and maybe the British were settling for being no more than jolly good losers, as happened so often in athletics, cycling, rowing and swimming. The rare exceptions were all Cambridge University-bred: Douglas Lowe again and Lord Burghley in athletics and yet another coxless four from Trinity College.

The elegant Lowe, a student of law, deserves recognition as Britain's finest Olympian athlete of the 1920s, twice winner of one of the most fiercely contested events in the athletics programme, the 800 metres, and on this latter occasion disposing of Séra Martin, of France, and Martin's two predecessors as world-record holder, Lloyd Hahn, of the USA, and Otto Peltzer, of Germany. Hahn was fifth in the final, Martin sixth, and Peltzer was eliminated in Lowe's semi-final. It was the third successive British Olympic triumph at the distance, and the sequence would be extended to four in 1932, by Tommy Hampson in world-record time, with a belated postscript in the form of another British win, by Steve Ovett, in 1980. There was a downside, though, to Lowe's pre-eminence. Guy Butler says that Lowe 'rarely trained more than twice a week and never throughout the winter'. The trouble was that such casual and nonchalant demonstrations of natural ability by British athletes such as Lowe, or as typified by Arnold Jackson's 1500 metres

In 1924 Douglas Lowe (*left*) won the first of his two Olympic titles at 800 metres, with Paul Martin, of Switzerland (*right*), in second place, one-tenth of a second behind. Lowe's other gold would come four years later by the much more decisive margin of a full second.

in 1912, were being rendered increasingly obsolete by the scientific training methods of others. Lowe retired after the 1928 season, served as honorary secretary of the AAA from 1931 to 1938, and eventually became a Queen's Counsel.

Lord David George Brownlow Cecil Burghley – the future Marquess of Exeter – had won the 400 metres hurdles in Amsterdam the day before Lowe's victory, ahead of the American favourites, Frank Cuhel and the defending champion and world-record holder, F. Morgan Taylor. Guy Butler has again left us an entertaining pen-portrait:

> Burghley's success was due not only to his courage and dash in competition.
> He worked extremely hard at the technique of hurdling, practising by himself
> on his lawn at home over a single hurdle. His style was an individual affair; the
> chief peculiarity being that he did not raise his front leg dead straight up to
> the hurdle but swung it up with a semi-circular movement. This indeed he was
> compelled to do by the fact that he had suffered an injury from a fall while out
> hunting.

As the family estate in Lincolnshire still to this day extends over more than 9,000 acres, His Lordship had plenty of space in which to practise his hurdling and to exercise his hounds. Oddly, at Cambridge during the previous three years Burghley had had no opportunity to compete at his gold-medal distance because it was not included in the annual match against Oxford, but he did set British records at 120 yards hurdles and 220 yards hurdles, as well as a world record at 440 yards hurdles which lasted only a matter of hours as it was beaten the same day in the USA. He went on to lead a highly distinguished public life as MP for Peterborough from 1931 to 1943, president of the AAA for 40 years and of the world ruling body, the International Amateur Athletic Federation, for 30 years, and as a member of the International Olympic Committee and chairman of the organising committee for the 1948 London Olympics.

The Trinity College crew that won Britain's third consecutive coxless fours gold (an Oxford crew had taken the gold in 1908 but the event was dropped until 1924) qualified for the final on the Sloten Canal in highly dramatic fashion, having trailed Germany by half a length with 50 metres to go to the finish of the 2000-metre course only for one of the German crew to collapse on his oars and bring the boat to a halt. In the final the curiously named Penn Barge Club crew, from the USA, led by three-quarters of a length some 250 metres from the finish until Trinity pulled ahead for another half-a-length victory. Rather uncharitably, *The Times* concluded that 'we would rather have won the eights', in which a University of California crew beat GB, including Jack Beresford.

David George Brownlow Cecil won the Olympic 400 metres hurdles of 1928 as Lord Burghley and later succeeded to the title of Marquess of Exeter. He became an eminent figure in public life and sports administration, including chairmanship of the organising committee for the 1948 London Olympics. Among other athletes in this photograph are (*left*) Thomas Livingstone-Learmonth (also GB), who was fifth, and (*right*) Frank Cuhel (USA), who was second.
TOPFOTO

In the years between the two world wars Jack Beresford was Britain's outstanding oarsman. He won three golds in three different events: the single sculls (1924), coxless fours (1932) and double sculls (1936). He competed at the Olympics on five occasions in all and won a medal at each, adding silver at single sculls in 1920 and eights in 1928.
TOPFOTO

Two days later the Games closed with the boxing finals and the remaining events in equestrianism, fencing and swimming. Italy won three of the titles in the ring and Argentina two, as Britain's last survivor, Fred Mallin, the younger brother of the middleweight champion of 1920 and 1924, lost the third-place bout in this same division. There was a tenuous British connection for New Zealand's welterweight champion, Ted Morgan, whose parents were English and had emigrated when the youngster was barely one year old.

The Americans won five swimming and diving golds, including one for future Hollywood screen Tarzan, Johnny Weissmuller, at 100 metres freestyle. The best that any member of the British team could do on this last day of Olympic competition in the 1920s was a second place for a 19-year-old Scotswoman, Ellen King, at 100 metres backstroke. In fact, it would be in that event that the next British swimming gold would be won … but not for another 28 years.

SIX

The Games of the 1930s

Blades almost clashing, and then the Germans crack as Hitler looks on

'THE SUNSHINE GAMES' was what Tommy Hampson called the Los Angeles Olympic Games of 1932. 'Everything was on the American scale,' he was to recall, 'but the warm soft air and brilliant sunshine of California was perhaps the greatest asset the organisers had. It undoubtedly led to the breaking of record after record.' Indeed, one of those record-breakers was Hampson himself, becoming the first man to run 800 metres faster than 1 minute 50 seconds.

Two successive Olympic Games have never been of such a different complexion, more widely separated in spirit, character, or politics. This is because four years after Los Angeles, the 1936 Games would be staged in the German capital, Berlin, just a few years after Hitler had come to power, and he was determined to capitalise on the event as a massive propaganda opportunity, and to highlight the prowess of the Aryan athletes and the power of a Germany with renewed vigour, confidence, and menace. One illuminating story of those Berlin Games comes from Bill Roberts, who was also an athletics winner for Britain, in the 4 × 400 metres relay, but who had his medal stolen from his home in Cheshire some 50 years later. Sir Arthur Gold, one of the leading athletics administrators, kindly arranged for a replica to be struck from the original moulds which had been taken to the USA after the Second World War, with the presentation to be made by the Princess Royal. 'The replacement medal was of much greater meaning to me than the original,' Roberts mused in his biography, published in 2002. 'You see, I knew where the Nazis had got their gold from to make those medals in 1936, and the action of Sir Arthur, himself Jewish, meant so much more to me.'

What these contrasting Games of the 1930s did have in common were serious concerns beforehand as to the extent of involvement of some countries or even whether they should compete at all. In 1932 the world was in a state of economic depression, and the burden of costs in sending teams to the USA showed up in the severely depleted list of Olympic entries: 1,281 from 37 countries, compared with 2,724 from 46 countries four years before in Amsterdam. As for Berlin, there was long and heated debate in the 18 months or so beforehand in the USA, Great Britain and France, in particular, regarding the savage repressiveness of the Nazi regime, with strong support being voiced for a complete boycott of the Games.

As usual the British were dependent on a public appeal for funds to send representative teams and despite the economic problems more than £10,000 had been collected in 1932 (£10,116 8s. 3d., to be precise), which was enough to afford 74 competitors, for whom 38 officials were deemed necessary, though some paid their own way. By far the largest contributor at £1,000 was the Sunday newspaper, the *News of the World*, which was an ardent sponsor of athletics and whose correspondent for the sport, Joe Binks, was a former British mile record-holder. The next most generous donor, at £500, was Sir Harold Bowden, who presumably felt he had to set a good example as he was chairman of the appeal committee. In 1936, in improved economic circumstances, barely £9,000 was raised – of which Lord Portal of Laverstoke, president of the British Olympic Association, and his business interests were responsible for £2,500 – which rather suggests that the British public did not take kindly to the idea of paying for competitions that would be held under the shadow of the swastikas.

The 800 metres gold-medallist in 1932, Tommy Hampson, was a master at St Albans public school and so was able to afford the time away to make the long journey to Los Angeles, departing aboard the liner *Empress of Britain* on 13 July and returning on 26 August; but others, equally worthy of selection, had to regretfully decline their invitations. This iniquitous situation was to be vividly described almost 70 years later by another of the British athletes at those Games, Jerry Cornes, who in conversation with the respected athletics historian and writer, David Thurlow, remembered the plight of one of his chief opponents in domestic one-mile races, Cyril Ellis, who had been three times the AAA champion:

> There is absolutely no comparison between then and now. In 1932 there
> were three places available for the Olympic 1500 metres after the AAA
> Championships. The RAF allowed Reg Thomas, the 1930 Empire mile
> champion, paid leave, and I had just left Oxford and had been appointed to the
> colonial administrative service, and they allowed me unpaid time off so that I
> could join a month later in Nigeria. But Ellis was a married man who earned his
> money as a miner by piecework. If he did not work, he did not get paid, and he
> could not afford to lose the money. Right from the beginning, when I started
> running, I believed that Baron de Coubertin had made a mistake by insisting
> that we should all be amateurs. I thought it was wrong that Ellis should miss
> out.

The bespectacled Hampson was an interesting late developer who made no great impression as an athlete at Oxford University but blossomed in 1930 with victory at 880 yards (804.67 metres) in the inaugural British Empire Games in Canada. He was the AAA champion for three successive years, but even so he improved his best time by the very substantial margin of two seconds to win the Olympic gold. His time of 1 minute 49.7

The historic 800 metres final at the 1932 Olympics. Tommy Hampson (*left*, wearing 199) wins the gold for Britain and becomes the first man to run the distance inside 1 minute 50 seconds, with Alex Wilson, of Canada, close behind. This completed a sequence of four successive British victories in this event since 1920. Hampson had also won the 880 yards at the inaugural British Empire Games in Hamilton, Ontario, two years earlier.

seconds would not be fast enough to rank in the top 40 in Britain by today's standards, but it was of immense historic significance in that byegone era. Hampson added a silver medal at 4×400 metres later in the Games, with Lord Burghley as one of his team-mates, and Jerry Cornes also had a meritorious second place at 1500 metres (109.35 metres short of a mile) and would return from Nigeria in 1936 to reach the final again on no more than a few months' training.

Very few others in the 1932 British team could match the increasing efficiency of the host country, which won 41 gold medals, nor of other traditional Olympic powers such as Italy (12 golds), France (10) and Sweden (9), or the most improved of all, Japan (7). Even so, Hugh Edwards, familiarly known as 'Jumbo', achieved the rare feat of collecting two gold medals in rowing, matched previously only by the American sculler, Jack Kelly, in 1920, succeeding first in the coxless pairs with his partner from Christ Church College, Oxford, Lewis Clive. The next day Edwards was in the winning coxless four, which also included Jack Beresford, but was something of a makeshift affair as Edwards was brought in late in the day when the original choice, Thomas Tyler, went down with flu in California.

There must have been some interesting exchanges of views between 'Jumbo' Edwards and Lewis Clive when they were out of the water because Clive, the son of a Grenadier Guards lieutenant colonel who had died on active service in 1918, was a committed socialist who served as a Labour member of Kensington Borough Council. At the age of only 27 he would be killed while fighting in the Spanish Civil War. Edwards had a chequered career at Oxford, sent down in 1927 for failing his exams but accepted back in 1930, and while studying for his degree he joined the RAF, did more flying than rowing and kept his private aircraft at the university. He became a well-known racing pilot, but it was his rowing ability which saved his life in 1943 when he was the only survivor from a bomber that crashed into the sea off Land's End and he steered his dinghy to safety for four miles through a minefield. He retired after the war with the rank of group captain and became an innovative rowing coach, advising his old university and the British Olympic eight in 1960.

The fourth of Britain's relatively meagre collection of gold medals could scarcely have been more deserved. At the age of 38 Tommy Green, the son of a retired police constable, and the father of four children, won the first 50 kilometres road walk to be held at the Olympics, and thus began a stalwart British tradition which would last until 1964, but nothing in his early life suggested that he could ever attain normal mobility let alone such sporting eminence. He was unable to walk at all until he reached the age of five,

Early stages in the 1932 Olympic 50 kilometres road walk – the first such event to be held at the Games – and Tommy Green is already at the head of the race which would bring him the gold medal. Behind his left shoulder is Janis Dalinš, of Latvia, who would finish second, although the difference between them would stretch to more than seven minutes. Further Olympic victories for Britain in this event would come in 1936 and 1960.

TOPFOTO

suffering from the bone-softening disease of rickets, and then as a 12-year-old butcher's assistant in 1906 he joined the Royal Hussars as a boy soldier by falsifying his age but was invalided out as a result of injuries suffered when a horse fell on him. Recalled in wartime, he was wounded three times and seriously gassed in France.

Employed at the Eastleigh railway works near his home in Hampshire, Green did not start race-walking until the age of 32, but he took to it so readily that he won the London-to-Brighton event in 1929, 1930 and 1931, reducing the record to 8 hours 2 minutes 55 seconds. In the Los Angeles 50 kilometres, according to the official report of the British Olympic Association, Green was a minute down on the leaders at three-quarters distance, suffering from the effects of the sun, but with a mile to go he and the Latvian, Janis Daliņš, were said to be together in the lead. However, as Green won by more than seven minutes it seems more likely that he was at the head of the race for rather longer. Green became a publican from 1934 onwards and continued to compete, winning his last race at the age of 54. The London–Brighton road walk had been first held in 1897, and a national 20 miles championship – which Green, incidentally, never succeeded in winning – had been contested since 1908. Green's first major success had been in the national 'junior' (based on experience, not age) 20 miles at Sheffield in 1927, and there were numerous other such distance races on the competition calendar during 1932. Green's record for the 37-mile Hastings–Brighton course was beaten by Harold Whitlock, of whom more would be heard in 1936, while the previous year's national champion at 50 kilometres, Tebbs Lloyd Johnson, also competed at the 1936 Games but would bide his time to make his Olympic presence more strongly felt, in London, in 1948.

The economic depression that foreshadowed the 1932 Games had reduced the number of competitors, and among other effects had also caused the cancellation of the football tournament, but overall the Los Angeles Games had been a rip-roaring success, with 16 world records set in athletics alone. One of these was achieved by a Ceylon-born Anglo-Irish graduate of Cambridge University, Bob Tisdall, in the 400 metres hurdles, although the rules in existence at the time meant that he was denied official ratification because he had knocked down a hurdle, and so the second man home, Glenn Hardin, of the USA, was given the credit instead. Like his predecessor, Lord Burghley, the versatile Tisdall had no opportunity to run his golden event at Cambridge and so had settled for wins at 440 yards flat, the 120 and 220 yards hurdles and the long jump in previous years at the Inter-Varsity match. Indeed, he had only run 400 metres hurdles or 440 yards hurdles three times before he travelled to Los Angeles.

Tisdall lived to the age of 97, latterly in Australia, having run in the Sydney Olympic torch relay only four years before. As Ceylon (now Sri Lanka) was a British crown colony until achieving independence in 1948, he could as readily have competed for Great Britain in Los Angeles, and only an hour after his Olympic triumph another gold medal was won for Ireland by Dr Pat O'Callaghan, successfully defending his hammer title from 1928. Dr O'Callaghan was the last of the Irish 'whales' in the throwing events to have been born under British rule, in County Cork in 1906, and was certainly the finest hammer-thrower in the world in the years between the wars, but all his achievements in the event were indisputably in the green vest of Ireland after the country's independence in 1921.

What turned out to be the most controversial of the Modern Olympic Games had in 1931 been awarded at the IOC congress to Berlin, while Germany was still a parliamentary republic under the presidency of Paul von Hindenburg. However, with the coming to power as chancellor of Adolf Hitler in 1933 the constitution was cast aside and the country quickly became the one-party totalitarian Third Reich. By the winter of 1935–36, when the true nature and intentions of the Nazi régime were becoming more widely recognised, there were calls on both sides of the Atlantic for an Olympic boycott, and the appeal for funds for the British team launched by Lord Portal with the support, among others, of the Olympic hero, Lord Burghley, had an apologetic tone to it: 'The British Olympic Council are convinced that in sending a team to Berlin they are acting in the best interests of the sport,' it was stated, and it was unprecedented in Olympic history that the note should be added that 'Great Britain's team will be chosen without any regard whatsoever to the origin, religious belief or political creed of the competitors'.

The strongest opposition to sending a team was voiced by the Trades Union Congress, and at the annual general meeting of the Amateur Athletic Association in March 1936 a resolution was put forward by the National Workers' Sports Federation that a boycott should be imposed. After a lengthy debate the resolution was eventually dropped, and one of the most influential contributions to the exchanges was made by Harold Abrahams, who as a Jew had more reason than most to loathe the Nazis but insisted that the presence of a British team in Berlin would be an 'influence for good'. One could only admire his magnanimity as he told the delegates: 'If I had been born in Germany, I doubt if I should be alive today, but I still think the right thing is for us to show the German people what Great Britain believes to be real sport.'

As a compromise, the matter was deferred to a further meeting of the AAA in May, where another esteemed Olympian, Douglas Lowe, now the AAA secretary, spoke in support of going to Berlin, stating that none of the 180 British competitors invited had declined the invitation. The idea of a boycott was overwhelmingly rejected. It is not readily apparent as to who the '180' were because, for instance, the 53 athletes (42 men, 11 women) who went to Berlin were not selected until after the AAA Championships and Women's AAA Championships held more than seven weeks later. However, in one of the most informative of the vast number of books written on the subject and entitled, evocatively, *Berlin Games: How Hitler Stole the Olympic Dream*, published in 2006, the author, Guy Walters, found no evidence of athletes in Britain having any interest in a boycott, or in some cases even any awareness that such a proposal had been made.

The arguments in the USA had been rather more strident and it had not been until the annual convention of the country's sports ruling body, the Amateur Athletic Union, in December of 1935 that the Berlin invitation had been taken up, but in a ballot, based on quarter-votes, the result was desperately close: 58.25 in favour and 55.75 against. It is known that some Jewish contenders for places in the US team decided against competing in qualifying trials, but two Jewish sprinters did go to Berlin, Marty Glickman and Sam

Stoller, only to be caught up in an internal dispute with US officialdom, which had anti-semitic overtones to it, over the composition of the 4 × 100 metres relay team.

Those AAA Championships which would decide the British athletics representatives in Berlin were held on a typical July weekend – in other words, amid constant downpours of rain – which nevertheless attracted 40,000 people to the ancient but refurbished White City Stadium which had been used for the 1908 Olympic Games. Whether it was the adverse weather, or the usual deadening effect of the clinging cinders through which the runners had to plough, or simply lack of talent, there was only one performance that held out any hope of a gold medal to come, and that was in the mile where a future world-record holder, Sydney Wooderson, beat a previous world-record holder, Jack Lovelock, of New Zealand, and formerly of Oxford University. Even so, the correspondent for *The Times* noted ominously that Wooderson was seen to be limping afterwards.

If any other British male athlete could be said to be regarded as a possible Olympic champion then it was Harold Whitlock, who the previous weekend in Derby had won the Road Walking Association's annual 50 kilometres championship in an exceptional time of 4 hours 30 minutes 38 seconds, with the 1932 Olympic champion, Tommy Green, now 42, missing out on re-selection in fourth place. The women would have only six events to contest in Berlin, but one of them was the high jump in which a 16-year-old, Dorothy Odam, had in June equalled the world record in the improbable setting of the playing fields belonging to Brentwood School, in Essex.

As previously pointed out, the public response to the British Olympic Association's appeal for funds was not over-enthusiastic, but sending off the teams by train and then by ferry from Harwich or Dover to the continent was considerably cheaper than the transatlantic voyage of four years before, and the total party consisted of 221 competitors and 86 officials. In fact, there were rather more gold-medallists among the latter group (ex-athlete Lord Burghley, ex-boxer Harry Mallin and ex-swimmer Rob Derbyshire) than among the former (rower Jack Beresford). In one particular sport which had brought so much honour in the past, hockey, there was no British representation at all, other than a single official, and the irony of this was that Great Britain had astonishingly won the gold medals in the version of the game played on ice the previous February at the Winter Olympics also held in Germany, at Garmisch-Partenkirchen – albeit not without some controversy. To the consternation of the Canadians, who had won the four previous Olympic ice-hockey tournaments, eight of the twelve British players had been emigrants to Canada with their families as youngsters and had been persuaded to return from as early as 1931 onwards by the wily secretary of the British Ice Hockey Association, J.F. 'Bunny' Ahearne, to play for English clubs such as those at Brighton, Earl's Court, Richmond, Streatham and Wembley. One of these eight recruits had arrived only weeks before the Olympics opened, and two others had not sought clearance from the Canadian ice-hockey authorities and were under suspension. In 1924, when Britain had won the bronze medals (losing 19–2 to Canada and 11–0 to the USA), the selection policy had been even more relaxed – eight of the nine players were Canadian-born; the only exception being the captain of the Cambridge University team.

Harold Whitlock retained for Britain the 50 kilometre walk title in 1936 after Tommy Green's success four years before. A motor mechanic by occupation, Whitlock tuned his performance to perfection, taking the lead at 35 kilometres and winning by almost 1½ minutes. Writing in the British Olympic Association's official report of the Games, Harold Abrahams said of Whitlock: 'He is the finest long-distance walker the world has yet seen.'

Great Britain's surprising ice-hockey gold-medal winners of 1936 were mostly immigrants from Canada, the country which had won the four previous Olympic tournaments. The team lined up as follows: back row, left to right – Jimmy Chappell, Archie Stinchcombe, Sandy Archer, Don Dailley, Percy Nicklin (coach), Jack Kilpatrick, Carl Erhardt, Johnny Coward, Gerry Davey; front row – Jimmy Borland, Art Child, Jimmy Foster, Edgar Brenchley. Not shown is Bob Wyman.

PHOTOGRAPHS: TOPFOTO

Objections were briefly raised by Canada's officials in Garmisch-Partenkirchen concerning the eligibility of the two suspended players but were dropped in a spirit of goodwill. This gesture might have soon been regretted because the British repaid it by winning 2–1 – which, remarkably, was to be Canada's only loss in 41 Olympic matches between 1924 and 1952 – and that was enough eventually to earn the gold, even though Britain also drew two of their seven matches and Canada won all their other seven. The oldest British gold-medallist, and still the oldest man from any country to win ice-hockey gold, was the team captain, Carl Erhardt, who celebrated his thirty-ninth birthday the day before the final. He had been born in Kent but learned the game at school in Germany and Switzerland and was an all-round sportsman who later founded the British Water Ski Federation. An 18-year-old team-mate, Jack Kilpatrick, is still the youngest ever ice-hockey winner.

The Summer Olympics opened on 1 August, and the first four days of competition produced no British champions in any sport, nor any medallists. So it was maybe with a sense of irony that the opening words from the correspondent for *The Times* in the edition for Thursday 6 August were the following: 'Great Britain won their first championship and Jesse Owens his third in the Stadium to-day'. While the great American sprinter was adding the 200 metres gold to those for the 100 metres and long jump already in his possession, Harold Whitlock was retaining the 50 kilometres walk title for Britain with his usual immaculate mode of progression. It was said of him that he was 'a very conscientious man who had made walking a real study' and that he was 'Guardsman-like in stride and action'.

On parade through the streets of Berlin, Whitlock had coped with both the showers of rain overhead and the slippery cobbles underfoot better than any of his 28 opponents from 16 countries, to win by some 1½ minutes in a time that was only three seconds different to that which he had achieved in the national championship a month before. Whitlock was a motor mechanic by profession, and after his first race-walking success of note in 1932 he had won the London-to-Brighton for four successive years, becoming in 1935 the first man to break eight hours in setting a time of 7:53:50 which would not be beaten until 1956 – and it would take Britain's next Olympic walking champion, Don Thompson, to do it. Whitlock also won the European 50 kilometres title in 1938 and returned after the war to compete again in the 1952 Olympics, placing eleventh as his brother, Rex, was fourth. Harold Whitlock remains one of the revered figures of race-walking, continuing to serve the sport for the rest of his life as secretary and then president of Britain's Race Walking Association, and writing a definitive manual about technique and training. Gratifyingly, at the age of 56, he would be chief judge for the 1960 Olympic 50 kilometres walk which brought a gold medal for Don Thompson.

Whitlock competed in an era when walking was a national pastime that could even make headline news. In 1932 a mass public trespass was organised of Kinder Scout, the highest point in the Peak District, which led to a confrontation with the Duke of Devonshire's gamekeepers, and access to the countryside became a popular issue, with a *Daily Herald* journalist, Tom Stephenson, among the leading campaigners and responsible for the eventual opening of the Pennine Way. A national council of walking enthusiasts had been formed in 1931 and this became the Ramblers' Association in 1935, with more than 300 affiliated clubs. A standard part of the training programme for British athletes was a Sunday walk, often lasting four hours, and Whitlock's fellow gold-medallist in Berlin, Bill Roberts, was a devotee. He worked in a timber-yard alongside the Manchester Ship Canal, eventually becoming manager, and he long remembered his regular weekend excursions to the Peak District:

> I'd go rambling out in the countryside beyond Manchester, and the reason so many of us did it was just to have one day away from all that grime and noise. When you got out there it was well worth it. On a Saturday night we'd catch the last train out of Hyde, and we'd walk all night and reach Kinder Scout just as it was getting light. If we got held up because of the weather we'd end up sleeping the Sunday night on the railway station at Glossop and getting the first train home in the morning. We'd take our lemonade and our sandwiches with us in a rucksack, and I suppose it all sounds very simple now, but very few of us had cars and we didn't have television. We made our own pleasures and they had to be cheap.

Roberts was the non-establishment odd man out in a British 4 × 400 metres relay team which astonished everybody by beating the Americans for Olympic gold, winning the final easily. His colleagues were Godfrey Brown, an undergraduate at Cambridge; Freddy Wolff, who was an executive in his grandfather's firm of London commodity brokers; and Godfrey Rampling, who was a lieutenant in the Royal Artillery. Roberts had left school at 14 to start his timber-yard work as an apprentice, and, inspired by the example of Walter Rangeley, who had won three medals at 200 metres and the 4 × 100 metres relay at the Games of 1924 and 1928, had joined the local Salford Athletic Club. Their training venue was the city's rugby-league ground until they were evicted and had to make do with the canal footpath instead.

In the individual 400 metres in Berlin the world-record holder, Archie Williams, had won for the USA by the narrowest of margins from Brown, while Roberts had lost the bronze equally slenderly to another American, Jimmy Lu Valle. Yet when it came to the relay neither Williams nor Lu Valle was selected, which was not entirely unexpected because the US team management had made a habit of bringing in reserves for this event ever since the 1924 Games, and as they had won the gold medals each time, including setting the current world record in 1932, the policy could be justified. On this occasion, however, they were to be proved over-confident.

Wolff, not at his best because of a tooth infection, was ten metres down on the leaders, Canada, at the end of the first stage, but Rampling ran magnificently to get to the front by two or three metres at halfway. Years later he was to recall fondly, 'On that day in Berlin I just seemed to float round the track, passing people without effort'. Then came Roberts, who gained more precious metres, and Brown was to pay him fulsome tribute: 'The film of Bill running the final bend is the most superb bit of quarter-miling I have ever seen.

Godfrey Rampling passes the baton to Bill Roberts, and the Great Britain team is on its way to victory in the 1936 4 × 400 metres relay. Roberts set the fastest time in the race, 46.4 seconds, and the British won by some 15 metres from the USA. Freddy Wolff had run the opening stage and Roberts would hand over to Godfrey Brown. Britain had won this event once previously, in 1920, but has not done so at any other Games since that 1936 triumph.

TOPFOTO

It really ought to be studied. So relaxed! So powerful! It just broke the American up and Bill came away, giving me about five or six yards.' That was enough to start with, and Brown crossed the line so far ahead – 15 metres or so – that it is questionable whether even at full strength the Americans could have seriously challenged for gold.

In 1986, half a century after their triumph, Roberts and Brown were re-united for the first time in many years at a press reception and their splendidly spirited conversation was thankfully recorded. Roberts said to Brown: 'I'm glad we've met again, Godfrey. I never thought we'd see each other until we got to heaven or the other place.'

Brown responded, 'Bill, you don't think the Almighty would separate us, do you? No, he'd thrust a golden baton in your hand and say, "Right, Roberts! Away you bloody well go!"'

Bill Roberts never forgot that day of glory in Berlin. He died in 2001 at the age of 89 and a few days beforehand he startled his stepson by suddenly sitting up in bed and copying a running action by swinging his arms vigorously backwards and forwards. 'This is how we won the gold medal,' he announced. 'I never looked back. Then it was up to him to take the baton from me.'

The Berlin quartet had done great credit to what was a solid tradition for the event – Britain had been third in 1912, first in 1920, third in 1924, second in 1932 – and there would be four more sets of silver medals and two of bronze to come in ensuing years, but never another Olympic victory. In 1991 the British did manage to beat the Americans again at the World Championships, which had been introduced eight years before, and the record-breaking anchor man, Roger Black, readily recognised his heritage. 'Perhaps the big difference between my era and that of the 1930s is that now we all train and race in favourable circumstances,' he later wrote. 'I had all-weather tracks, the lightest-weight shoes, expert coaching, full medical back-up, and the other great advantage of being good enough to earn a living in the sport which was denied to previous generations. I marvel at the fact that runners like Brown and Roberts could run as fast as they did all those years ago. Under 47 seconds on cinder tracks is good going by anybody's standards, and I was proud to follow in that succession.' The times of 46.68 and 46.87 by Brown and Roberts respectively in the individual event in Berlin were not beaten by another Briton until 1958.

Brown became headmaster of Worcester Royal Grammar School from 1950 to 1978, while Roberts managed his family's furniture business, with a profitable line in selling second-hand upright pianos to customers in the USA. The pair of them remain among the very finest 400 metres runners in British athletics history, as Brown went on to win the European Championships 400 metres and Roberts the British Empire Games 440 yards in 1938, and both resumed their disrupted track careers after the Second World War, with Roberts, at the age of 36, chosen to captain the British athletics team at the 1948 Olympic Games. Roberts was by no means dedicated monastically to athletics, playing the guitar and leading a dance band, Billy Roberts and his Collegians, in his spare time and having taken to smoking a pipe. The latter habit led to an unexpectedly dramatic interlude during his rousing speech at the Olympic team's headquarters at the RAF camp at Uxbridge, in Middlesex, as he waved his arms vigorously to emphasise a point and accidentally set light to a box of matches in his jacket pocket.

There was every good reason for British satisfaction regarding another track victory in Berlin. Jack Lovelock won the 1500 metres for New Zealand in world-record time and was to all intents and purposes a British 'product'. Born of an English father and brought up in New Zealand, he had arrived at Oxford University to take up a scholarship in 1931 with some modest reputation as a miler, having placed third in the New Zealand championships, and came under the wing of Jerry Cornes, the 1500 metres silver-medallist in Los Angeles. Within two years Lovelock had set a world record for the mile of 4 minutes 7.6 seconds, and when his diaries were published more than 70 years after his Olympic triumph, the editor, David Colquhoun, made the pertinent observation that Lovelock would have been 'unlikely to have become world-class had he stayed in the backwaters

New Zealand-born of English parents, Jack Lovelock won the 1500 metres gold for his native country in 1936 but had developed his talents to world-record level while studying medicine at Oxford University. In this photograph of the Berlin final Eric Ny (Sweden) leads from Lovelock, Glenn Cunningham (USA), Luigi Beccali (Italy), Phil Edwards (Canada) and Jerry Cornes (GB). Cunningham finished second and Beccali, who was the defending champion, was third.

TOPFOTO

of New Zealand athletics'. Lovelock's conqueror in the AAA mile a few weeks before the Berlin final, Sydney Wooderson, was indeed carrying an injury, as had been suspected, and finished last in his heat.

The teenage Dorothy Odam very narrowly lost the high-jump gold, clearing the same height of 1.60 metres as the Hungarian winner, Ibolya Csák, but was beaten in a jump-off. Had modern-day rules applied, Miss Odam would have been the winner as she had got over 1.60 at the first attempt in the competition proper and Miss Csák had done so only at her second attempt before both failed three times at 1.62. The same Briton, now Mrs Dorothy Tyler, would be second again at the 1948 Olympics to Alice Coachman, of the USA, both clearing 1.68, but the American doing so first time and Mrs Tyler second time. Competing also at the Games of 1952 and 1956, Mrs Tyler falls short of being one of Britain's greatest ever Olympic athletes – by almost nothing at all.

The other two British gold medals at the 1936 Games came in rowing on a tributary of the river Spree and in yachting at Kiel, and both were close-run affairs.

The British double scullers were Jack Beresford, appearing in his fifth Olympic Games, and Dick Southwood (PLATE I), a jeweller by profession whose oarsmanship had first been spotted at a local club by Beresford. Southwood had reached the Olympic single sculls final in 1932 but had suffered an attack of cramp and had finished last. By modern standards both he and Beresford were of puny build – Beresford weighed no more than 11 stone (70 kg); 60 years later in Atlanta Steve Redgrave would tip the scales at 16 stone (102 kg). In their qualifying heat Beresford and Southwood were beaten by a length or so by the Germans but then overwhelmed the opposition in the repechage for losing crews, already leading by seven lengths at 600 metres. Beresford, whose touch with the pen was almost as deft as with the oar, more than 30 years later recounted his swansong Olympic experience alongside Southwood:

We were both pretty tough and mature, with the confidence and will-to-win well ingrained in us, and with ten months' practice behind us and 2,000 miles in the boat, plus daily early-morning running and exercises, we were strong and fit. In our first race the Germans were very fast off the mark, and their tactics were to get ahead and then edge over and 'line' us, i.e. scull dead in front of us, giving us their wash. This they succeeded in doing, and the other four countries were so far behind that the single umpire in the launch wasn't able to control the course of the two leaders. At the finish we had to ease up or we would have bumped them and damaged our boat. So we just smiled and made no comment after the race.

In that final, beside Britain were Germany, Poland, France, USA and Australia. We were determined to stay with those Germans, but even at halfway they led by 1½ lengths, with the other countries out of the hunt. At this point we challenged for the lead and went on doing so until they 'blew up'. We literally gained foot-by-foot for the next 800 metres until at the 1800 metres mark we were dead level. And so we raced to the 1900 metres mark with blades almost clashing, as they had tried the old game of trying to 'line' us – but not again! Right in front of Hitler's box the Germans cracked and we went on to win by 2½ lengths.

Remarkably, Beresford and Southwood had not raced together at all until they went to Berlin because there were no double sculls events open to them in Britain, and they would only ever do so once more after the Games, at Henley in 1939. Germany had won all of the first five of the seven Olympic rowing finals that afternoon, including putting an end to the sequence of four successive British wins in the coxless fours, and then lost the eights by less than a second to the Washington University crew from the USA. Among the British journalists reporting on the regatta was Hylton Cleaver, whose writing in *Punch*, *Picture Post* and the London *Evening Standard* was highly regarded, and he said of Beresford, 'It did not matter what boat you put him in or what sort of rig you gave him, he seemed to have the flair for success'.

In 1936 the six-metre yachting, which Britain had won in 1908, was contested over a series of seven races, and though the British crew did not win any of them, and were beaten in five by the Norwegians, the latter's failure to complete the course on the opening day cost them the gold. Before the final race Britain had 56 points to 55 for Sweden and 54 for Norway, and Norway won again but Britain's second place pulled the gold out of the fire. The reaction of the gold-medal winners was surprisingly muted, hinting at some skulduggery. 'On the whole we did not form a high opinion of Olympic yacht racing in our own class [Six Metres] because, due to over-keenness, feeling tended to run high,' wrote the joint owner of the winning yacht, Charles Leaf, afterwards.

Leaf, who was of private means, had contributed an account of the yachting events for the British Olympic Association's official report of the Games, and considering the reticence of that era to discuss contentious matters in the press he was astonishingly

The six-metre yachting at the 1936 Games was held in stormy weather in the Baltic Sea off the port of Kiel. The British boat is on the far left of this photo and the crew went on to win the gold, despite not finishing first in any of the seven races. The owner, Charles Leaf, was of independent means and was a member of numerous yachting clubs. According to the official report, 'On the stormy days the six-metre boats had to struggle against great odds.'
PHOTOGRAPH FROM THE OFFICIAL REPORT OF THE 1936 GAMES

forthright in his criticism of Britain's yachting officialdom. Complaining bitterly of the lack of a non-sailing captain to deal with the myriad on-shore administrative matters, he stated: 'It is to be feared that the outlook of our national authority is no more than parochial, and this is greatly to be regretted nowadays when people are expected to be able to see an inch or two beyond the ends of their own noses. The lack of such a man put a most unfair strain on the personnel, who after a hard day's racing were kept running about on shore until late at night.'

Like Leaf, the other members of the winning 6-metre crew of five all came from a distinctly upper middle-class background. Miles Bellville, a gentleman farmer, was to win the Military Cross in 1942 as a major in the Royal Marine Commandos and was later appointed sheriff of Hereford. Christopher Boardman (namesake of but no relation to the 1992 British cycling gold-medallist) was a director of the family firm of mustard manufacturers known in every household in Britain, Colman's, and was helmsman in Berlin. Boardman, Bellville and a third crew-member, Leonard Martin, who worked in his family's wholesale tobacco business, had taken part in the America's Cup races of 1934, and Boardman had been a contemporary of Charles Leaf's at Trinity College, Cambridge. Russell Harmer was managing director of the wholesale clothing business established by his father, Sir Sidney Harmer.

The team events which had brought gold in the past – football, polo, water-polo – were of no great consequence for Britain at these Games. The footballers, returning to the tournament after staying away since 1920 because of differing opinions regarding payment to amateur players of compensation for loss of wages, beat China 2–0 but then lost to Poland 5–4 and were out of the tournament. The polo team came away with the silver medals, but as there were no more than five nations entered, and the standards varied so considerably that two of them, Germany and Hungary, were seeded only to contest third place, this was not the notable performance that it might have seemed – especially as Great Britain lost the final to Argentina 11–0. In water-polo the British team was beaten in only three of their seven matches and drew two but were swamped 10–1 by the eventual champions, Hungary, who had also won the gold medals in 1932 and would do so again on seven further occasions through to 2008.

The British water-polo team manager, John Hodgson, concluded sorrowfully in his official report that 'Hungary, Germany, Sweden, Holland and Czechoslovakia, by virtue of evolution upon British ideas and standards, brought fresh movements and intelligence into action which enabled them to succeed against countries where progress has not penetrated so rapidly'. Such 'fresh movements and intelligence' would provide hard lessons for Britain to learn in the years to come across a wide range of sports, but this would all have to wait for the time being. Three years after the Berlin Games closed the Second World War broke out and the proposed Olympic Games of 1940 (Helsinki) and 1944 (London) were, not surprisingly, cancelled.

No new facilities were built for the 'austerity' Games of 1948 in London. Instead, a track was installed for the athletics events at Wembley Stadium, famous as the venue for the annual FA Cup Final, and immediately taken up afterwards so that greyhound-racing – the lucrative main source of revenue for the stadium's owners – could be resumed.

TOPFOTO

84

SEVEN

The London Games of 1948

Oh, by the way, the man from *The Times* says he won the gold safely

T H E president of the International Olympic Committee, J. Sigfrid Edström, was generous to a fault in his appraisal. 'The great test was taken and the organisation rose gloriously to the supreme challenge,' he wrote in the official report of the 1948 Olympic Games. 'The visitors were housed and fed; the athletes were made at home in camps where every care was taken of their waking and sleeping hours.' He expanded his theme in ever more effusive mood, with even a touch of humour: 'Wembley Stadium itself, where day after day huge crowds assembled, surpassed in magnificence and convenience any previous home of the Games. All the other Olympic venues, too, were splendidly organised both from the spectators' and the competitors' point of view. Torquay I found much nicer than Nice; Henley recaptured the atmosphere of the old, old days; while at Aldershot and Sandhurst competitions went on in the friendliest manner.' His conclusion was unequivocal: 'On behalf of the International Olympic Committee and all participants at the Games I say a hearty "Thank You" to Great Britain.'

Perhaps it was with a sense of relief as much as euphoria that Edström penned these words, but he could be forgiven for that. In 1948, just three years after the end of the Second World War, London was still battered and bruised. In many ways it was neither a logical nor a sensible choice to stage the Games in that year. There were numerous other eager venues far better prepared, not least in neutral Sweden, which was Edström's country of birth, or Switzerland, where the IOC had its headquarters. Half-a-dozen cities in the USA were also clamouring for attention ... but none of these had the sentimental virtue of having stood alone against the onslaught of Hitler's Luftwaffe. Before hostilities had broken out London had already been chosen for what would have been the 1944 Games (which were cancelled, of course), and the date on the permit was simply altered by one digit. To all intents and purposes, Edström, sustaining the IOC almost single-handed during the war years, made the decision of his own initiative.

No new facilities were built for London 1948, simply because none could be afforded. Wembley Stadium was hired for the opening and closing ceremonies and a track temporarily laid for the athletics events, with the owner, Arthur Elvin, compensated handsomely for the lucrative greyhound-racing fixtures which had to be suspended in the interim. The seas off the Devon coast provided a ready-made setting for the yachting events, and the stretch of the Thames given over each year to the Henley Royal Regatta hosted the rowing and canoeing. Schools, colleges and military camps were turned into temporary hostels for the visitors. A potential debacle was narrowly avoided when the Games' organisers were finally persuaded, late in the day, by experienced gymnastics officials that it would not be a good idea in view of the unpredictable British summer weather to risk holding that sport outdoors at Wembley, and the events were hastily switched to the exhibition space at the nearby Empress Hall. The total cost of the Games was £761,688, equivalent to some £77 million in today's money, and a neat little profit of £29,420 (about £3 million now) was made.

Germany and Japan were not invited to take part. Perhaps from some points of view this appeared understandable, but at the very least it could be viewed as unethical according to Olympic ideals, and it may even have been illegal. The USSR stayed away, reportedly on Stalin's orders after he had been informed by the country's quaking sports leaders that they could not guarantee the Soviet team winning everything for which they were entered. Nevertheless, the women's long jump and nine other gold medals were won by Hungary (allies of Germany from 1941 onwards), and the women's javelin by Austria (annexed by Germany from 1938 to 1945), while a former German Army infantryman from Alsace – press-ganged into service – took a decathlon bronze medal for France. Another Frenchman, who was of Jewish origin, had survived the horrors of Auschwitz to compete in swimming as he had in 1936. A British bronze-medallist in weight-lifting, Jim Halliday, had endured four years in a Japanese forced-labour camp. Another German connection was that Britain's gymnasts, who were allowed to train with makeshift equipment in a London brewery basement, received technical guidance from a German prisoner-of-war, Helmut Bantz; in 1948 he went unlisted in the Games credits but was to earn a place in Olympic chronicles with an individual gold medal for his native land eight years later.

At the 1936 Games Great Britain had won 14 medals, ranking tenth overall. In 1948, with 59 countries taking part, which was ten more than in Berlin, the British had 23 medals, behind the USA (84), Sweden (44), France (29), Hungary and Italy (27 each). Considering the deprivations of the war, and the fact that most foodstuffs were still tightly rationed in 1948, this seemed a very fair return. Prospective Olympic competitors had actually fared a morsel or two better than the average citizen because they had been given extra ration coupons for some months beforehand. At least one of the medallists, however – the durable 48-year-old Tebbs Lloyd Johnson, who had been competing for 28 years and who won bronze in the 50 kilometres road walk – had not been regarded by the authorities as an Olympic contender and so had received no enhancement to his meal-time régime. Stoically he later remarked that, 'I honestly think that if the monotony of such a diet could be overcome, one could perfectly well train on bread, butter and jam'.

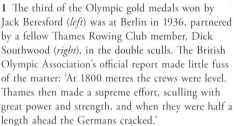

1 The third of the Olympic gold medals won by Jack Beresford (*left*) was at Berlin in 1936, partnered by a fellow Thames Rowing Club member, Dick Southwood (*right*), in the double sculls. The British Olympic Association's official report made little fuss of the matter: 'At 1800 metres the crews were level. Thames then made a supreme effort, sculling with great power and strength, and when they were half a length ahead the Germans cracked.'

2 Ken Matthews upheld the tradition of British success with his success in the 20 kilometre walk in Tokyo in 1964. By the time this photograph was taken he had left his nearest challenger, Dieter Lindner, of Democratic Germany, more than half a minute behind. Britain has had no further Olympic race-walking medals of any kind since the 1964 Games.

3 Seemingly with little excess effort Ann Packer wins the 1964 Olympic 800 metres from Maryvonne Dupureur, of France, and Marise Chamberlain, of New Zealand. Packer's time beat the official world record, even though she had had very limited experience of the event before the Games. She had also won silver at 400 metres and her husband-to-be, Robbie Brightwell, would add a relay silver, but both retired at the season's end. Amateur athletes in those days needed to earn a living elsewhere.

4 One of the most decisive victories in Olympic track history. That was the measure of David Hemery's win at 400 metres hurdles in the Games of 1968. Yet, although he finished six metres or so ahead of the German silver-medallist, Gerhard Hennige, he was still not sure as he crossed the finish-line that he had actually taken the gold. The one previous British winner of this event had been Lord Burghley 40 years earlier in a time more than five seconds slower.
BY COURTESY OF MARK SHEARMAN

5 Jim Fox, competing in his fourth Olympics, was the most experienced man in the British trio who won team gold for the modern pentathlon in Montreal in 1976, but the fencing – in which he is seen in action (*left*) – was a traumatic experience along the way. In a bout with Fox the double Olympic silver-medallist, Boris Onischenko, of the USSR, was found to have cheated. Before the closing cross-country race, Britain was still only fifth in the team standings, but Adrian Parker took first place and Danny Nightingale fourth, valiantly supported by Fox, to snatch the gold.
BY COURTESY OF MARK SHEARMAN

6 The 1500 metres – the final event of the decathlon in Moscow, 1980. The lesser athletes have finished, and Daley Thompson comes in only tenth fastest in this discipline with a time of 4 minutes 39.9 seconds, but it is more than enough to have won the gold medal by 164 points from Yuriy Kutsenko, of the USSR. Thompson's opening achievements over the two days of competition had been 10.62 seconds for 100 metres and 8.00 metres in the long jump which had already given him a healthy advantage over his twenty opponents.

BY COURTESY OF MARK SHEARMAN

7 Allan Wells won the 100 metres at the 1980 Games and very nearly completed the sprint double, losing the 200 metres by only 0.02 seconds to Pietro Mennea of Italy. Wells had taken the 100 metres gold even more narrowly, sharing the same time of 10.25 seconds as Silvio Leonard of Cuba. The Americans were missing from these Games in Moscow because of a political boycott, but Wells beat the best of them, Stanley Floyd, immediately afterwards. In this photograph Wells beats Don Quarrie, of Jamaica, the 1976 Olympic 200 metres champion, in the first-round heats of the 100 metres in Moscow.

BY COURTESY OF MARK SHEARMAN

8 Gold is won in Los Angeles, but even for Sebastian Coe, Olympic champion at 1500 metres for the second time, perhaps it takes some little while to realise the fact fully. His Olympic experiences had not always been happy ones – beaten by Steve Ovett at 800 metres in the 1980 Games after running a tactically naïve race.

9 Sebastian Coe wins the 1984 Los Angeles 1500 metres from fellow-Briton Steve Cram (almost obscured in this photograph), with the red-vested José Abascal, of Spain, a distant third and Joseph Chesire, of Kenya, fourth. Coe thus became only the second man to retain an Olympic 1500 metres title and, more significantly, the only one to do so since the very different era of 1904–06.

10 Moscow 1980. The satisfied smile of success. Steve Ovett had first run the Olympic 800 metres in 1976 when at the age of 20 he had finished a highly promising fifth. In Moscow Sebastian Coe had been the favourite for that event, but Ovett proved the master of strategy and took the gold, helping to explain the happy expression in this photograph. It was the sixth Olympic success by a Briton at 800 metres after the consecutive wins of Albert Hill (1920), Douglas Lowe (1924–28) and Tommy Hampson (1932), and then Ann Packer's victory of 1964.

11 Four years after his first Olympic triumph Daley Thompson was in even better decathlon form. At the 1984 Los Angeles Games he broke the world record. His effort in the shot was a personal best 15.72 metres, and he had earlier run 100 metres in 10.44 seconds and long jumped 8.01 metres to take an immediate lead, as he had in Moscow. His sprinting ability was such that he was also a member of the Great Britain team that reached the final of the 4 × 100 metres relay.

BY COURTESY OF MARK SHEARMAN

12 No British woman had ever placed better than seventh in the Olympic javelin throw, but Tessa Sanderson won in 1984, with Fatima Whitbread third. Enjoying the celebrations with Sanderson (*far right*) and Whitbread are Wilf Paish, coach to Sanderson, and Whitbread's mother, Margaret, herself a former Great Britain international in the javelin.

BY COURTESY OF MARK SHEARMAN

13 Jayne Torvill and Christopher Dean, with Ravel's *Bolero* as their iconic theme, transported ice-dancing to a higher plane. They were awarded maximum scores of 6.0 for artistic impression from all nine judges at the 1983 world championships and again at the Olympics the following year. A month later they became world champions for the fourth successive time in the same supreme manner and then turned professional.

14 Duncan Goodhew wins the 100 metres breaststroke at the 1980 Games, but there was neither proud flag raised nor stirring national anthem played at his medal ceremony because of the British government's opposition to the Soviet presence in Afghanistan. This, of course, was just one more example of the way in which, whether the Games organisers and competitors liked it or not, politics was intruding into sport.

15 Malcolm Cooper was another of Britain's double Olympic champions of the 1980s. Having won the small-bore rifle three positions event in 1984, he triumphed again in Seoul in 1988, and it was another Briton who pressed him closest. Here Cooper is joined by silver-medallist Alister Allan (*left*) and bronze-medallist Kiril Ivanov, of the USSR (*right*). The scores were desperately close: Cooper 1,279.3, Allen 1,275.6, Ivanov 1,275.

BY COURTESY OF MARK SHEARMAN

16 Britain had not won an Olympic hockey title since 1920, but in 1988 in Seoul the British performances gradually got better and Australia were beaten 3–2 in the semi-finals and Germany 3–1 in the final. Sean Kerly, seen here taking on two Koreans in a qualifying match that was drawn 2–2, scored all three goals against the Australians and 8 of Britain's total of 15.

BY COURTESY OF MARK SHEARMAN

17 The British seemed to have developed a special affection for breaststroke swimming. Adrian Moorhouse won at 100 metres in 1988, and of the 14 Olympic titles by swimmers from Great Britain since 1900 six were for this particular technique. Moorhouse was also the model of consistency: he set a world record of 1 minute 01.49 seconds in 1989 and equalled it twice the next year.

BY COURTESY OF MARK SHEARMAN

18 Oh so familiar a photograph! An Olympic rowing victory ceremony, and Steve Redgrave (*left*) and Matthew Pinsent (*right*) pose proudly with their gold medals. There were still more such occasions to come because this coxless pairs presentation was at Atlanta in 1996 – Redgrave's fourth gold medal, with another to add in 2000; Pinsent's second, with two more in 2000 and 2004.
TOPFOTO

19 Linford Christie wins the 1992 Barcelona 100 metres to become the third British Olympic champion in the event after Harold Abrahams in 1924 and Allan Wells in 1980. Christie said afterwards that at 60 metres he knew that the gold medal was his, and the intermediate times prove it. By then he led by 0.02 seconds. By 80 metres he led by 0.04 seconds. He won by 0.06 seconds.
BY COURTESY OF MARK SHEARMAN

What was odd about Britain's tally of medals was that fourteen of them were silver and only three gold, and a considered, reflective article in the political and current affairs weekly magazine, *The Spectator*, seemed to catch the national mood of phlegmatic acceptance: 'This time we were bound to be losers, just as we were due to be hosts, and it is perhaps not presumptuous to say that we showed up reasonably well in both capacities.' The near misses (literally so) had included no fewer than four in women's athletics, at 100 metres, 200 metres, 80 metres hurdles (all of them behind 'The Flying Dutchwoman', Fanny Blankers-Koen) and the high jump, plus the men's marathon and 4 × 100 metres relay. There were further second places in boxing (two), cycling (three), hockey and weight-lifting, but it was on the water that the gold was gained. At Henley the double sculls event was won by Richard Burnell and Bertie Bushnell, thus retaining for Britain the title from 1936, and the coxless pairs by Jack Wilson and 'Ran' Laurie; there was also a silver medal in the eights. At Torbay the Swallow class yachting title went to Stewart Morris, who had been a reserve for Berlin, and his crew-man, David Bond.

The Henley triumphs were achieved in the typically off-hand British manner which had somehow got them through the war. It was almost as if the small boats had sailed to the country's rescue again, just as they had done at Dunkirk in 1940. It helped, too, that the team manager had plenty of battle-front experience: Ewart Horsfall, gold-medallist in the eights in 1908 and silver-medallist in 1920, had occupied himself in between times by winning both the Military Cross ('an act or acts of exemplary gallantry') with the Rifle Brigade and then the Distinguished Flying Cross ('an act or acts of valour, courage and devotion to duty') with the RAF.

Burnell and Bushnell had come together merely five weeks before the Games. Only a couple of months earlier than that Wilson and Laurie (the latter was the father of the actor, Hugh Laurie, who was himself a junior international oarsman) had re-formed their successful partnership of a decade earlier. Burnell was the rowing correspondent for *The Times*, which was bizarrely no bar to his competing as an amateur, and his report the following day was a masterpiece of stiff-upper-lip under-statement. 'Bushnell and myself, of Great Britain, won safely': that was the sum total of his account of the final! Such was the complexity (some might say hypocrisy) of the rules regarding amateurism in rowing that while Burnell wielded oar and pen in the same cause, Bushnell had perforce to find employment elsewhere than in his family's Thames-side boat-yard business in order to be regarded as acceptable by the hierarchy: otherwise, as a boat-builder he would have been deemed a professional for the purposes of competitive rowing.

Burnell and Bushnell led all the way in their final, and the reporter for the *Manchester Guardian*, for one, was rather more expansive than Burnell had been, writing of 'Burnell supplying the horse-power and Bushnell the expertise, verve and watermanship'. There was some good excuse for Burnell's blasé attitude to his Olympic success, above and beyond the natural tendency of correspondents for *The Times* in those days not to get too over-excited. For winning gold was something of a family pastime: Burnell's father, Charles, had rowed in the eight at the 1908 Olympics; Burnell's father-in-law, Stanley Garton, had been in the eight of 1912.

The national anthem is played alongside the Thames as Richard Burnell (*left*) and the bespectacled Bertie Bushnell savour the moment after their Olympic double sculls victory at Henley in 1948. It was a successful defence of the title that had been won for Britain by Jack Beresford and Dick Southwood at the previous Games of 1936. The nearest approaches by Britons since in this event have been silver in 1976 and bronze in 2008.

Another rowing gold for Britain in 1948. Jack Wilson and Ran Laurie pass the packed Thames-side grandstands to win the coxless pairs with enough time in hand to look across at the opposition – the winning margin over Switzerland was almost three seconds, as Italy trailed third. It would be forty years before Steve Redgrave and Andy Holmes gained the next British gold in this event.

PHOTOGRAPHS: TOPFOTO

Even more exotic was the story of Wilson and Laurie. They had won the coxless pairs at Henley in 1938 while on leave from the Sudan Government Service which they had joined two years before, and in the course of their subsequent duties back in Africa they occasionally rowed together for fun on the nearest suitable river. Their hazardous diplomatic duties had included negotiations with the armed Abyssinian rebels who were opposing the invading Italian forces in 1940. Like Richard Burnell, who had been a member of the Oxford crew in the 1939 Boat Race, Wilson and Laurie were both 'Oxbridge' trained, having been together in the winning Cambridge boat in 1934/35/36. Laurie, whose four first names were William George Ranald Mundell, had also been in the Great Britain crew which had come fourth in the Berlin Olympic eights.

At the 1948 London Games the Henley Olympic rowing finals were held on the afternoon of Monday 9 August, and by then Britain had still not won a title in any of the 17 sports. The success of Wilson and Laurie in the second of the nine events, starting as favourites and beating Switzerland and Italy, was thus the victory that the whole nation craved, but the man from *The Times*, watching from the towpath as he awaited his own event, again refused to get over-excited. 'Their Olympic performance was a beautiful example of British rowing at its best,' he simply wrote. The old champion, Jack Beresford, commenting from his standpoint as a coach and umpire, was rather more voluble in his appreciation. Of the series of victory ceremonies he enthused, 'Weary shoulders were braced, tired legs straightened, as those lithe figures stood to attention in honour of their country. For weeks and months these young oarsmen had trained, had dedicated every moment of their lives that they might at Henley give of their best to strive to win the greatest rowing honours in the World.'

Torquay might be a considerable distance from London, but during the war it had also been in the thick of it, suffering no fewer than 700 air-raid alerts. The yachting courses in Torbay offered what was described by an expert writer, John Scott Hughes, in his Games preview as 'some special qualities which are not found in combination elsewhere; at any rate, not in British waters. For one thing, it is a splendid expanse of open water, freer than most yachting centres of tide, currents and obstructions of one sort or another which may be turned to helpful advantage by the seaman with local knowledge.' Recognising that his was also a highly sociable sport, Scott Hughes added helpfully, 'The towns close at hand – Torquay itself, Paignton, Brixham and historic Dartmouth – afford the accommodation and entertainment which visiting yachtsmen would wish to enjoy'.

The favoured British entrants were Durward Knowles and Sloan Farrington, who had won the world title for the Star class in 1947 and had then been first home in four of the five selection races in Torbay. Yet neither of them had been born in Britain, nor ever lived there. They were from the crown colony of the Bahamas, but as their native islands did not have an Olympic Committee of their own the pair was free to compete for Britain as welcome Empire recruits. As it happens, Knowles and Farrington's star was slightly on the wane and they ended up fourth as not a single gold in any of the five classes was decided until the last of the seven days of hectic racing. None of these classes was more furiously contested than that for the Swallow, a class being held for the one and only time at these

Games, in which 14 crews started – from Argentina, Brazil, Canada, Denmark, France, Great Britain, Holland, Ireland, Italy, Norway, Portugal, Sweden, Uruguay and the USA.

Having placed third, first, third and first again in the opening four races, Stewart Morris and David Bond seemed to be on safe passage to gold, but then the Bello brothers, who had been born in Portuguese East Africa (later Mozambique), narrowed the British lead from 949 points to a mere 100 going into the closing race. Morris and Bond needed to finish at worst in fourth place to take the gold, and this they did – but only by 14 seconds after languishing eleventh earlier on. In their seven outings the Britons had been on the water for a total of 95 hours 13 minutes 3 seconds. Yet even though this was but the third victory by Britain at the Games the media response was tepid. The *Daily Mail* gave only the results and no description. *The Times* allocated three terse sentences. The *Manchester Guardian* briefly extolled Morris's 'unconcerned consistency'.

Television coverage went almost entirely unremarked at these Games. By this date in Britian only some 48,000 television licences had yet been issued, although the single viewer in the Channel Islands, where reception was erratic, wrote later to the BBC complimenting them on their 'pictures of excellent entertainment value'. BBC Radio provided an altogether more immediate service, rising to its biggest outside-broadcasting challenge since its foundation in the 1920s, and with some 11 million homes to serve. No fewer than 32 commentary positions were set up at Wembley Stadium alone, and scheduled programmes were regularly interrupted between 3 p.m. and 6.45 p.m. to bring listeners the highlights of the Games. Harold Abrahams was one of the athletics commentary team, while the urbane Max Robertson excelled in describing races fluently and at great tempo.

Stewart Morris, then aged 39, had been competing successfully since 1932 and had won the European Finn title in 1938. He had served as a commander in the Royal Navy Volunteer Reserve during the Second World War, awarded the OBE for his part in the 1944 Normandy landings, and now managed the family hop-growing business. He would continue racing into the 1960s and served the sport in many administrative capacities, having been a member of the Yacht Racing Association Council since 1935. In one particular respect, he was almost the last of a long line – the twenty-third graduate of Trinity College, Cambridge, to have won an Olympic gold medal (eleven in rowing, three each in polo and yachting, two in rackets, one each in athletics, boxing, lawn tennis and shooting), and there would only be two more, Harry Llewellyn and Derek Allhusen, in equestrianism in 1952 and 1968 respectively. Morris's crew-man, David Bond, was an Old Harrovian who served in the RAF ranks as an aircraftsman during the war, later working for the British Aircraft Corporation, from which company he took eight weeks' unpaid leave to prepare for and compete in the Olympics. He then set up as a yacht-builder in his native Cornwall.

The closing ceremony to these 1948 Games bore no resemblance to the orchestrated cavortings and trumpetings to which on these occasions we have now become accustomed. Instead, the simplicity of the afternoon's proceedings served a sterling purpose in banishing all memories of those tarnished militaristic Nazi Olympics of a dozen years and a world war before. The Olympic flame was extinguished and the Olympic flag lowered, folded, and handed on to Helsinki's dignitaries for raising again in four years' time. The British press were almost all delighted with what they had witnessed over the previous fortnight:

'Magnificent in sportsmanship, superb in athletic performance, and admirable in organisation, these Games will pass into a high place in sporting history.' – *Sunday Times*

'It is the guests as much as the hosts who make a party, but we may well feel proud of our share in the wonderful success of the Olympic Games of 1948.' – *The Observer*

'On the athletic track, as on the cricket field, we have in these times to content ourselves with being good losers, taking what consolation we can from these Olympic trophies which we won last week on the river and in the sea. But our recent visitors would, it is believed, readily grant us laurels for the successful organisation of the Games and the way in which Britain's resourcefulness overcame those obvious material difficulties which faced us.' – *Daily Telegraph*

'Great days, great nights – a fortnight of them. We shall think of them, you and I, many times in the years to come. And in our memories we can rightly include the satisfaction of a task well done.' – *World Sports* magazine

Those final words of praise were penned by Denzil Batchelor, one of Britain's most respected sports-writers There was, though, at least one authoritative dissenting voice among his peers. It was that of Hylton Cleaver, who in an entertaining book of memoirs published three years later reflected at length on the ethos of the Games: 'We know that nearly every other country taking part is semi-professional, heavily subsidised by its governments, and as often as not will create an uproar if defeated. But in our own quiet, phlegmatic, insular and almost arrogant way we will pursue our own ideals. No sport is subsidised. Only those who can afford to meet their own expenses can attain championship rank. We start too late to get ready, and we are obsessed by the belief that to win is not the object of taking part.'

Talking of 'taking part', the organisers of the next Games commendably announced in 1949 that 'it is the ardent desire of the Finnish people that at least 64 nations, including Russia, Bulgaria, Romania, Germany and Japan, will compete in Helsinki in 1952'.

Lieutenant Colonel Harry Llewellyn was not the best of Britain's trio of riders in the 1952 equestrian Prix des Nations event, but he was the last of them to enter the arena and he and his mount, 'Foxhunter', jumped a clear round to bring team victory – the only British gold medal of the entire Games and achieved on the closing day. Wilf White was 5th individually, Duggie Stewart 14th and Llewellyn 15th to win by five faults overall from Chile, 40.75 to 45.75, and 12 other countries.

TOPFOTO

EIGHT

The Games of the 1950s

A last-gasp triumph on horseback as the days of the dilettante finally come to an end

THE TEAM MANAGER was most anxious to set the record straight. 'It's only fair to all concerned to make the following point. Mr W.H. White, on "Nizefella", was the outstanding performer for Britain,' wrote Captain Tony Collings in the British Olympic Association's official report of the 1952 Helsinki Olympics. It was a forlorn gesture, for, by then, several months after the Games, the press clamour had swept Harry Llewellyn to eternal fame.

Britain's victory in the Prix des Nations show-jumping event was the saving grace: the one gold medal to be won in the 16 sports, and achieved on the very last day, followed promptly by the closing ceremony. Two dozen other nations had done better overall at the Games, led by the USA (40 golds) and the USSR (22), as the superpowers faced each other for the first time in Olympic competition. There were actually not that many more medal-winning countries in Helsinki than there had been four years before in London – 43 compared to 37 – but the state-aided Eastern Europeans proved to be the significant new factor in the equation.

As the Finnish hosts had hoped, the USSR did attend the Games, as did the Germans, Japanese, Bulgarians and Romanians. The Iron Curtain phalanx of the USSR, Hungary and Czechoslovakia between them won 45 gold medals and 126 medals in all. Emil Zátopek, the invincible Czech distance runner, was the 'Man of the Games' for his remarkable three victories at 5000 metres, 10,000 metres and the marathon. Germany, divided geographically and politically, was represented only by the Federal Republic (West) and not the Democratic Republic (East), winning no golds but 7 silvers and 17 bronzes. Excluding the flawed St Louis Games of 1904, Britain's single gold, two silvers and eight bronzes was the country's worst ever Olympic display.

In the individual show-jumping Wilfred White finished in fifth position and very close to a gold medal, with the same number of faults registered against him as the French winner. Major Douglas Stewart was fourteenth and Lieutenant-Colonel Harry Llewellyn fifteenth. Very last to enter the arena, however, was Llewellyn and 'Foxhunter'; their faultless clearances took his team from seventh place to first. Hence the British media's outburst of relieved patriotism. Captain Collings, instinctively calling to mind a military metaphor, summed up neatly how the situation appealed to the national psyche: 'It was a question of "sticking it", and as has happened so often in our history it was a matter once again of winning the last battle.'

Harry Llewellyn, from a prosperous South Wales colliery-owning family, was the first Welsh gold-medallist since Jack Ainsworth-Davis in athletics and Chris Jones in water-polo in 1920, and he was yet another British Olympian who had studied at Trinity College, Cambridge. He had been an outstanding steeplechase jockey, finishing second in the 1936 Grand National and fourth the next year. He then served as Field-Marshal Montgomery's chief liaison officer during the war, for which he was awarded the OBE. At the 1948 Olympics he had won show-jumping team bronze.

Knighted in 1977 for services to Wales, Llewellyn rode 'Foxhunter' in 35 competitions for Great Britain. He became chairman of the British Show Jumping Association and a steward of the Jockey Club and frankly admitted that had he prepared his horse more carefully the Helsinki gold would have been won rather more readily. Of 'Foxhunter' he said, 'He was raring to go and jumped a beautiful clear round with great ease, which, of course, he could have done in the morning if I'd had him properly stoked up'.

Wilf White, a Cheshire farmer who was 48 years old at the time of his Olympic success, had a dozen other international team wins between 1949 and 1959 riding 'Nizefella'. Also to be a member of the bronze-medal team at the 1956 Olympics, he continued competing to the age of 70 and was a successful National Hunt trainer and a steward at the Royal Show for 21 years. Duggie Stewart had competed in the three-day event at the 1948 Olympics and had been commanding officer of the Royal Scots Greys in the latter months of the Second World War.

In his brief summary of the various competitions at the Games, the BOA's secretary, Sandy Duncan, himself a former international long jumper and an Inter-Varsity winner for Oxford, was apologetic in every one of the seven paragraphs. The press and the public expected too much, he complained. It's a major achievement even to reach a final, he pleaded. Our facilities and funding are inadequate, he bemoaned. His key criticism maybe needed further explanation than he was prepared to put into print: 'Our governing bodies must decide whether they will, or can, make the all-out effort to train their Olympic teams. The day of the dilettante in international competition is finished.'

None of Britain's medallists could be accused of failing to take their sporting pastimes seriously, and the Trinidad-born sprinter, Emmanuel McDonald Bailey, for instance, lost 100 metres gold by a mere four one-hundredths of a second and had to make do with bronze instead. However, some of the other results were far below what might have been expected at Olympic level in former years. The football tournament was won by the government-supported team from Hungary which would the following year humiliate the full England professional XI, but Great Britain's amateurs could hardly complain of un-level playing fields as they lost their opening match 5–3 to lowly Luxemburg. Hungary also took the water-polo title, while the British, once the masters of the game (that is, more than 30 years before), went out in the first round; the official report said that 'they were obviously individually fit, but what they needed was sufficient team preparation'.

Yet lack of preparedness was not the explanation for failing to win a single medal in a sport in which Britain had done so well in the past. British oarsmen reached five rowing finals, which was an improvement on any previous Games ... but then they came fourth in all of them. Hylton Cleaver, the doyen of rowing correspondents, was mystified: 'The pill was a very bitter one to swallow, for never before had we trained so long and so sensibly for any Olympic regatta.' Nor was it a matter of newly subsidised rivals forging ahead, as only two of those, Czechoslovakia and Yugoslavia, each won a title and the others went to Argentina, France and the USA (two). Nine other countries collected medals, of which the USSR had but two.

The melodrama surrounding Britain's belated show-jumping success in Helsinki obscures the fact that six months before in Oslo Great Britain had already won a gold medal at the Winter Olympics. Jeannette Altwegg was the 21-year-old figure-skating daughter of a British mother and a Swiss father (the latter now a naturalised British citizen) and she was in the privileged position of being able to train as much as seven

Tracing sedate and intricate compulsory figures on the ice to the satisfaction of eagle-eyed judges was once an integral but tedious part of the figure-skating programme and worth 60 per cent of the total score. Such figures were eventually incorporated into the short programme introduced in 1973. At the 1952 Winter Games in Oslo Jeannette Altwegg was 'the embodiment of accuracy', according to the British Olympic Association summing-up. She then held her own in the free skating to win the gold ahead of Tenley Albright, of the USA, by 161.756 points to 159.133.

TOPFOTO

hours a day, five days a week, at the Streatham ice rink in south London. Such diligent preparation earned her the accolade from Dr Willy Meisl, an Austrian-born pre-war refugee from Nazism who had become one of Britain's foremost sports writers, that she was 'the embodiment of accuracy in the compulsory figures and her free-skating was of the finest standard'.

Miss Altwegg had been the bronze-medallist at the 1948 Olympics and world champion in 1951, and she spent ten months of the year figure-skating and the other two months playing tennis, in which sport she was good enough to have reached the Wimbledon junior final in 1947. Yet despite her gracious figure-skating skills she refused what Dr Meisl described as 'fabulous offers' to turn professional and retired immediately after the Games, devoting her time to modestly paid employment at a centre for war orphans in Switzerland. She was, strictly speaking, the first Briton to win an individual gold medal at the Winter Olympics because the 1908 success of Madge Syers, also in figure-skating, had actually been achieved at an autumnal sequel to the Summer Games that year.

The disappointments of Helsinki were followed four years later at Melbourne by the most successful Olympic showing since 1924, and there was no obvious reason why there should have been such a rapid transformation in the country's Olympic fortunes. The six gold medals in 1956 came in athletics, boxing, fencing, swimming and equestrianism. In fact, there were some surprising similarities with what had happened at the 1924 Games. Cambridge University provided the 1956 athletics winner, while in 1924 it had been responsible for two of the three golds in that sport. There were two boxing golds and a women's swimming gold at both the 1924 and 1956 Games. Even an historic first win in fencing had some precedent, because silver had been won in the same event, women's foil, in 1924 and again in 1928 and 1932.

To the frustration of Olympic historians seeking a trend, and journalists striving for a headline, there is often no logical explanation to be found in such swings of fortune. In gold-medal terms Britain was the equal seventh most successful nation alongside Germany (Federal and Democratic Republics combined) and behind the USSR (37), USA (32), Australia (13), Hungary (9), Italy and Sweden (8 each).

Although the Games of 1956 had been awarded to Melbourne, it was decided that the equestrian events would be held in Stockholm because of the severity of Australia's equine quarantine laws. Oddly, for a country so enamoured of horses in any guise, the show-jumpers in Helsinki had been the first British equestrian champions at any Games. Four years later, in 1956, another gold was won, albeit in a form of horsemanship for which Britain had only recently begun to show an aptitude: three-day eventing, which comprised an endurance course (steeplechase and cross-country), a dressage test and a show-jumping event undertaken on successive days. As it happens, some years earlier, in 1936, Britain had won the team bronze-medal in the three-day event, although that had been achieved by sheer perseverance rather than brilliant comportment in the saddle. Germany's trio had won very easily from Poland, and Britain's Captain A.B.J. Scott, Lieutenant E.D. Howard-Vyse and Captain R.G. Fanshawe had placed third, but with more than 9,000 penalty points to the winners' 676.65. What distinguished the British performance was that the luckless Captain Fanshawe had fallen off his horse and chased it on foot for more than two miles before he could re-mount. Luckily, the only other complete team, Czechoslovakia, could present no challenge because one of its riders took more than 2¾ hours to complete the eight kilometres of the cross-country course, for which the time limit was 17 minutes 46 seconds.

The 1948 Olympic three-day event had been the first ever such competition held in Britain. It was won by the USA, with the hosts among the non-finishers, but the next year the British Horse Society inaugurated the annual 'Badminton Trials' on the Gloucestershire estate of the Duke of Beaufort, president of the British Olympic Association. Such was the progress of Britain's riders that the bronze medals in Helsinki three years later were lost only because one competitor, dazed by an earlier fall, missed a marker flag by three metres and was eliminated. Again we have Captain Collings to thank for explaining Britain's past reluctance: 'the British, well content with their wonderful hunting, their polo and their steeplechasing, had taken little or no interest in the various forms of advanced horsemanship; in fact, were apt to shun "competition riding" and look upon it as the peculiar prerogative of the foreigner', he wrote in *World Sports* magazine.

The 1956 winning Olympic team was Bertie Hill, Laurence Rook and Frank Weldon. Rook was the very same rider whose minor and understandable lapse in Helsinki had caused Britain to miss out on bronze. Four years on, and the British had progressed from promising outsiders to favourites, as all three riders had in turn won the European individual title in 1953/54/55, and Britain had taken the team prize in each of those years. In Stockholm the competition actually lasted four days, as the dressage took up the first two, at the end of which Britain already had the lead. This was extended after the endurance phase, and the British trio went into the show-jumping with the enviable advantage of being able to knock down 12 more fences than their nearest rivals, Germany, and still win overall.

Lieutenant-Colonel Weldon, of the Royal Horse Artillery, placed third individually. Rook, who had retired as a major in the Royal Horse Guards the previous year, having won the Military Cross in 1944, was sixth. Hill, a West Country farmer, was twelfth. Britain won commandingly with 355.48 minus points to Germany's 475.91. Weldon's bronze was the first individual Olympic medal by a British rider. Hill had also placed seventh in the 1952 Olympic three-day event and he was to become the first Briton to take part in Olympic equestrianism on three occasions when he competed again at the 1960 Games, placing twenty-fifth. He was in a position to win the individual gold in Stockholm but lost valuable marks when he had to dismount at a water-course fence, described by expert onlookers as 'a dangerous obstacle', and push his horse backwards over it. He later turned his inestimable experience to full use as a highly successful trainer to the British team.

Admirably, the British Olympic Association's official report, while heartily commending the gold-medal performance, did not hesitate to criticise the conditions of the competition where it was thought appropriate. Of the cross-country it was stated, 'The spectacle of tired horses galloping over the second part of the course, with its variety of fixed obstacles, must also move any horse-lover to pity. Stewards should be appointed to flag down exhausted horses.' Of the veterinary inspection before the show-jumping, the writer concluded, 'No horses were failed, although in my opinion some should have been. By being lenient towards the riders, the inspection allowed unsound animals to suffer the discomfort of jumping.' The opinion carried weight – the author was Harry Llewellyn.

The Olympic Games 'proper' began five months later in November in the warmth of the Australian summer. Britain's fund-raising had been launched much earlier, headed by the esteemed former Olympic champion, Lord Burghley, now the Marquess of Exeter, and administered from conveniently sited offices in the West End of London that had been provided free of charge by Rolls Royce. Some £146,000 was raised from the general public, business, commerce and industry. More than 60 companies provided gifts for the competitors, including all the uniforms and other useful supplies such as Horlicks, Lucozade, boiled sweets, 'Rose Coral' lipstick, plastic raincoats and 'Radian-B' liniment. In a nice reversal of the bygone Irish antipathy towards acknowledging the British flag, the doctor who offered his services as honorary medical officer was Denis Cussen, holder of the Irish 100 yards record since 1928 and a competitor for Ireland at the Olympics that same year.

Britain's only athletics gold-medallist in Melbourne was Chris Brasher in the 3000 metres steeplechase. Yet two years before the 1956 Games a trio of Britons had joined forces to break through the 'barrier' of the four-minute mile, and no one then could possibly have imagined that Brasher – the dogged and selfless pacemaker for the first two laps – would be the only man in that race to win an Olympic title. Roger Bannister was the one who became the first sub-four-minute miler, but had placed fourth in the Olympic 1500 metres of two years before and by 1956 had retired from competition to pursue what was to become an eminent medical career. The second of the trio, Chris Chataway, had set world records at three miles and 5000 metres but was now past his best. The achievement of Brasher, Britain's number three steeplechaser, in winning that event in Melbourne, was still being described months later in a mystified manner by the usually forthright Harold Abrahams, himself an Olympic champion of 32 years before and now a respected athletics correspondent. 'If a genius really is one who has the capacity to take infinite pains, then Brasher is a genius,' Abrahams wrote.

Brasher had been a moderately successful distance runner at Cambridge University but was not even the best in his college, St John's. Sensibly, having run no faster than 4 minutes 15.8 seconds for the mile, he had turned his full attentions to the steeplechase, to such good effect that he reached the Olympic final of 1952, in which his British team-mate, John Disley, won the bronze medal. Without decrying such sterling efforts, it is a fact that in the 1950s the steeplechase, with its 28 solid wooden barriers and seven water-jumps to clear, was a viable option for those who lacked the speed to succeed at the highest level on the flat but who possessed an abundance of determination. Yet Brasher deserves every credit for being one of the first to prove that the 'plodder' can sharpen his pace as well as his stamina by dedicated endurance training. By the summer of 1956 he had reduced his mile time by nine seconds, and in a warm-up meeting in Australia shortly before the Games opened he ran the equal eighth fastest ever time in the world for two miles on the flat.

Even so, his victory was the most surprising in any of the 33 men's and women's athletics events and was made all the more dramatic by an initial announcement that he had been disqualified for obstruction. This matter took three hours to resolve before the jury of appeal voted in Brasher's favour. His was the first distance-running Olympic gold by a Briton since another steeplechaser, Percy Hodge, 36 years before, and there was an obscure but thought-provoking link with even earlier times in that Brasher had been educated at Rugby School, which had provided so much inspiration for the founder of the Modern Olympics, Baron de Coubertin. Brasher was not actually the first Old Rugbeian to strike gold, because Major Duggie Stewart had done so four years before

The most surprising win in athletics at the 1956 Games was that of Chris Brasher in the 3000 metres steeplechase. Having been one of the pacemakers in the first sub-four-minute mile by Roger Bannister two years before, Brasher went to Melbourne only as Britain's number three in his event but had judged his training peak to perfection to take the gold medal. Later, with his fellow steeplechaser, John Disley, he founded the London Marathon.
TOPFOTO

(also over obstacles but with a horse to carry him). Brasher later became a distinguished sports writer and with John Disley co-founder of the London marathon.

Britain could also take some credit for gold in another event which it had already won twice at the Olympics. Norman Read had first competed in race-walking at the age of 14 in his home village of Steyning, in Sussex, and had been the AAA junior champion for the one-mile walk in 1950. Enterprisingly, but without too much forethought, he then decided to emigrate to New Zealand three years later to achieve his ambition of competing at the Games. To his dismay he discovered when he arrived in Auckland that the only races to be had were much shorter events on the track, and when at last national championships were held at 20 and 50 kilometres on the road in March of 1956 he won the former by over 11 minutes and the latter by over 20 minutes. His times were still not good enough for Olympic selection – ten men were faster in the English Road Walking Association's 50 kilometres event, for example – but he went off to Australia, anyway, eight months before the Games, trained furiously by walking more than 100 miles a week, won the Australian open 50 kilometres title, and then to the astonishment even of his New Zealand team-mates defeated the favoured Soviet walkers for the Olympic gold.

Of Britain's contingent of 201 competitors in Melbourne for all the sports, 26 (or 13 per cent) were women, but they won two of the country's five gold medals, through Judy Grinham (swimming, 100 metres backstroke) and Gillian Sheen (fencing, foil). Two other golds came from the boxers, Terry Spinks (flyweight) and Dick McTaggart (lightweight), and as the seven-man boxing team also won a silver and two bronze they massively exceeded the norm – contributing more than 20 per cent of Britain's total of 24 medals from less than four per cent of the manpower. The USSR led the medal count for the first time, combining the Stockholm and Melbourne results. Total medals were: USSR 98, USA 74, Australia 35, Germany and Hungary 26 each, Italy 25, Great Britain 24. Gold medals: USSR 37, USA 32, Australia 13, Hungary 9, Italy and Sweden 8 each, Germany and Great Britain 6 each.

By coincidence both British gold-medallists in the ring had a connection with the butchery trade. McTaggart was a 21-year-old RAF corporal from Dundee serving as a butcher, whose five brothers were also boxers, and he was awarded the prize for the most stylish boxer at the Games. Spinks, 18, was an ex-apprentice jockey from the East End of London who had given up his job as a butcher's assistant to train for the Games and relied throughout the tournament on what Britain's most knowledgeable boxing correspondent, George Whiting, colourfully described as a strategy of 'pop and hop it' – dart in, hit the opponent with a left jab, and step sharply back.

The swimmer Miss Grinham was born in the north London borough of Neasden six months before the outbreak of the Second World War. She was living proof, one could say, of the inaccuracy of Sir John Betjeman's later puckish description of Neasden as 'the home of the gnome and the average citizen'. She had gone to Melbourne rated among the favourites, and hers was one of only two European wins in the 13 men's and women's races in the pool. She subsequently added British Empire and European titles and remains one of the finest of all British swimmers, although the times which she achieved have

Terry Spinks (*left*) and Dick McTaggart (*right*) both won Olympic boxing gold medals in Melbourne in 1956 – Spinks at flyweight, McTaggart at lightweight – but the impressive trophy belonged to McTaggart, awarded to him as the supreme stylist of the Games. The foremost boxing writer of the day, George Whiting, wrote admiringly of McTaggart, 'This brush-topped Scot from a fighting family in Dundee has a boxing brain'.

Judy Grinham won the 1956 100 metres backstroke in world-record time and in 1958 became the first woman to hold simultaneously Olympic, European and Commonwealth titles in swimming. Training in public pools, with no lane separated off for her, and receiving no sponsorship, she was financed by her family. She retired from the sport on her twentieth birthday.

PHOTOGRAPHS: TOPFOTO

long been surpassed. She won the 1956 final in 1 minute 12.9 seconds and the men's title at those Games was won in 1:02.2. At the 2008 Olympic Games 25 *women* from 18 countries swam faster than 1:02.2 in the first-round heats, and the final was won in 58.96 seconds, with Gemma Spofforth, of Great Britain, setting a European record of 59.38 in fourth place.

In their home water Australia took eight of the swimming titles, and Murray Rose became an immediate national hero with his wins in three of the freestyle events. Rose had been born in Scotland in 1939 but had emigrated to Australia with his family soon after the end of the Second World War. The entire Australian swimming team for the 1956 Games had trained together for three months beforehand under the supervision of four coaches – undeniably legitimate practice but perhaps no less a liberal interpretation of the rules of amateurism than the state aid being lavished upon the East Europeans in these years. Such politically motivated benevolence had taken the Soviets far ahead of the Americans in the Olympic 'cold war', but it would be another quarter of a century at least before the realities of modern sport would at long last force the Olympic hierarchy to abandon their outdated views and embrace professionalism. The anomalies were obvious to all – state-sponsored athletes, or athletes in the armed forces who were allowed time and facilities to train – but the abandonment of amateurism in the official charter and

Gillian Sheen (*left*) remains Britain's only Olympic fencing champion, having won the women's foil at the 1956 Games. British women had also been silver-medallists in this event at the successive Games of 1924, 1928 and 1932. Joining Sheen in this photograph is Mary Glen Haig, whose best Olympic fencing performance was a more modest eighth in 1948 but who became only the third woman member of the International Olympic Committee in 1982 and was created Dame Commander of the British Empire in 1993.

TOPFOTO

regulations of Olympic competition was a drawn-out and often contentious process. Eventually by the 1970s and 1980s the rules were gradually liberated until after 1988 in Seoul professionals were allowed to take part in most sports. Today wrestling and boxing are still amateur-only events at the Olympics.

By chance the fencing gold-medallist Gillian Sheen had been born on the same day, 21 August 1928, as Chris Brasher. Her birthplace was Willesden, no more than a couple of miles away from Judy Grinham's birthplace of Neasden. Unlike Miss Grinham, she was not thought of beforehand as a potential Melbourne gold-medallist, nor was she still even after reaching the foil final. She had been British champion seven times and had competed in the 1952 Games, being eliminated in the second round, and only got through the semi-finals in Melbourne by beating the world champion, Lydia Domolki, of Hungary, in a deciding *barrage* after losing three of her five bouts.

The final involved eight competitors, from Austria, Denmark, France (two), Great Britain, Italy, Romania and the USA, and went to another *barrage* in which Miss Sheen beat Olga Orban, of Romania, 4–2 after both had won six of their seven bouts, including the Romanian taking their previous encounter by the same score earlier in the day. Miss Sheen was a dental surgeon by profession and later moved to New York to set up in practice with her husband. Another of the finalists, Ellen Müller-Preis, of Austria, had first competed in the 1932 Games foil when Judy Guinness Penn-Hughes had won a third consecutive silver medal for Britain after Gladys Davies in 1924 and Muriel Freeman in 1928.

Terry Spinks was also an unexpected winner, though there the comparisons with Britain's first fencing champion ended. Disconcertingly he looked little more than 14, and as he had lost to Vladimir Stolnikov, of the USSR, earlier in the year in a contest in Moscow that was succinctly summed up by George Whiting as an 'unmitigated trimming', Spinks was given no chance when the two met again in the flyweight quarter-finals. Yet Spinks went on to the gold 'by means of swift consistency over five strenuous contests', according to Whiting, although the fighter himself seemed to have achieved it all by instinct. Interviewed forty years later, he readily admitted, 'I had no idea what a big thing it was I'd done. I was a boy from Canning Town on the other side of the World. It was like going to the moon.'

'Time will tell whether Spinks can prosper over the longer courses of professionalism,' Whiting had predicted in his Olympic summary, and Spinks stood the test of time well in the ring. He won 41 of his 49 professional engagements and became British flyweight champion, but he had problems in other areas of his life. Addiction to alcohol cost him two marriages and several business ventures, but he eventually recovered and was belatedly awarded the MBE 45 years after his Olympic success.

His fellow champion, lightweight Dick McTaggart, was a rarity among British Olympian pugilists in that he never turned professional, competing again in the Games of 1960 (where he won bronze) and 1964, and reputedly having 634 contests during his career of which he won 610. He was coach to the Scottish boxers at the 1990 Commonwealth Games.

Returning home to the back streets of the deprived London docklands borough of Canning Town, Terry Spinks receives a hero's welcome from his neighbours. The diminutive Spinks had won the flyweight (51 kilogrammes limit) title at the 1956 Melbourne Games against all the odds. According to George Whiting in the British Olympic Association's official report, Spinks's 'prospects could hardly have been described as either cosy or rosy'.

The disappointments of Britain's Olympic endeavours in Australia included the fact that the football team lost 6–1 on the same day that Gillian Sheen was winning fencing gold, and there was not a single finalist in rowing, compared with five in 1952 and at least one gold at every Olympics from 1908 to 1948, except for 1920. In a damning indictment of British ineptitude, *The Times* concluded of the Olympic rowing: 'There were two features common to all the successful crews – a rigorous, studied training programme of hard work in and out of the boat and a background of regular experience as settled combinations, both notably absent in British rowing.' The writer was Richard Burnell, gold-medallist of 1948.

At long last the engrained British attitudes of dilettantism and slipshod training and preparation were gradually changing, but at the same time worldwide competition was growing ever stronger, and improved methods would not be promptly rewarded with more medals. The number of British wins in Melbourne would not be exceeded at an Olympic Games for another 44 years.

NINE

The Games of 1960 and 1964

Hag-ridden by complexes, and so two gold medals must suffice under the Roman sun

D ID we loyal band of youthful British athletics supporters really spring to our feet and bawl out in discordant chorus, 'Keep right on to the end of the road! Keep right on to the end!', when Don Thompson came striding gallantly into the Rome Olympic stadium one sun-baked afternoon in August of 1960 to win the 50 kilometres walk? After half a century of nostalgic reflection, I can't be sure. As Sir William Golding, famed author of *Lord of the Flies*, once wrote in another context, 'Our memories become imaginations and our imaginations memories'.

Certainly, the Italians surrounding us in the crowd on the back straight seemed for once a shade subdued, but was it our impromptu welcome for Britain's only athletics gold-medallist that cooled their ardour? Rather, it might have been the fact that the diminutive Thompson looked to them the most unlikely of champions in his baggy white vest and shorts, sensible black leather shoes, rolled-over grey socks and a floppy hat which might have been more appropriate to lazing away Bank Holiday Monday in a deck-chair on Brighton beach. By way of contrast, only a few days previously a suave and sophisticated Italian, in designer sunglasses and hip-hugging blue-and-white uniform who could have featured in an advertisement for Giorgio Armani, had won the 200 metres.

Many of the other athletics events at the 1960 Olympics were a disaster for Britain's competitors. Their officials had decreed that the best way to deal with the unaccustomed heat of a Roman summer was for each member of the team to be sent out just a couple of days before his or her event. It was the wrong decision. None of the Britons in the men's 800, 1500 or 5000 metres even reached the final. Nor did the favoured Arthur Rowe in the shot. Mary Bignal had led the qualifiers in the long jump with a British record but eventually placed ninth. Only the 100 metres runners had prospered with the sun on their backs: Peter Radford third and Dorothy Hyman second.

The first woman since 1932, and the first swimmer, to carry the British flag at an Olympic opening ceremony was Anita Lonsbrough in 1964. Four years previously she had won the 200 metres breaststroke. Only two other women have been Britain's flag-bearers at the Summer Games: Lucinda Green (equestrianism) in 1984 and Kate Howey (judo) in 2004. Three women have done so at the Winter Games: Mollie Phillips (figure-skating) was the chosen one in 1932, Rhona Martin (curling) in 2006 and Shelley Rudman (skeleton) in 2010.
TOPFOTO

Defying the critics, the old champion, Harold Abrahams, wrote at length later on in the British Olympic Association's official report, analysing the achievements in great detail by comparing them with pre-Games form, and came to the conclusion that the team 'deserve considerably more appreciation than they have received in many quarters'. Further, he defended the authorities by claiming that the late arrival of the athletes in Rome had not been crucial: 'in a very small number of cases this *was* a factor – but only one of several – affecting performances.' As Abrahams was Cambridge University's BOA representative and an official of the British Amateur Athletic Board and the AAA, he had a duty to defend the establishment position, but he knew his statistics and so he could justify his assessment.

The fact is that the athletes won eight of Britain's twenty medals in Rome, while the others came from swimming (five), boxing (three), fencing (two), equestrianism and weight-lifting. The USSR again led the USA in the medals table (and even the BOA's official report published that), 43 gold medals to 34, 103 medals in total to 71. Britain's two gold medals ranked the country equal twelfth with Denmark and New Zealand, which was maybe not over-inspiring, but in total medals gained Britain was eighth; and was there really any significant difference between their 20 and the 22 for Australia (of which 13 were in swimming), and 21 each for Hungary and Poland? Ominously, however, what could further be gleaned from a close study of the detail was that Britain did not win a medal in 12 of the 18 sports and in two of the sports which had formerly been so dependable for Britain – rowing and yachting – did not even come close to doing so.

The story of how Don Thompson prepared for the Games has become part of athletics folklore. Each night after work as an insurance clerk he would spend hour upon hour energetically knee-lifting on the spot in a home-made heat-acclimatisation chamber that had been constructed in his bathroom to simulate the humid conditions in Rome, plus up to five hours' fast walking every Sunday. What is mostly overlooked is that like so many other Olympic champions – of most recent memory, Chris Brasher in Melbourne – Thompson had the chastening experience of a previous Games to guide his thinking. In Melbourne he had been in fifth place with only eight kilometres to go but had collapsed in the heat and failed to finish. In Rome it was the defending champion, English-born Norman Read of New Zealand, who was among those who fell by the wayside as Thompson walked the perfect race.

On a winding course through the streets of the city he was already in the lead by more than a minute at halfway, but it was not by design: two Australians and a Soviet walker who had been ahead of him had been disqualified for 'lifting' (failing to keep contact with the ground), while a precocious novice from India had slowed to a shuffle. With no television coverage beamed back to the stadium, the press and spectators had to rely on occasional messages flashed up on an electronic scoreboard – in itself a major technological advance – and as Thompson's lead at 45 kilometres was said to be a mere one second over the champion from 1948, John Ljunggren, of Sweden, there was, as Abrahams put it, an 'agonising wait' (and we eager British fans would have heartily agreed with that sentiment) until the valiant little Thompson, only 5 feet 5½ inches (1.66 metres) tall, materialised into the stadium sunshine from the gloom of the tunnel connecting to the road outside to complete the race with a vigorous lap of the track.

When Thompson crossed the line, 17 seconds (no more than 50 metres) ahead of Ljunggren, he was much less demonstrative than we ecstatic supporters. Interviewed at great length three months later by Phil Pilley, the astute editor of *World Sports* magazine, Thompson recalled, 'This may sound funny – I wasn't wildly excited. What I mean is that I didn't feel like kicking my legs in the air with joy. A lot of the glamour of winning had been dulled by the strain, first of leading, then of the struggle with Ljunggren. I didn't feel elated. Just pleased.' Yet Thompson's achievement was great. It was Britain's fifth walking gold over the years after George Larner (two in 1908), Tommy Green (1932) and Harold Whitlock (1936), plus others for British-born George Goulding (for Canada in 1912) and Norman Read (for New Zealand in 1956). The only athletics discipline which had proved almost as profitable for Britons was the 800 metres. Thompson was still competing 30 years after his Olympic triumph, finishing second in the national 100-miles championship at the age of 57.

The slight and unassuming Don Thompson, nicknamed 'The Mighty Mouse', prospered in the heat of Rome in 1960 while others wilted and became the fourth British-born Olympic champion for the 50 kilometres walk in the six Games since 1932. A key part of his preparations for the weather conditions had been to set up a home-made heat-chamber in his bathroom where he exercised vigorously every night.

Taking unpaid leave from her Huddersfield Town Hall clerical duties to train harder, Anita Lonsbrough beat the state-aided East German favourite, Wiltrud Urselman, by half a second for the 1960 200 metres breaststroke title. It was the first swimming gold for Britain since Lucy Morton had won the same event 36 years before. Times had advanced somewhat in the interim: Morton 3 minutes 33.2 seconds; Lonsbrough 2:49.5!

PHOTOGRAPHS: TOPFOTO

Anita Lonsbrough, at 19 years old, became the third British woman to win individual swimming gold, in the process breaking the world record for the 200 metres breaststroke and beating the previous holder, Wiltrud Urselmann, of Germany. Pat Besford, the diva of British swimming writers, described the situation thus: 'Lonsbrough did not go to Rome with an immaculate racing record. She had lost two of her four big races before the Games and lost her World Record – to Urselmann. But came the final, and while the German prowled anxiously, fretfully, around the starting area the calm British champion sat on a chair with her bath robe like a cloak around her shoulders. There was no doubt who was frightened of whom.' The recollections of Lonsbrough were as down-to-earth as one might expect of a Yorkshirewoman: 'Don't think I'm big-headed, but I never thought of losing. All I wanted was to get it over. And then, as I was on the starting line, I saw a fly on the water in my lane. I remember thinking, "I hope I don't swallow it when I dive in". You think of the daftest things at times like this.'

No doubt Fräulein Urselmann would have been astonished to discover that in order to fit in enough training in the lead-up to the Games Miss Lonsbrough had requested and been granted unpaid time off from her work as a clerk in the treasurer's office at Huddersfield Town Hall. In the Communist-led German Democratic Republic they did things rather differently, lavishing on their sports stars such as Urselmann sinecure appointments at colleges or in the armed services, providing them with palatial training facilities, superior diet and accommodation, and a medical back-up system which could perhaps most euphemistically be described as highly sophisticated. Miss Lonsbrough (whose time of 2 minutes 49.5 seconds would have left Britain's 1924 winner of the same event, Lucy Morton, a full 50-metre length behind) also won European and Commonwealth titles and after retirement from competition was able to give up her clerical duties and become a national newspaper and radio swimming correspondent.

The wait for Britain's next women's Olympic swimming victory would last 48 years, until Rebecca Adlington won both the 400 and 800 metres freestyle in Beijing. A sound reason for that hiatus was explained by Neil Allen, correspondent of *The Times*, whose thoughtful and entertaining diary of the 1960 Games was published in book form later that year. He was the first national-newspaper writer in Britain to develop a profound knowledge of and a passion for international sport in all its forms, equally at home beside a running track, a swimming pool or a boxing ring, and he bewailed the fact that attitudes towards sport in Britain were still, as he put it, 'cursed by an obsession with parochial matters that is encouraged both by snobbery and hack journalism … hag-ridden by complexes – one must win casually, hard training is not done, physical education is just "PT".'

One of the most stunning victories in Rome had been achieved by the almost unknown Ethiopian marathon runner, Abebe Bikila. As Neil Allen wrote:

It is revolution time in international sport. A series of upheavals has caused old standards of performance to be thrown aside, useless and out of date. The social revolution of the World, in which many under-privileged countries have begun to lift their heads has formed the backcloth to the sweeping changes in sport … through newspapers, radio or television we have had drummed into us the vast strides that Man – and Woman – is making in every sport where there can be comparison with the past. The barriers are thrown down, first by one pioneer and then by scores of other eager young men and women. Some, admittedly, compete for personal or party gain, but the vast majority do so simply because they wish to prove themselves to themselves. We can ignore the 1890s or the 1920s with their handfuls of wealthy games players. *THIS* is the golden age of sport.

Four young men and women in Britain (one of the men actually not *that* young) who did thrust aside old prejudices and trained hard would be rewarded with athletics gold medals four years later.

The British had made a habit of picking up the occasional gold at the Winter Games to interrupt the interminable sequence of victories by those countries that enjoyed rather greater expanses of ice and snow on which to hone their skills. After curling in 1924 (though that award would still not be properly recognised for more than another 40 years), ice-hockey in 1936 and figure-skating in 1952, there was a further unlikely success in Innsbruck in 1964. Tony Nash steered the number one British bobsleigh, with the Honourable Robin Dixon (later to be Lord Glentoran) as brake-man, over its four runs just ¹²⁄₁₀₀ths of a second faster than the Italian favourites. This was a complete reversal of Olympic form, because the last time that the event had been held at the Games, in 1956, Italian pairs had finished first and second, with Great Britain tenth and eleventh, but at the 1963 world championships on the same Igls course Nash and Dixon had placed third. Nash was a director of his family's engineering firm and so one of the leading lights in the technological development of bobsledding in the 1960s, and the pair went on to be world champions in 1965 and an honourable fifth in defence of their Olympic title in 1968. Britain had enjoyed something of a pre-war bobsledding tradition, with second place in the four-man event in 1924 and third in 1936.

The 1964 Summer Games had been awarded to Tokyo, which made for an historic first venture into Asia for the Olympic movement. In order to raise money for the British team, there took place the now familiar mundane round of dances, whist drives and garden fêtes and the canvassing of banks, breweries, property developers, insurance companies, the stock exchange, civil service and armed forces. Some £170,000 was needed, and the Foreign Office broke new ground by providing grants totalling £30,000. No doubt a contributory factor was that the prime minister of the Labour government, Harold Wilson, had been a capable 440 yards runner at Oxford University in the 1930s and he had appointed the country's first minister for sport, Denis Howell, one of whose useful credentials for the job was that he was a qualified football referee. To put the sums into context £170,000 in 1964 is equivalent to £2,570,000 in 2011 (based on the retail price index). Thus, one might calculate that Britain's 18 medals in Tokyo (four gold, twelve silver, two bronze) cost £142,770 each in today's terms. As the Games drew to a close the prime minister clearly thought – or at least publicly pronounced – that the country had got good value for money. He sent a congratulatory telegram to the team members in Tokyo, enthusing that 'you have given us our most successful Olympics for 40 years', but he was too quick off the mark. The facts didn't support the claim. The medal total was two fewer than it had been in Rome (there was no subsidy from the Conservative government in power at the time), and this downturn couldn't as yet be readily blamed on increased competition. Medals were gained by 41 countries in Tokyo as against 44 in Rome. Great Britain's total of four golds ranked tenth. The USA led with 36, from the USSR (30), Japan (16), Germany, Hungary and Italy (10 each), Poland (7), Australia (6) and Czechoslovakia (5). Leaving aside the unrealistic prospect of challenging the USA and USSR, Britain had still not won as many gold medals as Australia, Hungary or Italy in 1952, 1956, 1960 or 1964. The Soviets still led when it came to overall medals, with 96 to the USA's 90, and Great Britain, tallying 18, sharing eighth place with Australia.

The issue was clouded by the fact that all of the Tokyo golds for Britain, and 12 of the 18 medals of every description, came in the Olympic discipline with the highest profile – athletics. The most complimentary term which the British Olympic Association could find to describe the overall performance in all sports was 'creditable', which could have been interpreted as damning with faint praise, and their apparent satisfaction that 'seven of the 16 sports brought back one or more medals' might more accurately have read that, apart from athletics, six sports (equestrianism, fencing, rowing, swimming, weight-lifting, yachting) managed one medal each and thirteen other sports (basketball, boxing, canoeing, cycling, football, gymnastics, hockey, judo, modern pentathlon, shooting, volleyball, water-polo, wrestling) none at all. The reason for the disparity in figures is that the BOA made no mention in its summing-up of four others among the twenty sports (basketball, football, volleyball and water-polo) in which Great Britain was not represented.

Despite this, there was no question that the athletes had performed magnificently. Gold for Ann Packer at 800 metres, Ken Matthews in the 20 kilometres walk, Lynn Davies and Mrs Mary Rand (the former Miss Bignal) in the long jumps; silver in the marathon, 4×400 metres relay, 400 metres hurdles, steeplechase, 50 kilometres walk and the women's 400 metres and pentathlon; bronze in the women's 4×100 metres. The full measure of it is that in the 48 years since no Olympics for Britain's athletes has matched that success, and it would be a major achievement if more than a quarter of that total of medals were won in 2012. Of course, the competition was not so universal in 1964, but there were 93 countries involved, ten more than ever before, and the warning signs were there that the Olympics were expanding at a breakneck rate, just as Baron de Coubertin must have first feared at the start of the twentieth century.

The editor of the BOA official report was the late Doug Gardner, one of the most respected of British sports writers, and, although he headlined his summary of the Tokyo Games as 'A Pleasure and a Privilege', he wondered, 'How much bigger, how much more elaborate, how much more expensive can the International Olympic Committee allow what was once a simple festival of celebration involving only 13 nations, ten sports and fewer than 300 competitors to become?' There were 5,140 competitors in Tokyo from the 93 nations taking part, 14 of them for the first time. The number of competitors was not a record for the Games, probably because of the travel costs involved. The accounts had not yet been closed, but Gardner reckoned the cost might have been as much as £400 million. For those days, this was big money, although by today's standards it now appears like small change.

A distinguishing feature of the British team in Tokyo was the further eroding of once prevalent social distinctions. A fair illustration was the presence in the equestrian three-day event of Sergeant Ben Jones, the first non-commissioned officer to represent Britain at that level, and of Lance-Corporal Jim Fox and Sergeant Ben Finnis in another military-slanted sport, the modern pentathlon, a multi-discipline event comprising horse-riding, fencing, shooting, swimming and running, on successive days. Other than sports governing bodies, only Cambridge and Oxford Universities had representatives at the BOA (Harold Abrahams and the *Guinness Book of Records* founder, Norris McWhirter, respectively), but of the 24 competitors who won medals, including relay and team events, the sole Oxbridge product was the 4 × 400 metres runner, Adrian Metcalfe. Even the coxless four oarsmen, who took the silver to maintain an illustrious tradition in the event which continues to this day, came not from the universities but from the Tideway Scullers club situated along the Boat Race course at Chiswick.

The quartet of athletics champions – the new generation of British athletics – was a press-man's dream: Ann Packer and Mary Rand, strikingly attractive, articulate, joyous; Lynn Davies, unassumingly handsome and immaculately groomed; Ken Matthews, lean and gaunt, valiantly defending an unfashionable legacy (PLATE 2). Had it been a West End musical, Ann and Mary would have been the chorus girls suddenly thrust to stardom, Lynn the dashing matinée idol, Ken the respected character actor. In purely athletic terms, they were a well-rehearsed cast, benefiting from a sense of purpose and pride stemming from the national coaching scheme that had been put in place soon after the Second World War and forcefully directed by the charismatic Geoff Dyson. Regrettably, Dyson had resigned and gone off to Canada in 1961, frustrated by the conservatism and ill-regard of the team officials, but his influence remained.

Yet there was an anomaly regarding the reaction to those athletics triumphs. Packer, Rand and Davies duly received awards in the New Year's Honours List – each with MBEs – which in the twenty-first century has now become a rite of passage for the country's Olympic champions. Yet Matthews was ignored, or overlooked, for 14 years until at last the omission was corrected. How to explain it? Could it be that the graceful form of Britain's Olympic champions on the track and long-jump runway was more readily appealing in those 'Swinging Sixties' than the angular, hip-waggling gait of the road-walker? Even Neil Allen, that most open-minded of athletics observers, had shared in the popular mood when he summarised Don Thompson's road-walking win in Rome: 'I could make a longer rhapsody of Thompson's feat, but it would be dishonest to do so for though I admire his gameness not even a British success in walking can stir me at all. For me this sport is a complete blank spot. I believe that 70 per cent of the walkers I see are really "lifting", and I cannot imagine what purpose there is in a "race" where you are using a slower method of progression than running. The reaction of myself, and several other British journalists, when Thompson entered the stadium was to laugh at this quaint little figure waddling along. We laughed with some pleasure, but we laughed.'

Sadly, this is a view that is widely shared to this day. The victory in Tokyo by 30-year-old Ken Matthews, a power-station electrician by occupation, was supported by a second place for another British walker, Paul Nihill, at 50 kilometres, but Matthews commented ruefully, and prophetically, 'I don't think I'm far off the limit of speed with fair walking. There'll be someone coming along who's larger than me and stronger.' In the 48 years since then the rules of race-walking – which perhaps should now more accurately be described as 'power walking' – have been amended radically, and Britain has slid into

Olympic long-jump champion in 1964, the lithe and graceful Mary Rand was also an outstanding all-rounder and here she sprints to the fastest 200 metres time in the pentathlon at those Games. It was not enough to win another gold – this went to the rather more sturdy Irina Press, of the USSR – but sufficient for silver, and Mary added a bronze in the 4 × 100 metres relay. The others in this photograph are Ulla Flegel, of Austria (*left*), who pulled up injured, and Helen Frith, of Australia.

BY COURTESY OF MARK SHEARMAN

almost total obscurity in the sport, apart from one valiant woman, Jo Jackson, who was twenty-second at the 2008 Games, where there was not a single Great Britain competitor in the men's events, though 39 other countries thought it worthwhile to take part, including Costa Rica, Ecuador, El Salvador, Guatemala, Kazakhstan, Moldova, Serbia and Tunisia. The men's 20 kilometres in Beijing, aided by more liberal interpretations of legal race-walking technique, was won in 1 hour 19 minutes 1 second, and Matthews' 1:29:34 in Tokyo would have left him 2.5 kilometres behind.

Coached by his father, Matthews had led after five kilometres in the 1960 Olympic event but had been forced to retire in the latter stages, suffering from a leg injury and the effects of a heavy cold. Two years afterwards, and fully fit, the strategy had worked when he won the European title by taking the lead at around the same early juncture and steadily applying the pressure from then on. In Tokyo he employed his familiar tactics again to perfect effect. His successive five-kilometre 'split' times were a model of consistency – 22:19, 22:04, 22:29, 22:42 – and he crossed the finish-line almost 40 seconds ahead of an East German, Dieter Lindner, with the defending champion, Vladimir Golubnichiy, of the USSR, third. Golubnichiy was to regain his title four years later.

The first of the British successes in Tokyo was that of Mary Rand. Born and brought up in Wells, Somerset, her voice had an enticing West Country burr, while Neil Allen once described her persona as a 'shimmering mixture of health and cheerful sensuality'. She had first made her mark as a scholarship pupil at the sports-orientated Millfield School, where she excelled at several disciplines, including hurdles and both long and high jump. As a long jumper she had an instinctively confident technique that had been moulded by her faithful coach, John Le Masurier (not the almost identically named comic actor in *Dad's Army*), and her six jumps in Tokyo all ranged between 6.56 metres and her world record of 6.76 in the fifth round.

Mary Rand's autobiography eventually appeared in 1969, and she was fortunate in that her agent, Bagenal Harvey, chose a New Zealander, Norman Harris, to help her compose it. Harris remains one of the finest of all sports writers, with an acute ear for a meaningful quote. The description of the completion of her winning jump pulsates with excitement and captures perfectly a disarming degree of naïvety on her part:

> You stand up, skip out of the pit, look back for the flag. A white flag. They're measuring. On to the board flashed '6.76'. A roar's going up from the stand. 'My God, what have I done?' You can't think, with these centimetres. You'll have to check with the programme, back in the bag. You're running back and the crowd's going stark mad. In the programme at the top of the page the figure for the World Record. The figure down there is 6.70. Back on the board they've got 6.76. There must be some mistake, there must be. Any minute they're going to correct it and it's going to read 6.67, or 6.66, and not 6.76. But it doesn't change. It's funny. It didn't feel all that long. But then that's the way with the best ones, you don't realise it.

Four days later came the men's long-jump final, which held out no great promise for Britain as in the morning Lynn Davies had only qualified for the final with the last of his three efforts, and that was 7.67 metres compared to 8.03 by the American world-record holder and defending champion, Ralph Boston. But in the afternoon's final the persistent rain inhibited everyone – even Davies, from showery South Wales – and although Boston led after four rounds it was with no more than 7.88 to 7.80 for Igor Ter-Ovanesyan, of the USSR, and 7.78 for the Welshman. In his biography six years later Davies, who was a good enough sprinter to have run in the 100 metres earlier in the Games, recalled his fifth jump. He waited at the end of the runway for the wind to drop and then set off: 'I gave it the gun. I went down the runway faster, I'm sure, than I've ever moved in my life and I hammered into that board. I knew it was going to be one of the best of the afternoon.'

The jump was measured at 8.07 metres (26 feet 5¾ inches). It was not only the best of the afternoon but the best of Davies's life so far. Maybe the familiar weather helped, and certainly it was too much of a temptation for the media to resist saying so. Perversely Davies recalled that before the morning's qualifying 'people were saying how delighted I should be that this was real South Wales weather, but all I could think of was that it was still tipping down and that I was wet and miserable'. What was immeasurably in Davies's favour was that he had trained immensely hard under the guidance of an exuberant national coach for Wales, Ron Pickering, later to gain wider public renown as a television

The leap of Lynn's life! The last time Britain had won Olympic long-jump gold had been … four days before, but the odds seemed set against Lynn Davies emulating Mary Rand's success in Tokyo in 1964. In the final he was in third place, with the world-record holder, Ralph Boston, of the USA, leading, but then in the fifth of the six rounds Davies produced a best-ever jump of 8.07 metres, which was more than enough in the relentless rain to ensure gold.
BY COURTESY OF MARK SHEARMAN

commentator. Pickering had first spotted Davies as an untutored 19-year-old and he drove his protégé hard: flat-out sprints of 60, 150 or 220 yards; charging up sand-hills for 40 minutes at a time; repeatedly long jumping to within a few centimetres of his competitive best. Davies also swam, did up to 1½ hours of continuous gymnastic exercises, and lifted huge weights – 245lbs power clean, 240lbs bench press.

All this activity was fitted into a teacher's career. In the 1960s there was rarely any lucrative future in prospect, no cashing in on Olympic gold, no touring round Grand Prix meetings, no collecting generous appearance fees or lavish prizes. Athletics would remain strictly amateur – or at least supposedly so – for the best part of another two decades, and Pickering realistically forewarned Davies of a rather more prosaic post-Tokyo schedule: 'I tried to tell him about the enormous problems I thought would lie ahead of him when he got home to Britain. Every women's institute in Wales would want him to speak to them, every church to open their bazaar. The advertisers would be after him, too, quite apart from the well-wishers, and if he accepted their offers it would mean the end of his athletics career.' Davies shunned the big-money temptations, eventually jumped even further, and won European and Commonwealth golds, but his career ended in anti-climax, swept into the oblivion of ninth place at the 1968 Mexico City Olympics, demoralised by Bob Beamon's shattering world-record leap of 8.90 metres, which would not be bettered for 23 years.

On the day that Mary Rand became long-jump champion, her friend and team-mate, Ann Packer, won her first-round heat of the 400 metres. The next day she won her semi-final, and the day after that she was second in the final to Betty Cuthbert, of Australia, 52.01 to 52.20. As Miss Packer's pre-Games best had been 53.4, this would have been a perfectly satisfactory conclusion to her Games, neatly rounded off on the final day by seeing her husband-to-be and Britain's team captain, Robbie Brightwell, collecting another silver medal in the 4 × 400 metres relay. In between times, though, the future Mrs Brightwell had kept herself rather busy.

There had seemed to be a good chance of reaching the final of her subsidiary event, the 800 metres, and maybe even challenging for the bronze. Her best time of 2 minutes 5.3 seconds was far behind that of a North Korean, Sin Kim Dan, and slower than all of the three entrants from the Soviet Union, plus a Frenchwoman and a Hungarian. However, this was an event still feeling its way at international level. It had been contested at the Olympic Games of 1928 and immediately dropped from the programme by the exclusively male bastion of officialdom, persuaded despite much evidence to the contrary that it was too long a distance for women to contend with. Since then womanhood had proved rather adept at numerous strenuous pursuits once conveniently regarded as beyond its powers, and the 800 metres had at last been restored in Rome in 1960. Unfortunately, after they had arrived in Tokyo, Sin Kim Dan and the entire North Korean team had been sent home, refused permission to compete for no better reason than that they had taken part in an unsanctioned Games in Indonesia the previous year. So much for the Olympic spirit!

Struggling heavy-legged after her earlier endeavours at 400 metres, Ann Packer got through her heat and looked much better in the next day's semi-final. Even so, it was to general astonishment another day later that she swept past all seven opponents in the last 100 metres or so (PLATE 3). This was an Olympic final unlike any other, which even the articulate Neil Allen found hard to put into words that evening:

> When we write of great races it is words like 'tense', 'strain', 'pain', 'effort'
> which come to mind quickest. But not with Ann's 800 metres victory which so
> moved the thousands here today. Rather the demand is for 'ease', 'grace', 'joy',
> 'freshness'. Neither gold medal nor World Record seemed to put any burden on
> Ann as she crossed the line, arms raised, a half smile on her lips.

Ann herself was matter-of-fact about passing the French leader of the race to go on to gold: 'I knew at last I really had a chance and I came up to Dupureur expecting her to fight back. But she didn't and I went by. It all seemed so easy.' The winning time was 2 minutes 1.2 seconds (Sin Kim Dan had run an authentic but unratified 1:58.0), but it was only the seventh 800 metres race of Packer's life – the first of them the previous May. Her true potential might well have equalled that of the North Korean, but that we shall never know: she ran one more race soon after the Games, before retiring at the age of just 22. She married Robbie Brightwell and had three sons. Her mentor was Denis Watts, yet another product of Geoff Dyson's national coaching scheme, but even he had underestimated her capabilities, and the most heartfelt tribute came from the silver-medallist, Maryvonne Dupureur, who reflected, 'Your Packer was much too good. I did the best I could, but she is a true champion and I am very happy for her.'

Did anyone but know it, this was one of the last flings of the true amateurs. Of the 63 athletes in the British team, 16 were at college or university, 3 still at school, and 11 were teachers or lecturers: at least they had the long summer holidays to fit in their major competitions, although as the Tokyo Olympics were held in October term-time they would still have needed leave of absence to answer their country's call. Another 17 worked in offices, managerial or clerical. There were four engineers, two electricians, two fitters, a police officer, a soldier, a medical practitioner, an estate agent, a research chemist, a fireplace tiler and a housewife (Mrs Rand). Only one described his occupation as 'athletics', and he was the 5000 metres runner, Mike Wiggs, competing in his second Olympics, and even he admitted to being also a part-time sales representative. There was money to be made in athletics, as there had been as long as anybody could remember, and the surreptitious exchanges of little brown envelopes would eventually have to give way to full-blooded professionalism, but not for the time being. Eminent Olympic athletes had been disqualified for accepting money ever since the great Native American all-rounder, Jim Thorpe, had been deprived of the two gold medals he won in 1912. The finest of all distance runners in the inter-war years, Paavo Nurmi, of Finland, had also been banned for professionalism, and from the 1940s onwards illegal payments became commonplace. How else could it be explained that, for example, Olympic medal-winners would tour Europe throughout each summer, competing almost every day for more than two months, moving on each night from one town to the next? Of course, they loved athletics, but how could any 'amateurs' – other than the independently wealthy, or perhaps university students for whom it might be regarded as an inexpensive way to spend the holidays – afford to indulge their passion for the sake of travel expenses and lodging alone?

As a postscript to these Tokyo Games, there was a number of performances in 1964 that would, with hindsight, appear of great significance in subsequent Olympic Games: for example, Miss M.E. Peters had a fourth place in athletics, J.R. Braithwaite had a seventh in shooting, R.J.H. Meade was eighth and R.S. Jones ninth in equestrianism, while J.R. Fox was twenty-ninth in the modern pentathlon. All would do rather better in Olympic celebrations to come.

TEN

———

The Games of 1968, 1972 and 1976

All of them still amateurs, but some are more amateur than others

I T might seem perverse to group the Games of 1968 with those of the 1970s rather than the 1960s, but there is sense in doing so. For these three Games shared certain characteristics and stigmas: Mexico City, with its problems of high altitude, to which the Olympic delegates had seemed oblivious when they cast their votes; then Munich and its terrorist debacle; and then Montreal and its African-inspired boycott. These events provided tangible evidence of the increasing politicisation of the Games. In the purely sporting context, the balance of power shifted dramatically over the same time frame, although some would contend there was very little that was 'sporting' about it.

None of this transformation ought to have come as a surprise, and the frankest admission of it was to be found in an obscure but important publication in 1964 in which the author reviewed the development of the Olympics over the previous dozen years. 'The meeting in Helsinki in 1952,' he wrote,

> marked a new era in the history of the Olympic Games – the epoch of gigantic Olympics. But it was certainly not in the way that Coubertin had imagined it. The Helsinki Olympics far outgrew the significance of sports events. The Games became an international and social matter in which victory, and not participation, was the most important. And as far as pure amateurism was concerned, perhaps that should not even be mentioned! Everyone behaved as if he did not know, but everyone knew. And everyone knew that the person he had just been speaking to also knew. So it is perhaps best not to broach the subject of amateurism.

Remarkably, this was not published as a thoughtful leader article in *Le Figaro*, *The Times* or *New York Times*; instead, it came from the pen of one of the most influential figures in state-funded Eastern European sport and appeared in a compact history of the Olympics published in Budapest and translated into English. He was Sándor Barcs, politician, journalist, administrator. During his long lifetime – he lived to the age of 97, dying in 2010 – he was president of the Hungarian Football Association and of the Hungarian state news agency and radio network. He was a member of the country's parliament and a vice-president of FIFA, the ruling body of world football. He was also a pragmatist with an acute sense of history. The Hungarian footballers had inflicted that humiliating 6–3 defeat on England's professionals at Wembley in 1953, and afterwards Barcs had famously remarked, 'Jimmy Hogan has taught us all that we know about football'. Hogan was a Lancashire-born coach largely unappreciated in England, who had mainly worked on the Continent and in particular in Hungary in the 1920s.

At the 1968 Games Hungary achieved its highest ever placing in the medals table, fourth to the USA, USSR and Japan, but the advance of real significance was made by the German Democratic Republic. The Communist-ruled eastern part of divided Germany was allowed for the first time to compete in its own right at the Winter Olympics in Grenoble and then in the Summer Games, where it won 30 medals in all to Britain's 13. From a country with a population of no more than 17 million, this was a spectacular return, and yet it was only the beginning. In 1972, Winter and Summer, there would be 80 medals for the GDR; in 1976 there would be 109, and in 1980 (admittedly boycotted by around 60 countries, including the US, following the Soviet invasion of Afghanistan) that figure had risen to 149.

This remarkable ascent to Olympic prominence was achieved by the simple process of spending as much money on elite sport as Britain did on its entire education programme. From the age of seven onwards youngsters were picked out to attend specialist schools where their physical and psychological potential were assessed to identify for which sport they would prove most suitable. The proof of the comprehensiveness of the planning was that at the 1980 Games the GDR would win gold in six different Winter Sports disciplines (biathlon, bobsled, Nordic skiing, figure-skating, luge and speed-skating) and in ten in the Summer (athletics, boxing, canoeing, cycling, gymnastics, handball, judo, rowing, swimming and diving). In seven of these branches of sport Britain was scarcely or not at all represented.

All of the Eastern European countries, as well as China and Cuba, were developing state-aided sports systems as a propaganda tool, but the GDR was proving rather more adept at it than anyone else. A comprehensive study in 1980 by two British researchers, Simon Freeman and Roger Boyes, suggested the following reasons: 'They are better at selecting young athletes, more ruthless in training them, totally uncompromising when faced with failure. They are driven, too, by a desire to win that is matched only in the Soviet Union. There the enemy is America: in East Germany it is West Germany.' There were reckoned to be 20 such schools in the GDR, and more than 20,000 pupils aged eight to ten in 'training' (30 hours sport, 15 hours academic studies each week) at any one time. Whatever the youngsters themselves thought about ideological differences, the long-term attraction for them was rather more materialistic – and denim-clad. 'Paid by the state to train, compete and of course win, they clearly enjoy the fruits of success,' wrote Freeman and Boyes, '… the most treasured privilege of all is the freedom to travel to the West, a right granted to only a handful even amongst the country's elite. With just one careful shopping trip in London or New York an athlete can easily double his annual income.' Authentic blue jeans fetched astronomical prices behind the Iron Curtain.

By contrast, Britain had Loughborough University – where neither sporting talent nor blue jeans were in short supply – which had provided half a dozen of Britain's athletes in Tokyo, but strenuous practice sessions in the swimming pool or on the rugby pitch for the budding PE teachers who studied there were not necessarily the best preparations for running, jumping and throwing at Olympic level.

Some of the runners and jumpers from the 112 competing nations revelled in Mexico's conditions; others didn't. With less resistance to encounter in Mexico City's thin air, the leading athletes in the explosive events thrived – there were world records for men at 100, 200, 400, 800 metres, 400 metres hurdles, 4 × 100 and 4 × 400 metres relays, and in the long jump and triple jump; and for women at 100, 200, 400 metres, 100 metres hurdles, 4 × 100 metres and long jump. Conversely, the distance runners from the low altitude countries suffered tortuously with less oxygen to take in, and Britain's Ron Hill (seventh in the 10,000 metres) and Bill Adcocks (fifth in the marathon) deserve far more credit than such worthy finishing positions usually earn.

The one golden British contribution in athletics was exceptional even by the supreme standards required to attain such heights, and from a personal point of view I would have no hesitation in saying that of the six Olympic Games at which I have been present the only track victory that I have seen which was as commanding and as aesthetically satisfying as David Hemery's at 400 metres hurdles in Mexico was that of Herb Elliott, of Australia, eight years earlier in the Rome 1500 metres. Hemery broke the world record and won by a huge margin, seven-tenths of a second (PLATE 4). Yet his account of the last few metres of the race, in which he was in lane six, reflects none of this majestic superiority so obvious to those of us eagerly watching:

> Maddeningly, my legs just would not change pace. To make matters worse, I was sub-consciously waiting for the 'ooh' of the crowd when a leader is being caught by a fast finisher, and I could not understand why there was no crowd noise. With every muscle in me, I forced my stride length and speed to be maintained to the tape. I dipped at the line and two strides afterwards tipped my head to the right to see if Whitney was coming by. I could not see him and my hands went to my knees. I had not looked left and was still not 100 per cent sure I had won.

He need not have worried. The American he had feared in lane seven, Ron Whitney, was ten metres behind, and it was a German, Gerhard Hennige, who distantly took the silver and another Briton, John Sherwood, the bronze from the outside lane.

Hemery had some advantage in his preparations because he came from an academic background and had time to spare for his training as he had completed his degree studies with the Games approaching. But his methods of preparation for hurdling were unusual in that he had spent his upbringing from the age of 12 in the USA, where his father had pursued a chartered accountancy career, and he had one coach at Boston University, Billy Smith, who looked after his strength and stamina, and another in London, Fred Housden, who took care of technique when Hemery made his summer visits. The two coaches were only ever to meet once, and that was four years later. Housden was a 78-year-old retired Harrow School mathematics teacher who had a quaint habit of sending Hemery doggerel verse to inspire him on the eve of a major race. His pre-Mexico exhortation was thus:

> Come off, H, ten
> With speed and then
> Sprint like the devil's own.
> If you'd be great
> Just *concentrate*
> And be the first man home.
> Then, should you win the highest stand,
> It won't be good, it will be grand!
> All the best, Fred.

Hemery himself was a rather unlikely champion – tall, almost gawky, fair curly hair, and a soft-spoken manner untainted by any transatlantic twang, which gave him the guise of perhaps a trendy young clergyman rather than what the Russians would call a true 'Master of Sport', the honorific title that brought with it so much material benefit. Like all great champions, though, he was intensely focused and an accurate judge of his abilities – at the beginning of 1968 when the world record stood at 49.1 seconds he had written in his diary '48.0' as his seemingly wildly ambitious target time at the Games; in the event he ran 48.12. He had won the shorter hurdles race, at 120 yards, at the 1966 Commonwealth Games in Jamaica and would continue to the 1972 Olympics, where he had very reasonable hopes of winning again over the full lap. But he then came up against a revelation in the form of John Akii-Bua, of Uganda, who beat Hemery's world record, with the defending champion a gallant third. Akii-Bua owed his emergence entirely to British expertise, as Malcolm Arnold had been Uganda's national coach for four years. Arnold would later return home and number among his future charges another hurdler, Colin Jackson, who would win everything but an Olympic gold, and a sprinter, Jason Gardener, who would win gold as a relay runner.

Hemery was a committed amateur in an era of sport when it was becoming increasingly difficult to achieve the highest honours without some form of financial support, and any such support could push the bounds of the existing rules for Olympic eligibility. The year after the Mexico Games, in conversation with Neil Allen, the most informed of British athletics writers, Hemery explained,

> I can understand that my personal attitude will seem very strange to others.
> I simply feel that to make money in any way from amateur athletics would

Bob Braithwaite and his trusty rifle return home after his gold medal at the 1968 Games in clay-pigeon shooting, then known as 'Olympic Trench' and now as 'Olympic Trap'. Winning Britain's first gold medal on the range since 1924, Braithwaite hit all of the last 187 clays in succession to score 198 points out of 200. He won by two points, having missed bronze by the same margin, in seventh place, in 1964.
TOPFOTO

completely spoil for me what is fun. I agree there are those who need money much more – perhaps a young male athlete who, for example, has a wife and young child to support and is hoping to buy his own house. But I hope you will understand that I myself am only an unemployed student with a small allowance who will *have* to work in 1969.

Other British champions in Mexico had been giving thought to the very same subject.

The success of Bob Braithwaite has been described in the context of his sport, shooting, as 'one of the last occasions that a gifted amateur with steely determination and great skill won over a field consisting predominantly of commercially sponsored and government funded professionals'. Braithwaite became Britain's first gold-medallist on the range for 44 years by hitting 198 of the 200 4¼-inch clay targets fired from a trench into the air at more than 100 miles per hour, including the last 187 in succession. In the process he beat 58 other marksmen from 31 different countries.

Braithwaite had placed seventh in Tokyo, but his duties as a veterinary surgeon at Garstang, in Lancashire, had so much restricted his opportunities to make the journeys to the only available Olympic-standard clay-pigeon practice ranges at Hull or Bournemouth that he set up a makeshift device in a field at the family farm near Lancaster, with the obliging parish vicar volunteering to operate the release mechanism. Now aged 43, and having been a vet for more than twenty years, Braithwaite had considered becoming a full-time marksman, but in an interview with Alan Hubbard, of *World Sports* magazine, a year after his golden triumph, he pointed out the drawback of a Briton doing so:

> With our outlook, of course, I would automatically forfeit Olympic status.
> But it's all wrong, you know. We and the Spaniards must be the only
> shooters in Europe who are not professional. The Frenchman who won
> the European title two years ago is a government-sponsored coach to their
> association, and this year's champion, another Frenchman, works full-time for
> a cartridge-manufacturing company. I've had offers to do the same, but I prefer
> my independence.

Taking the gold by two points from Sergeant Thomas Garrigua, of the US Air Force – in a contest in which 193 hits out of 200 for a Frenchman, an Italian and a Romanian were not even good enough to make the top ten places – was akin to winning the 1500 metres on the track by 20 yards ... just as Herb Elliott had done in Rome. 'Shooting,' Braithwaite explained, 'is as much a mental thing as physical. You can liken it to driving. One day you can purr down the M1 like Jackie Stewart and the next like some old woman.' Stewart, being a handy man himself with a sporting rifle when not winning Grand Prix motor races, would have understood the analogy perfectly.

Braithwaite was noted for his forthrightness, and four years later, when he just missed out on Olympic selection for the third time, he fired off a scathing verbal broadside in the direction of the man who had been the autocratic president of the International Olympic Committee since 1952, Avery Brundage: 'The Games are completely "shamateur". How that man Brundage can get up on the podium and talk about amateurs when all his American shooters are employed by the United States Army, Air Force or Marines purely to shoot [for competitive sport], I can never understand.'

In Mexico Great Britain took five gold medals in all, and the only higher total since 1924 had been in Melbourne in 1956. Braithwaite's had been Britain's eleventh shooting gold in Olympic history, though the first since 1924, and the other 1968 successes also came in familiar sports – boxing, equestrianism and yachting. Chris Finnegan was Britain's twelfth winner in boxing, Rodney Pattisson and Iain Macdonald-Smith the twelfth in yachting, while the horsemen (and a horsewoman this time) contributed a third team success in the last five Games. Athletics, admittedly with rather more events to choose from, still far out-stripped every other sport. Hemery was the forty-first British gold-medal winner in track or field events.

The middleweight boxing gold-medallist Chris Finnegan came from the small Buckinghamshire town of Iver (where the pseudo-Cockney *Carry On* film actor, Sid James, was a fellow resident), and Finnegan expressed himself in much the same forthright manner, being a hod-carrier on a building site by trade. He beat Aleksey Kiselyov, of the USSR, in the middleweight final and breezily described the contest thus: 'I went out and thought "He's a big sort of boy, so I'll get me jab going". But I was a bit tensed because I'd seen him whang down some stick-and-run boys like me before. When I got back, me corner gave me a bit of a telling off. But the Russian was huffing and puffing when I got in close and I could feel his old lungs going.' Finnegan dealt with the issue of money in the practical manner of other post-war Olympic boxers by turning professional soon afterwards, and he became British light-heavyweight champion in 1971 and European champion the next year. He challenged for the world title at Wembley later in 1972 and was stopped in the fourteenth round by Bob Foster, of the USA, in a contest described by the authoritative magazine, *The Ring*, as the 'Fight of the Year'.

Jane Bullen (later to be Mrs Holderness-Roddam), of the winning equestrian three-day event team, came from rather different stock to Chris Finnegan, having been educated privately by a governess to the age of 14, and she was to become joint owner of a 1,000-acre stables in Wiltshire. By 20 she was qualifying as a state-registered nurse and required special leave from Middlesex Hospital to go to Mexico. She was the first British woman to compete in the three-day event. One of her team-mates was Ben Jones, a staff-sergeant in the Royal Army Veterinary Corps who in 1964 had been the first non-commissioned

The equestrian team that won the three-day event title for Great Britain in 1968: from left to right, Derek Allhusen, Jane Bullen, Richard Meade and Ben Jones. Allhusen, aged 54, took the individual silver medal, with Meade fourth, Jones fifth and Bullen eighteenth. The British success was based on outstanding performances over a cross-country course that was described by their manager as 'the most dangerous I've seen'.

TOPFOTO

Richard Meade is the most successful horse-rider in British Olympic history, with three-day event team gold in 1968 and then team and individual gold in 1972 riding 'Laurieston'. By 1972 Britain had thus won the team title for the third time, having also done so in 1956, but Meade's was the country's first individual success. He was practically born in the saddle – his parents were joint Masters of Hounds in Monmouthshire.

officer to represent Great Britain in the sport and subsequently was in charge of schooling for the King's Troop of the Royal Horse Artillery. The team captain was 54-year-old Major Derek Allhusen, who was yet another Olympian educated at Eton and Trinity College, Cambridge, and a past high sheriff of Norfolk who bred horses for a living. The fourth member was Richard Meade, an insurance broker by occupation who had also been at Cambridge and had then served in the 10th Hussars.

That is not to suggest for one moment that their gold medals had been easier won than that of Finnegan. Both Jones and Meade were riding their horses for the first time in competition, and Allhusen – rather in the manner of Harry Llewellyn 16 years before – clinched the gold with an unexpected clear round in the show-jumping finale. Allhusen narrowly missed the individual silver and Meade was fourth, Jones fifth and Jane Bullen eighteenth. Yet it is worth pointing out that had any of this quartet been a paid coach in such sports as athletics, boxing or swimming, for instance, they would not have been allowed to compete for Britain at the Olympics. Such a full-time occupation as those of

Staff-Sergeant Jones or Major Allhusen was perfectly acceptable if you rode a horse, and this, of course, once again made a complete nonsense of the antiquated Olympian concept of amateurism. Allhusen, incidentally, is one of the few Olympians from any country to have competed in both Summer and Winter Games, though a pentathlon competition consisting of cross-country skiing, downhill skiing, shooting, fencing and horse-riding, in which he was sixth in 1948, was classified only as a 'demonstration' event.

At the ill-fated 1972 Munich Olympics, Britain was to win the three-day event team competition again, and Richard Meade took the individual gold to become Britain's most successful equestrian rider. His colleagues this time were Captain Mark Phillips of the 1st Queen's Dragoon Guards, Mary Gordon-Watson and Bridget Parker, but as yet the idea had not filtered through to the Olympic hierarchy that each team member deserved gold – after all, they had ridden more than 50 miles (80 kilometres) apiece to achieve their victory. Only one medal was presented at the victory ceremony, for which the duties were performed by Prince Philip, conscious no doubt of the irony that his daughter, Princess Anne, the future wife for 19 years of Captain Phillips, was missing out because injury to her horse had forced her to withdraw from the selection short-list after winning the European title.

Rodney Pattisson, the victorious helmsman in the 1968 Flying Dutchman class, could well have been dubbed 'the David Hemery of the High Seas', or – to be more nautically precise – Acapulco Bay. Pattisson and his crew, Iain Macdonald-Smith, won five of the competition's seven races and were second in another to achieve the greatest winning margin in Olympic yachting history. The name of their speedy craft was *Superdocious*: presumably the additional 'cali-fragilistic-expiali' to complete the title of the song from *Mary Poppins* was omitted because the full name would barely have fitted into the length of the 6.6 metre hull. Pattisson was a Royal Navy submarine lieutenant at the time of his success but took advantage of the relaxed attitude regarding the amateur status of Olympic sailors by resigning his commission soon after the Games and joining a Dorset boat-building firm as their European sales manager to aid his preparations for the next Olympics in 1972.

The plan worked because Pattisson, renowned as a demanding perfectionist who was expert at tuning his yacht to its racing optimum, remains one of Britain's most successful Olympic competitors in his sport. Having won in Mexico with Macdonald-Smith, Pattisson successfully defended his title in Munich four years later in the grand manner, winning four of the six races, partnered by Chris Davies, who held a managerial post with the boat-building company Vosper-Thornycroft. Then in Montreal in 1976 Pattisson would take the silver with Julian Brooke-Houghton as his crew. Pattisson's first international success had been as a 17-year-old in 1960 when he won the World Cadet class title. It was in this same year that the Flying Dutchman class had been introduced to the Olympics and it would continue until 1992.

Macdonald-Smith, aged 23, and a recent Cambridge University graduate who was now a solicitor's clerk by profession, had only come together with Pattisson a year before the Mexico Olympics, when they were second in the British championship, but such

The Flying Dutchman sailing class in 1968 and again in 1972 was won by a 'Flying Scot'. Rodney Pattisson (*left*) took the gold on the first occasion with Iain Macdonald-Smith (*right*) as his crew and on the second with Chris Davies alongside. In 1976 Pattisson added a silver with a third partner, Julian Brooke-Houghton.
TOPFOTO

was the rapport they struck up that they were also world champions on three occasions. Macdonald-Smith competed again in the 1976 Olympics on his own merits, placing thirteenth in the Soling class.

Pattisson and Macdonald-Smith were succeeded as gold-medallists in comparable manner at those 1976 Games by Reg White and his brother-in-law, John Osborn, who similarly won four of the first six races in the newly introduced International Tornado catamaran class to take the title without even needing to start the seventh and final race. No one knew better than White the capabilities of the craft he sailed, as he was a boat-builder by profession and had helped in the design of the Tornado in his home town of Brightlingsea on the Essex coast. The son of an oyster merchant, White was world champion in 1979, as his son, Robert, was to be in later years, and even at the very end of his days he was inextricably linked with the water. Having just completed a race with his 19-year-old grandson as crew, he died of a heart attack at the age of 74 just a few feet away from where he had first set sail. Robert White junior remembered, 'When I was five or six I was asked what I wanted to be, and I said, "A tiller man, like my dad"'.

Like Pattisson, Britain's only athletics winner in Munich in 1972 took part in the Olympics on three occasions. In 1964 Mary Peters had placed fourth in the five-event two-day pentathlon – 80 metres hurdles (later replaced by 100 metres hurdles), shot, high jump, long jump and 200 metres – and in 1968 she was ninth. Had she retired then, as she might well have done at the age of 29, she would have been remembered as a fine athlete but not a great one.

The crucial deciding 200 metres in the Olympic pentathlon of 1972. Heide Rosendahl, of Federal Germany, wins and Britain's Mary Peters (number 111 in late 3) finishes far behind, but it's times that count, not positions, and Mary has run just fast enough to take the gold overall by 10 points, a world record 4,801 to 4,791. The others in the photograph are (from the left) Karen Mack (Federal Germany), seventh overall; Valentina Tikhomirova (USSR), fifth; Nedyalka Anghelova (Bulgaria) sixth; Burglinde Pollak and Chistine Bodner (both Democratic Germany), third and fourth.

But then, at Munich in 1972, in her eighteenth year of competition, Mary Peters was transformed into a household name. Before the Olympics she had ranked fifth to three German women and one from the Soviet Union, but she then proceeded to set personal bests in the hurdles and high jump and lead by 97 points at the end of the first day. By the time that the leaders came to line up for the closing 200 metres Peters was still ahead, but Heide Rosendahl, competing for the German Federal Republic on home ground and in third place, was much the better sprinter; the difference in personal bests was 1.1 seconds. Rosendahl won and the electronic scoreboard showed that she had run her best ever, 22.96. Peters was at least eight metres behind. Fevered reference to the scoring tables revealed that she needed at worst 24.18 to win the gold … and at last the figures flashed up. It was 24.08 for Peters to claim overall victory, with a world-record total score.

It wasn't a tabloid newspaper but the august British publication for the sport's enthusiasts, *Athletics Weekly*, which described Mary Peters as 'the bouncy blonde with the flashing smile and cheery wave', and it fitted to perfection. Her background, in fact, singled her out as an unlikely champion. She was the first female gold-medallist in any sport to have come from Northern Ireland, though actually born near Liverpool. The Troubles in Northern Ireland had broken out a few years earlier, and just a few months before the Games Bloody Sunday had marked a particular low-point in the province's history, when 26 protesters had been killed by the British army on the streets of Londonderry. Yet on 5 September it was political violence from a very different quarter that erupted to ruin the sporting celebrations in Munich. Just two days after Mary Peters had won her pentathlon gold medal the 'Black September' Palestinian terrorist group attacked the Israeli team in the Olympic village, leading to the deaths of 11 competitors and officials. Understandably, Dame Mary Peters, as she was to become, preferred not to be drawn into statements on political matters, but she later expressed the belief that it was right that the Olympics should have continued. Sport, she said, was not as important as people's lives, but even so it would have been wrong to capitulate and bring the Games to a halt.

Her recollections of her decisive 200 metres to win the pentathlon gold were appealingly simplistic for someone who would go on to forge a career in public life as, among numerous other activities, an inspirational speaker, British women's team manager and national federation president, founder of the Ulster Sports Trust and nomination as lord lieutenant of Belfast. 'I went out there and ran and ran,' she mused, 'and about 50 metres from home my legs were like jelly and I thought I'd never make it to the tape.'

Dame Mary had moved to Northern Ireland at the age of 11. She had first competed in a pentathlon in 1955 at the age of 15 without even having tried some of the events before and had become a British international by 1961 despite having only one decrepit track in Belfast on which to train, spending £100 of her own money so that she could have a foam landing in the high-jump pit. Weight-training up to three days a week, and capable of bench-pressing 140lb, she had won the Commonwealth Games shot put and pentathlon in 1970. Spurred by those successes, and by now working as a secretary in the health studio owned by her coach, Buster McShane, she set about her Olympic task in a fervently resolute manner. 'I went for gold,' she recalled. 'There was nothing else in my mind but gold.'

The by-now recurring theme of amateurism crops up once again when considering the careers of the four British gold-medallists at the 1976 Winter and Summer Games. All of them did comply fully with the Olympic regulations regarding eligibility, but to some extent they all recognised that the amateur ideal was being tested and strained: the rule seemed clear enough, but it could be bent in all sorts of ways.

John Curry won the figure-skating in Innsbruck. Then in the summer at Montreal there were triumphs for the modern pentathlon team, for David Wilkie in swimming, and for boat-builder Reg White and John Osborn, as previously mentioned. Curry and Wilkie both turned to the USA for the coaching and training facilities they needed. Of the winning modern pentathlon trio, Jim Fox was an army sergeant competing in his fourth Olympics in what had once been an exclusively military discipline (PLATE 5).

Curry was truly a ground-breaker, as the previous highest placing by a Briton in men's figure-skating had been fourth in 1908, and Curry's consummate balletic artistry in winning Olympic gold transformed the concept of the sport. But he estimated that his final year's preparations for the Games had cost the best part of £10,000, and when he was asked at a post-Olympic press conference whether that came close to making him a professional he responded diplomatically, 'I am an amateur as described by the rule books'. At the 1972 Games Curry had placed eleventh but was then offered sponsorship by an American industrialist who was a skating enthusiast and joined the training group in Denver, Colorado, of an esteemed coach, Carlo Fassi. After his Olympic victory Curry turned professional, forming his own ice-dance company, but died of an AIDS-related heart attack at the age of 44.

John Curry returns from Innsbruck after his 1976 figure-skating victory. It was said of him that he 'gave one of the greatest performances in skating history to take the Olympic gold medal … graceful, athletic, and with a perfectly co-ordinated programme, he completely outclassed the rest of the world's finest skaters.' This was still the era of amateurism, and after winning the world title Curry turned professional and set up a spectacular touring ice show.
TOPFOTO

In 1976 David Wilkie became the first British male swimmer for 68 years to take an Olympic title. And he did it in the grand manner, breaking the world record for the 200 metres breaststroke. Of Scottish parentage, though born in Sri Lanka, Wilkie had been the Olympic silver-medallist in 1972 and then took up the offer of a scholarship at the University of Miami to improve his chances at the next Games. The Florida climate obviously helped.
TOPFOTO

Wilkie, Britain's first male swimmer to win Olympic gold since 1908, had been the silver-medallist in the 200 metres breaststroke in Munich in 1972. The following January he had left his Edinburgh home for Florida to study marine biology at the University of Miami and he won the world title that year. He took the 1976 Montreal gold by almost exactly the same margin of two seconds or so as he had lost to the same man, John Hencken, of the USA, four years before. Seven of Wilkie's Great Britain team-mates in Montreal stated their intention of taking up US college scholarships, and one of the four going to Wilkie's *alma mater* was Kevin Burns, from Sheffield, who spoke for all when he spelled out the reason: 'Why shouldn't we accept the scholarships? I gave up a £4,000-a-year job in computers to go on the dole because I needed the time for training.

Now I'll be getting further education and good swimming.' Apart from Wilkie, Americans won all the other 12 men's swimming titles in Montreal.

Danny Nightingale, of the modern pentathlon team, spoke for all when he said: 'The only way to win an Olympic gold medal in any sport now is to make it your whole goal for a limited time. You have to do it full-time, worrying about nothing else. And to do that you need somebody to support you, not just a few hundred pounds but perhaps thousands.' Nightingale, a 22-year-old engineering student at the University of Sussex, had kept body and soul together during his Olympic preparations by working as a part-time gardener, and fortunately for him and his fellow gold-medallists there was financial backing for the last three months from the Sports Aid Foundation, which had been formed in 1976 to raise money from the private sector (now known 36 years later as SportsAid it still, commendably, keeps alive the principle of encouraging voluntary donations from the public).

After three of the modern pentathlon segments had been completed, Great Britain was back in eighth place in the team standings, but Adrian Parker won the 300 metres swimming and he, Nightingale and Jim Fox all recorded their fastest ever times. Britain was now fifth and Parker had another victory in the closing 4000 metres cross-country race by 18 seconds, again magnificently supported by his team-mates, to turn a deficit of 537 points to Czechoslovakia into overall victory, 15,559 points to 15,451. Fox, who had been persuaded out of retirement after the Games of both 1968 and 1972, had suffered the disturbing experience of being involved in the fencing bout which led to the sensational disqualification of Boris Onischenko, of the USSR, for tampering with his epée in order to register hits to which he was not entitled. Onischenko, who had won team gold and individual silver in 1972, was bundled off home by the Soviet authorities and, stripped of his army colonel's rank, he eked out a living as a taxi-driver. Fox was commissioned as a captain, retired to a renovated barn in Oxfordshire, became chairman of Britain's Modern Pentathlon Association, and when he attended the annual Sports Writers' Association dinner in 1998, Alan Hubbard, writing for *The Independent*, described him in forgivably nostalgic terms as 'a swashbuckling Corinthian hero in an age when sportsmen were men and women seemed happy to be ladies … his dignified presence a sobering reminder of a gentler more romantic era before the pursuit of sporting glory became suffused by greed, drugs and duplicity.' Sadly, Fox still had his own problems to deal with, battling Parkinson's Disease.

Of the 235 gold medals on offer at the 1976 Games, both Winter and Summer, the Soviet Union had taken 62, the German Democratic Republic 47 and the USA 37, and these three countries were far ahead of all the rest. Great Britain was equal thirteenth with its four. Altogether, 134 titles went to the state-aided Eastern Europeans. The British monthly magazine, *Sportsreview*, the successor to *World Sports*, enterprisingly produced tables showing the distribution of Montreal gold medals in relation to the size of each nation's population. The GDR, not surprisingly, won by a street with 2.36 golds per million people. Great Britain was 'rather shamefacedly' twenty-second with 0.05.

ELEVEN

The Games of the 1980s

Two titles each for Coe, Thompson, Redgrave, Holmes ... and hot-shot Cooper

Boycotts were nothing new at the Olympics. In 1956 Holland, Spain and Switzerland had withdrawn in protest at the Soviet-led suppression of the Hungarian uprising three months before. Then in 1976 twenty African nations, supported by Iraq and Guyana, pulled out of the Games because of New Zealand's continuing rugby-union relations with the apartheid regime of South Africa. Commendable as these actions might seem, they had none of the impact that the mass walk-out before the Moscow Games was to have 1980.

In December 1979, just a few months before Moscow was due to stage the XXIInd Olympiad, 100,000 Soviet troops entered Afghanistan to bolster a faltering Communist faction there. Immediately protests flooded in from around the world, and President Jimmy Carter of the USA took the controversial step of initiating a boycott of that summer's Moscow Olympics. In the end a total of 65 nations, including Canada, West Germany and Japan, decided not to attend the Moscow Games, nearly all of them in protest at the Soviet invasion. The Americans were, of course, the most obvious of all the absent friends, but who could fail to be left with the impression that denying the country's amateur sporting elite their medal chances was nothing more than a cynical political gesture on the part of President Carter? None of the economic sanctions which surely could have been more effective were applied. Four years later, in spiteful retaliation, the USSR led 14 of its fellow Communist-bloc countries in staying away from the Los Angeles Games. The excuse this time was equally spurious – that the safety of Soviet athletes in California could not be guaranteed.

Ironically, the first Olympic competition of 1980 had taken place in the USA – at Lake Placid, in New York State, where the Winter Games were held in February. There the men's figure-skating gold was taken for the second successive time by a Briton. Robin Cousins, 22 years old and originally from Bristol, had won his first national title at the age of 12, and his vivid recollections of his years of dedicated training in London which led to Olympic gold were of 'getting up at four o'clock in the morning to practise for two hours on Queensway ice rink before the public session, then going to stack shelves at Whiteley's, living in a £9-a-week bed-sit at Notting Hill, with a Bunsen burner instead of a stove'. After his Olympic triumph Cousins led an altogether more affluent life, becoming a show-business star, promoting his own 'Ice Capades', and playing in theatre and pantomime.

Having thus achieved a gold medal in a Winter Sports event in which the USA was third, fourth and fifth, Great Britain could reasonably have been expected to do rather better at the Summer Games in Moscow in 1980 than in Montreal four years before. After all, the Americans, West Germans and Japanese had won 53 gold medals between them in 1976, and the boycott by these countries meant that these were now up for grabs. The main beneficiaries were inevitably the Soviet hosts, increasing their total from 49 in 1976 to 80. The British score improved from three wins to five, but the Italians and French did better, moving from two apiece in 1976 to eight and six respectively. The question which naturally arises is whether any of that British gold could be directly attributed to the absence of US opposition. Were the British wins devalued in any way as a result of less severe competition in Moscow? The answer, in a word, is 'no'.

Four of the golds came in athletics, just as in 1964, and Allan Wells (100 metres), Steve Ovett (800 metres), Sebastian Coe (1500 metres) and Daley Thompson (decathlon) were unquestionably among the very best athletes in the world. (PLATES 6–11) The closest challenge if the US team had been there would have been faced by Wells. The foremost of the American sprinters that year was Stanley Floyd, who achieved the rare feat of winning his country's national, national collegiate and 'Olympic trial' races, but it has to be said that 1980 was not a vintage year for US sprinting. Wells, becoming the first British Olympic champion at 100 metres since Harold Abrahams in 1924, and the first Scottish athletics gold-medallist since Eric Liddell the same year, was a truly worthy winner who came very close to completing the double at 200 metres. In the longer event he lost by just two one-hundredths of a second – not much more than the thickness of his vest – to the Italian world-record holder, Pietro Mennea.

Even without the Americans, the 100 metres was also a desperately close-run affair; the measure of which is that Wells and the Cuban, Silvio Leonard, drawn as far apart as they could be in lanes eight and one respectively, shared the same time to one-thousandth of a second (each one-thousandth representing no more than a centimetre or so's difference). (PLATE 7) It was the Scotsman's neatly timed dip at the line which showed him ahead on the automatic-timing photograph, and even then the judges took several minutes to make up their minds. Wells, at 28, was the oldest man to win an Olympic 100 metres and had only turned to sprinting four years earlier, having previously been merely the twenty-seventh ranked long jumper in Britain. His laconic comment afterwards was that 'I only saw Leonard in the last 20 metres and knew then that I had to do something special'. His wife and co-coach, Margot, watching from the stands, and herself an international sprinter, gasped with relief, 'I never want 10 seconds like that again. Allan's never beaten Leonard before, and I didn't think he had this time until I looked at the re-run.'

The form book in 1980 was torn up sensationally by two of Britain's other gold-medallists: Steve Ovett beat Sebastian Coe at 800 metres, and Coe beat Ovett at 1500 metres. (PLATES 8–10) Three weeks or so before the Games Coe had set a world record for the 800 of 1 minute 42.4 seconds and Ovett a world record for the 1500 of 3 minutes 32.1 seconds. So the way in which both athletes competed and responded made for one of the truly great sporting rivalries of modern times. At the Games Coe would be second at 800 metres and would then win the 1500 metres both there, with Ovett third, and in Los Angeles in 1984 – the only man in Olympic history to do so in that event twice, other than the American, James Lightbody, in the very different era of 1904 and the unofficial Games of 1906. During their careers Coe, Ovett and a future Olympic silver-medallist, Steve Cram, would between them set 20 world records, reducing the 800 metres from 1 minute 43.4 seconds to 1:41.73, the 1500 metres from 3:32.2 to 3:29.67 and the mile from 3:49.4 to 3:46.32 – equivalent in distance to some 12 metres, 15 metres and 20 metres respectively.

How, then, did it come about that Britain should produce three such outstanding middle-distance runners in the same era? The answer is two-fold, and in both cases tradition had a great deal to do with it. Firstly, over the decades a pattern had developed for various countries in turn to dominate these events – Finland in the 1920s, the USA and Great Britain in the 1930s, Sweden in the 1940s, and then Britain again, Hungary, Australia and New Zealand in the 1950s and 1960s, usually with two or three exceptional runners in each country spurring others on. Secondly, for the British the half-mile (actually some six yards further than 800 metres) and the mile (1,609 metres), with their blend of speed and stamina, had been of particular appeal ever since the mid-nineteenth century. Walter George had run a remarkable 4 minutes 12¾ seconds for the mile in 1886. The idea of breaking four minutes was already being voiced before the First World War by George Hutson, the AAA winner in 1914 but who was killed in action only two months later. That four-minute barrier, referred to above (page 98), had eventually been breached by Roger Bannister in 1954.

Almost invariably some form of advanced training methods over the previous 40 years or so had given each country in succession the advantage over its opponents, devised by the innovative coaching expertise of Gösta Holmér in Sweden, then Mihály Iglói in Hungary, Percy Cerutty in Australia and Arthur Lydiard in New Zealand. Coe had his father, Peter, as a mentor, bringing the precision of his background as an engineer to the process of producing a world-beating athlete, first envisaged when the youngster was barely into his teens. Ovett was guided by the wisdom of the affable Harry Wilson, who had competed with reasonable success at every event from the sprints to the marathon. The English Schools' championships had provided the first major wins for the future Olympic champions, but interestingly at other distances: Ovett at 400 metres in 1970, aged 14; Coe at 3000 metres in 1973, aged 16. Coe and Ovett had been surprisingly outpaced by an East German, Olaf Beyer, in the 1978 European Championships 800 metres, although Ovett won the 1500 three days later.

In Moscow Coe got the 800 final totally wrong, leaving himself far too much to do in the final straight. Ovett beat him by several metres, gold to silver. The last time that

The finish of the 1980 Moscow 800 metres. Steve Ovett wins by a couple of metres from Sebastian Coe. The others (*left to right*) are Andreas Busse and Detlef Wagenknecht, the East Germans who were fifth and sixth respectively, and Nikolay Kirov, of the USSR, who took the bronze medal. The winning time was relatively modest, 1:45.40, compared with Coe's world record from the previous year of 1:42.33, but gold was the target, whatever pace it took.

Britain had won both such medals in an Olympic athletics final had been 60 years before when Albert Hill and Philip Baker (later Lord Noel-Baker) were first and second at 1500 metres. Coe won the Moscow 1500 six days after the 800 against all expectations, but there was not another British 1–2 because he and Ovett were separated by another East German, Jürgen Straub. In Los Angeles four years on, when there was every prospect of Britain taking all three medals in the 1500, Ovett was unwell and Coe, having previously been second again in the 800 (to Joaquim Cruz, of Brazil), won from Steve Cram. Athletes representing Britain, or living and training in Britain, including in 1896 Teddy Flack (Australia), in 1920 Bevil Rudd (South Africa), in 1936 Jack Lovelock (New Zealand) and in 1948–52 Arthur Wint (Jamaica), had now won 29 Olympic medals in the men's 800 and 1500 metres.

The rivalry between Coe and Ovett – though they largely avoided each other in competition – was eagerly fanned by the British media, presenting them simplistically as a sort of Prince Charming (Coe, of course) and the dastardly Baron. Of course, their relationship was more complex than that. In 1981 Coe collaborated with the chief sports writer of the *Daily Express*, David Miller, on a biography entitled 'Running Free'. In his introduction Miller suggested in relation to Coe, 'It is the family ethic which has helped endear him to the people at a time when the decline of the family, and of trust and respect between parents and children, is contributing to debility in the Western world'. This interesting theory was then extended by Miller to link the successes of all five British gold-medallists in Moscow, including the swimmer, Duncan Goodhew. Miller wrote as follows:

> While Soviet and East German medals are heralded by their leaders as being symbols of the supremacy of the mother state, it did not pass notice that in the gaining of many of Britain's medals there was an element of family achievement. Not only was there Sebastian Coe and his father Peter – his constant coach and companion – but Allan Wells and his altruistic wife Margot. There was also Sebastian's great rival Steve Ovett and his ever attentive mother Gay, while Daley Thompson acknowledged his debt to his Auntie Doreen, who had nurtured him since he was a child ... and Duncan Goodhew walked to the start wearing a cap belonging to his father who sadly did not live to see his son's triumph.

It was a neat journalistic train of thought rather than a serious sociological study, but it did make some sense.

If you were looking for the Olympic athletics event with the least sense of history for the British, and therefore at the opposite end of the scale to the middle-distance races, the decathlon would readily fill the bill. Admittedly, back in 1904 the 'all-around' competition had been won by Tom Kiely, but he had been adamant that he was Irish not British, and the best that any Great Britain decathlete had done was a ninth place by Geoff Elliott, primarily a pole vaulter, in 1952. In 1964, when Mary Rand had placed second in the pentathlon in addition to her long-jump gold, there had not been a single British competitor in the decathlon. In 1972, when Mary Peters won the pentathlon, a British decathlete was no better than fifteenth. At the 1976 Games some promise had been shown by Francis Morgan Thompson, familiarly known as 'Daley' as an abbreviation of his father's Nigerian name, in finishing eighteenth of the 28 competitors, celebrating his eighteenth birthday in the process.

Daley Thompson could have had his choice of any number of events in which to specialise and maybe reach world class. In 1976 he was the second best junior in Britain at 100 metres, fourth at 400 metres, third in the pole vault, first in the long jump, fourth in the shot, and in the top ten in the high hurdles, discus and javelin. Yet even he, with his analytical mind for all things athletic, was surprisingly vague when it came to explaining his eventual preference for the 10-event decathlon, which involved the punishing succession of 100 metres, long jump, shot, high jump and 400 metres on the first day, and then 110 metres hurdles, discus, pole vault, javelin and 1500 metres on the second.

Thompson's decathlon potential was spotted early in 1975 by his mentor at the Essex Beagles club, Bob Mortimer, who arranged a meeting with Bruce Longden, a future national multi-events coach. Thompson set a British junior decathlon record that year, but in his biography published in 1983 he would recall,

> All the time I was training with Bruce before the first decathlon I was still thinking of myself as a sprinter. Then at some time after that I didn't any more. But I don't remember when that was … I wasn't just leaving sprinting. I was leaving something I'd found was really good for me … there was never a conscious decision to leave sprints for the decathlon. I did one, did another, did a third. Then it was time to do the decathlon.

The doing of it would lead to the most illustrious career of any man in decathlon history, and it was quite astonishing that a Briton should have achieved this in a discipline long dominated by the Americans and East Europeans. In chronological sequence Thompson won every type of honour open to him: European Junior Champion in 1977, Commonwealth Champion in 1978, Olympic champion in 1980, European champion in 1982 (having been second in 1978) and world champion in 1983 – and he won the Commonwealth title again in 1982 and 1986, the Olympic title again in 1984 and the European title again in 1986. His margins of victory in Moscow and Los Angeles were decisive and uncannily similar – 153 points ahead of Yuriy Kutsenko, of the USSR, and then 152 points ahead of Jürgen Hingsen, of West Germany. The first of his four world records was set in 1980 and the last of them with his 1984 Olympic win. It was not until 1992 that his record was beaten. In any judgment as to the identity of Britain's greatest Olympic athlete – and therefore greatest athlete – then the choice between Sebastian Coe and Daley Thompson would be a difficult one to make.

Coe's relationships with the press were rather more cordial than either Ovett's or Thompson's. Coe was ever the diplomat, charming and articulate. Ovett preferred to avoid what he called 'the media minefield', not attending press conferences. Thompson, as dauntingly forthright off the track as on it, even targeted his own biographer, who was an American named Skip Rozin: the unabashed Rozin wasn't one to miss a good 'quote' and delighted in relating the conversation in full when Thompson started talking to him during one of their interviews about 'life with the decathlon', making reference to his constant training companion, the Cyprus-born Pan Zeniou:

> Apart from Pan, who has a three-quarter understanding, nobody really understands. Even people who try. Even you. You have a little bit of understanding, but you only know it from the outside. You know what it's about, but you don't know the inside. Even people who do other sports seriously, they don't understand. It's that different from what they do. And there's no way

I can explain it to someone who only does sport for recreation … it's a whole lifestyle. It's everything.

In effect, what Thompson was saying was no blinding revelation. He was simply claiming that 'no one understands me except me'. Many another Olympic champions would share the sentiment.

The athletics purists might argue that Tessa Sanderson is the one British gold-medallist from 1980 or 1984 who might have benefited from the absence of boycotting nations. Sanderson won the javelin at the latter Games with an Olympic record of 69.56 metres, and the missing future world-record holder from East Germany, Petra Felke, had eight throws better than that during the year. Even so, Sanderson took the title ahead of the reigning world champion, Tiina Lillak, of Finland, and there's good reason to suppose that she could have beaten Felke, too, on the day, had the German been there. In third place was another Briton, Fatima Whitbread, who would herself break the world record two years later, and this was to constitute a rivalry over the years in the mould of Coe *v.* Ovett, but in this instance unaccountably so. No British woman had previously placed higher than seventh in an Olympic javelin final. This time Sanderson won in the grandest possible fashion, producing her best throw in the first of the six rounds, although Lillak got uncomfortably close, throwing only 56 centimetres less. (PLATE 12)

Coe and Thompson were two athletes now making a very substantial living from their sport, as the outdated rules regarding amateurism were at last abandoned and large sums of money came to be available. For example, the then administrators of athletics in Britain, the Amateur Athletic Association and the British Amateur Athletic Board, belied their misleading titles by negotiating deals through their newly appointed agents headed by a former Olympic hurdler, Alan Pascoe, with such household names as Pearl Assurance, Peugeot Talbot and Kodak, among others. The Kodak agreement alone was worth more than £2 million over five years, and a £10.5 million contract was agreed with Independent Television, also running through to the end of the decade. As much as £330,000 was additionally coming into British athletics each year from government funding via the Sports Council for Great Britain.

On a universal scale, the International Amateur Athletic Federation (another misnomer) set up its first Grand Prix series covering 15 major meetings during 1985, with individual top prizes of $10,000 per event and $25,000 to overall winners. The money was paid into trust funds set up for the athletes by their national federations. It represented a tentative but crucial official start towards full-scale professionalism.

One contest that neither Coe nor Thompson won during 1984 was that of 'BBC Sports Personality of the Year'. That award went jointly to two other Olympic gold-medallists who *were* required to beat opposition from the USSR. Jayne Torvill and Christopher Dean not only did that, in the ice-dancing event at the Winter Olympics in Sarajevo that year, but achieved perfect 6.0 scores across the board. Their interpretation of Ravel's *Bolero* was a masterpiece not only of beauteous artistic interpretation and choreography but of compacted musical arrangement, as the original 17-minute piece was reduced to 4 minutes and 28 seconds to comply – only just – with competition rules. (PLATE 13)

Torvill and Dean both came from Nottingham, and the US Olympic historian, David Wallechinsky, has wittily remarked that they have 'brought the town more glory than D.H. Lawrence, though not quite as much as Robin Hood'. On the ice it is Fred Astaire and Ginger Rogers who make the most apt comparison. Junior champions who met up in their teens and had their first win together in 1976, Torvill and Dean were provided with funding by Nottingham Council which enabled them to give up their jobs (insurance clerk and police officer respectively), although in order to retain amateur eligibility for the Olympics they were unable to earn money from their sport. Having placed fifth at the 1980 Olympics, they turned professional after their 1984 triumph and made a comeback to the Games when the rules had changed to take the bronze medals in 1994. In all they won four world titles as amateurs and five as professionals.

It seems no coincidence that in addition to Coe and Thompson there were three other Britons who were double Olympic champions in the 1980s: the oarsmen, Steve Redgrave and Andy Holmes, and the rifle marksman, Malcolm Cooper. Of course, there had been multiple gold-medallists for Britain in the past such as the swimmer, Henry Taylor, and the water-polo players, George Wilkinson and Charlie Smith, in the early years of the twentieth century, and then the outstanding rower of the pre-Redgrave era, Jack Beresford, in the 1920s and 1930s. Each of them had, in fact, won three or more gold medals over a lengthy span of years, but there had never been so many British Olympians with such protracted careers as there were in the 1980s. Thompson would compete in four Olympics. Tessa Sanderson, Britain's first Jamaican-born athletics gold-medallist, would outlast even him, appearing in all six Games from 1976 to 1996. Redgrave, as we now know, would win gold at five successive Games through to 2000.

The reason was simple: amateurism had finally come to an end. Olympic hopefuls and competitors were now free to earn a living from their sporting endeavours, though by no means all of those selected for the Games could actually do so. Of Britain's 1988 Olympic team, which numbered 349 in all, 28 proclaimed themselves as full-time professionals – 12 in athletics, 4 each in equestrianism, table tennis and tennis, 2 in judo, and 1 each in rowing and swimming. Another 34 were sports students or had sports-related jobs. By 1996 the team of 404 included 111 professional sportsmen or sportswomen and at least 37 others with sports-related occupations. The proportion of professionals or semi-professionals had thus doubled in eight years, from 18 per cent to 36 per cent. In athletics, badminton, canoeing, cycling, equestrianism, rowing, table tennis and tennis the 1996 figures ranged from 50 to 100 per cent.

Duncan Goodhew's 1980 success at 100 metres breaststroke (PLATE 14), following on seventh place in the 1976 final, was also bound to invite comparisons, as the 'absent friend' on this occasion was Steve Lundquist, winner of the US national title a week later. Goodhew's time was 1 minute 3.44 seconds, Lundquist's 1 minute 2.88 seconds – rather less than a metre's difference in distance. Lundquist, incidentally, was to win gold in this event four years later. To reinforce the idea of family bonds, as propounded by David Miller in his Coe biography, Goodhew's mother was an excited spectator in the stands, though his step-father, who was an air vice-marshal in the RAF, stayed away in support of Prime Minister Margaret Thatcher's vociferous opposition to British participation in the Games. Goodhew's was the first gold won by Britain in Moscow, and yet no Union Jack was raised at the victory ceremony, nor any national anthem played. In deference to official British sensitivities regarding the Soviet presence in Afghanistan, an Olympic flag was displayed instead at all of the British award ceremonies, accompanied by the Olympic hymn.

Mrs Thatcher also found allies in the persons of Britain's shooting officialdom, who decided not to send any representatives to the Moscow Games. Among those therefore deprived of a medal opportunity was Malcolm Cooper, but he made up for the disappointment by winning the gold for the cumbersomely titled 'small-bore rifle three positions' event (prone, kneeling, standing) in both 1984 and 1988. (PLATE 15) This competition involved 40 shots with a .22 rifle in each of the three stances at a target 50 metres away for which the innermost of the ten concentric rings measured five millimetres in diameter. For his 1984 gold Cooper scored 1,173 out of a maximum 1,200 and won by ten points – in shooting terms, that represented a commanding victory. Four years later it was a much closer contest under different regulations as he trailed his Scots-born team-mate, Alister Allan, by one point in the qualifying round, 1,181 to 1,180, but eventually won 1,279.3 to 1,275.6. It was the first 1–2 for Great Britain in the sport for 80 years and there has been no other since.

Cooper had learned his shooting as a teenager in New Zealand, where his father was stationed with the Royal Navy, and had competed at the 1972 and 1976 Games; in has case the length of his sporting career could not really be attributed to the advent of professionalism because he already earned his living from the sport. He had set up his own rifle manufacturing and supplies business, Accuracy International, in 1978, with customers that included the British army, and which was to win the Queen's Award for Export. He had the full support of his wife for the simple reason that she was also an expert shot and shared a Commonwealth Games team gold with her husband in 1986. Cooper set 17 world records during his career and collected 61 medals in all at Olympic, world and European level. Sadly, he died of cancer in 2001 at the age of 53.

Rowing was a sport that had regularly supplied Britain with Olympic success in the past – 14 gold medals in all by 1984. By that date, though, there had not been a gold for 36 years, although four silvers had been accumulated (including pushing the German Democratic Republic close in the eights in both 1976 and 1980) and two bronzes. Great Britain's eight in the latter year had shown no great form prior to the Games, and a promising 18-year-old had been considered as a late replacement, but it was probably for the best that he was sent to the World Junior Championships instead. Had young Steve Redgrave gone to Moscow, a mere silver would have spoiled what was going to become over the next 20 years a perfect record of a gold a Games, ignoring an odd bronze also picked up on the way!

The coxed fours event had not produced a single medal for Britain in 17 finals since 1900, and it was a close-run thing for the crew of Martin Cross, Richard Budgett,

Andy Holmes and Redgrave, with Adrian Ellison as cox, to end that sequence, as they eventually got past the USA only in the last few metres to win by half a length. The words that Redgrave recalled best from the numerous interviews conducted afterwards were those of Richard Burnell, gold-medallist in 1948 and now the long-established rowing correspondent for *The Times*, who confided, 'You're World Champion for one year. You're Olympic champion for life.' Redgrave's team-mates were hugely impressed by him. Martin Cross said that he exuded 'power which I hadn't felt in a boat before'. Richard Budgett, a future British Olympic Association senior team doctor, said that Redgrave 'is not arrogant – he is absolutely, very quietly, sure that he is the best'.

Redgrave himself was oddly unemotional. 'You would imagine that after winning an Olympic final the excitement would be overwhelming,' he related in his biography written in the year 2000. 'All I felt was relief. A sense of blessed belief that what I believed we could do, what the crew believed, and the coaches believed, we'd actually achieved.' Maybe the reason was that Redgrave realistically acknowledged that the absence from his event of the GDR, USSR and Poland, who had taken the first three places in 1980, had made a difference. 'That medal was definitely tainted,' he was to conclude 16 years later.

By the time of the 1988 Games in Seoul he had linked up with his fellow Los Angeles gold-medallist, Andy Holmes, as a coxless pair, and they had won the world title the previous year. In Seoul they gained the fourth of Britain's gold medals in the event, after those of 1908, 1932 and 1948, and also competed in the coxed pairs, taking the bronze despite a schedule that required them to race in two semi-finals within an hour. Tragically Holmes's continuing enthusiasm for sport was eventually to cost him his life as he died, in 2010 at the age of 51 and by then the father of five children, from a rare water-borne disease after competing in a 26-mile sculling race.

The winners of that Seoul coxed pairs final were the Abbagnale brothers from Italy, who were apparently awarded the equivalent of £15,000 each by a grateful nation. Redgrave remarked ruefully, 'We received a thousand handshakes and nothing more'. Apart from benefiting from the setting-up of trust funds approved for Olympic competitors, Redgrave had been given valued support by the Leyland DAF truck company (and free meat from his local butcher), but even after two Olympic golds his sport was far from providing a lucrative income. 'I was just about surviving,' he recalled. 'I was always in the red, but I had a standard of living with which I was happy. The rewards were just about sufficient to justify me carrying on.'

Teamwork was obviously an essential factor in the success of Redgrave and Holmes, and when it came to full-scale team sports the British victory in men's hockey in Seoul in 1988 was the first at the Summer Games since the hockey and water-polo players had won in Antwerp 68 years earlier. In 1920 the hockey title had been gained with some ease, beating Belgium, Denmark and France by an aggregate of 17 goals to 2. In 1988 there were no Belgians, Danes or French. India had won the Olympic title every year from 1928 to 1956 and again in 1964 and 1980. The other champions had been their neighbours, Pakistan, in 1960, 1968 and 1984, Germany in 1972 and New Zealand in 1976. Holland had won four of the six World Cup tournaments since 1974.

Having only drawn their opening match with Korea, and lost to Germany, the British seemed to be offering no challenge to the game's masters. They still got through to a semi-final, although in prospect it looked a lost cause because Australia had won their five matches in the other group, aggregating 19 goals to 3. Yet the British triumphed 3–2, with all their scoring due to Sean Kerly, and then beat Germany 3–1 in the final. Kerly was one of nine players in the squad who had also been bronze-medal winners in 1984 and his spectacular ability to find the net – 57 goals in 74 Great Britain matches – had brought him unusual fame for a hockey-player but no fortune. (PLATE 16) The game remained strictly amateur in Britain and he had even lost his job as a fashion-buyer because of the time he needed for training and competition. Britain's part-time players also included a newsagent, a hairdresser, a computer consultant, a quantity surveyor and a doctor.

The two other golds among Britain's five from Seoul came in swimming and yachting, now popularly termed sailing. The swimmer was Adrian Moorhouse, regaining for Britain the 100 metres breaststroke title that Duncan Goodhew had won eight years before. (PLATE 17) Thus six of the nine British men and women who had won individual golds in the pool since 1900 (chronologically, Fred Holman 1900, Lucy Morton 1924, Anita Lonsbrough 1960, David Wilkie 1976, Goodhew and Moorhouse) had done so using the breaststroke technique. Moorhouse, also winner of four European and three Commonwealth titles in the event, had become an international at 15 and number two in the British team to Duncan Goodhew. Moorhouse's Olympic success was achieved by the smallest margin since the event had been introduced to the Olympics in 1968 – one-hundredth of a second over Károly Güttler, of Hungary. In a race almost invariably won by the proverbial finger-nail, no other Olympic final has yet been closer. Moorhouse then went on to break the world record in 1989 and equalled it twice the next year.

The winning sailors at the Busan Yachting Centre were Mike McIntyre and Bryn Vaile, victors in the International Star class of keel-boat for which the only previous British medal had been a silver in 1932, though the winning helmsman in 1956 for the USA, Herb Williams, had been born in Hove, in Sussex, and the 1964 gold-medallist for the Bahamas, Durward Knowles, had represented Britain at the 1948 Olympics, finishing fourth. Knowles was among the seafarers again in 1988, aged 70. McIntyre and Vaile needed to win the last of their races, and their immediate rivals, the USA, needed to finish worse than sixth for Britain to take the gold. The Americans, striving their mightiest, broke their mast and the title was decided among the splintering of wood.

McIntyre, a Glaswegian who had been seventh in the 1984 Olympics Finn class, and Vaile, Enfield-born despite his Welsh christian name, were of contrasting physical build, although both proved that winning Olympic gold on the open seas requires brawn and muscle as well as acute seamanship. McIntyre was 6 feet 3 inches (1.91 metres) tall, weighing 14st 3lb (91kg). Vaile was 5 feet 11½ inches (1.81 metres) but much the heavier at 16st 2lb (107kg). Even so, McIntyre was by no means the tallest man in the British yachting team or in the regatta … or even, for that matter, among Olympic sailors originating from Glasgow: Mark Covell, silver-medallist in the Star class, was 6 feet 7 inches (2.01m) in height and 20½ stone (130kg) in weight.

Successive Summer Games since 1964 had produced respective totals of four gold medals, five, four, three, five, five and five again for Great Britain, which seemed to suggest that the British were respectably holding their own even as the competition hotted up. Actually, there was a big difference to be found in any comparison of achievement over the years: while there had been 5,140 competitors from 93 countries competing for 163 gold medals in Tokyo in 1964, when the Olympics returned to Asian soil 24 years later there were 8,447 competitors, 159 countries and 241 gold medals.

In other words, there were now 64 per cent more competitors and 70 per cent more countries contesting 48 per cent more gold. Among Britain's numerous Olympic sponsors in 1988 were the insurance brokers, Minet, who had alone committed £1.5 million, and that was 900 per cent above the total team budget for Tokyo. In scale and cost the Modern Olympics just kept on getting bigger and more ambitious.

TWELVE

The Games of the 1990s

Right from the 'B' of the Bang!
And the 'S' of every single stroke

IN THE 20 years up to 1988 the German Democratic Republic had won 32 Olympic rowing titles. Great Britain had won merely two, and Steve Redgrave had a role to play in both. Then the Berlin Wall came down, and one of the most successful of the East German technical experts was recruited by Redgrave's club, Leander, and then appointed Britain's chief coach. Despite the Marxist origins, it seemed a marriage of talents made in heaven, and so, eventually it was to be proved. The new adviser to Leander, Jürgen Grobler, arrived in January 1991; his contribution to the GDR's rowing domination had been as coach to the national women's team which had won five Olympic golds and 21 world titles. His name was soon anglicised to un-accented Jurgen Grobler, but his grasp of English was rudimentary, and Redgrave was at first wary of what the new arrival could contribute. But looking back on the relationship years later, Redgrave was to write admiringly in his autobiography: 'When they present the medals at championships I believe that the coaches should be there on the podium as well, receiving their recognition.' Grobler eventually got his reward: an honorary OBE in 2006.

The partnership between Redgrave and Andy Holmes, which had brought the Olympic coxless pairs gold among numerous other honours, had come to an end. At the time Redgrave was planning a four-year schedule aimed at the next Games, while Holmes was not. Redgrave's newly acquired shipmate for Leander and then Great Britain to share those four years of sweat, pain and total dedication was the right size for the task, at 6 feet 5 inches (1.95m) and 17 stone (110kg), but not otherwise the obvious choice. Firstly, Matthew Pinsent was only 20, eight years Redgrave's junior. Secondly, he was an Oxford undergraduate, and Oxbridge had long since ceased to be the automatic production line for British Olympic rowers. Early in 1991 Pinsent was otherwise committed to what Redgrave described, perhaps a shade insensitively, as 'a Mickey Mouse event' – the Boat Race.

When Pinsent arrived to start training with Redgrave for the coxless pairs, Grobler took the radical decision to put the younger man in the stroke seat, traditionally the guiding force in a boat, and move Redgrave to bow. To the layman this might have

Steve Redgrave carried the British flag at this opening ceremony for the 1992 Games in Barcelona and then won his third gold medal and was flag-bearer again in 1996. He was thus the country's first competitor to have been awarded this particular honour twice, but this is still one Olympic record which he no longer holds. At the Winter Games Mike Dixon, who competed in the biathlon, has carried the flag three times, in 1994, 1998 and 2002.

seemed as risky as asking triple-jumper Jonathan Edwards to change his lead-off leg, but within three weeks the re-shuffle had proved itself and the two men were never to swap back seats after that. Redgrave continued to give the commands, and as he explained, 'In fact, it's easier reading a race from the bow than the stroke seat. You can see more of what's going on, and it's much easier to talk to the oarsman who's in front of you rather than turning over your shoulder.' That summer Redgrave and Pinsent won the world title in Vienna. It was Pinsent's first, and Redgrave's third.

Their Olympic preparations in the first half of 1992 were by no means perfect. Tell the truth, they were not far short of disastrous. Redgrave suffered severe stomach problems which took months to diagnose. There was defeat in the national trials by an inexperienced pair of brothers, Greg and Jonny Searle – of whom more would be heard – and then in Cologne by the Slovenians who had been the world championships silver-medallists. But the British team management kept faith. Redgrave and Pinsent were selected for the 1992 Barcelona Olympics, with Redgrave given the added honour of carrying the British flag at the opening ceremony.

In contrast to all the pre-Games setbacks, the Olympic final on Saturday morning, 1 August, was as near to being an anti-climax as such an occasion could be. 'By the time

146

Matthew and I crossed the 250-metre mark we had taken over the lead and continued to extend our advantage,' Redgrave was to relate in distinctly matter-of-fact terms. 'It was obvious that no one was racing us. They were merely competing for minor medals. It was a joyful moment. Matthew thrust his right arm into the air, one finger erect. I confined myself to patting him on the shoulder.' Redgrave had equalled Jack Beresford's pre-war record of three Olympic gold medals – and in precisely the same manner: calm, cool, collected, the epitome of British restraint. (PLATE 18)

The Searle brothers had been selected instead for the coxed pairs, with Garry Herbert to guide them, and they, too, won their final the next morning. If anything theirs was the more historic success. Certainly, theirs was the more emotional, with Herbert – displaying what might have been construed as uncharacteristic emotion for a future barrister – crying his eyes out during the victory ceremony. This was the twentieth time that the event had been held at the Games, and Britain had previously won only one medal for it (bronze four years earlier). The elder brother, Jonny Searle, like Pinsent, had been a member of two winning Oxford crews in the Boat Race and had been in the Great Britain eight which had taken bronze in the world championships of 1989 and 1991. Greg had joined him on the latter occasion. They were the first brothers to win Olympic gold in any sport for Britain since the polo-playing Charles and George Miller in 1908.

In between these successes – the first double gold in Olympic rowing for Britain since 1948 – and some eight hours after Redgrave and Pinsent had completed their 2000 metres, the runners came to their marks that evening for the men's rather briefer 100 metres final on the track at the hill-top Montjuic Stadium. The eight of them, in order from lane one, were Bruny Surin (Canada), Ray Stewart (Jamaica), Frankie Fredericks (Namibia), Dennis Mitchell (USA), Linford Christie (GB), Leroy Burrell (USA), Davidson Ezinwa (Nigeria) and Olapade Adeniken (also Nigeria). Burrell had run the fastest semi-final time less than 1½ hours before, 9.97 seconds, but as all of them except Surin had broken ten seconds in one race or another there was not a great deal to choose between them. It had all the makings of an historic contest.

Yet the winner's recollection is not much different to the way Redgrave had felt earlier that day. 'I was going to give it everything, right from the "B" of the "Bang!",' Linford Christie reminisced in 1995. 'I made a good start and when I got to 60 metres I knew I had won. There were still 40 metres to go, but I just knew I was heading for the gold medal.' Even after he had crossed the line, in 9.96 seconds, there was no unbridled outburst of emotion: 'There was supposed to be a cloud nine feeling, a sense of walking on air. I was waiting – but nothing was happening. Of course, I was very very happy. I was happy for Ron, for all my friends and sponsors, all the people who had been supporting me. This was what they had been dreaming of. To be honest, it was more Ron's dream than mine.'

'Ron' was Christie's coach, Ron Roddan, a former club sprinter whose competitive highlight had been to once reach the Middlesex county 100 yards final, and he had had an even more significant influence on Christie's career than had Jurgen Grobler on Steve Redgrave's. Eight years earlier Christie had been just another runner with a fair turn of speed, and if you had cared to search for his name in the *International Athletics*

Annual published by the Association of Track and Field Statisticians – the *Wisden* of the sport, with its 600 or so pages crammed with facts and figures – you would have found that, of the 194 men in the world who had run 10.44 seconds or faster for 100 metres in 1984, Christie was ranked 194th. At the age of 24, that seemed to be the sum of his achievements.

Roddan's training group met at the West London club, Thames Valley Harriers, which made for a neat link with Steve Redgrave and the Searle brothers. Redgrave came from Marlow, in Buckinghamshire, and the Searles had been at school at Hampton, in Middlesex, both also in the valley of the river Thames. Jamaican-born Christie's previous club, improbable as it might seem, was London Irish. There his name was often mistakenly recorded in results as 'Christy Linford', reportedly because that seemed to be more Irish. Similarly, it is said, one of his relay clubmates, Ade Mafe (pronounced 'Addy Maffy'), of Nigerian background, was thought by some of those Irish expatriates who hadn't seen him run to be 'Paddy Murphy'.

The shortcoming in Christie's make-up in those earlier years was that he was not entirely dedicated to the hard slog of training, and Roddan told him, as Christie himself was to readily admit, 'Get down to work, like I know you can do. But don't waste my time any more.' Christie responded and was European champion within two years and then given second place to Carl Lewis in the 1988 Olympic 100 metres final after the Canadian winner, Ben Johnson, had been stripped of his title within hours for drug abuse. Another European gold had followed for Christie in 1990 and then fourth place in the next year's world championships final to the American triumvirate of Carl Lewis, Burrell and Mitchell. Lewis, unquestionably the greatest sprinter/long jumper in the sport's history, challenged only by Jesse Owens, missed the Barcelona Olympic 100 metres because he happened to be ill at the time of the USA sudden-death qualifying trials.

The blue riband event, the men's 100 metres, was as old as the Modern Olympics itself, the first title in 1896 having been taken by an American, Thomas Burke, in 12.0 seconds. The USA had won the event on 14 further occasions, and Britain was the only other country to have done so more than once (Abrahams 1924, Wells 1980, and now Christie). (PLATE 19) The Ancient Greeks had different ideas regarding the true test of sprinting, and their shortest event had been held over a distance of 192 metres. As the average speed of the world record for 200 metres – until the advent of first Carl Lewis and later Michael Johnson in the 1990s and then Usain Bolt in the twenty-first century – was actually faster than that for 100 metres, perhaps the Greeks were proved right.

Britain's other athletics gold medal in Barcelona was achieved in an event with a much shorter history. The 400 metres hurdles for women had not been introduced to the Games until 1984, and it was a fact that women athletes had been consistently short-changed ever since the 800 metres had appeared briefly in 1928 and then, as previously related, been promptly banned as an Olympic event. It had eventually been revived in 1960, and the 400 metres was brought in four years later. Then came the 1500 (1972), the 3000 (1984) later replaced by the 5000, the 10,000 (1988), the marathon (1984), the 10 kilometres walk (1992) then updated to the 20 kilometres walk, and the steeplechase (2008). The

The joy of victory. Sally Gunnell's 400 metres hurdles win in Barcelona was followed by a bronze medal as she ran 50.4 seconds on the flat in the 4 × 400 metres relay. She had been a fine pentathlete and long jumper as a youngster and her first international success had come at 100 metres hurdles in the Commonwealth Games of 1986. It was her astute coach, Bruce Longden, who persuaded her to switch to 400 metres hurdling.

BY COURTESY OF MARK SHEARMAN

field events would not be expanded until 1996 to include the triple jump and until 2000 to take in the pole vault and hammer.

By 1992 the women's world record for the 400 hurdles had been reduced to 52.94 seconds by the Russian, Marina Styepanova (whose surname among journalists and others was inevitably corrupted to 'Step-on-over'). Britain had a strong contender for Barcelona gold in Sally Gunnell, who had started out nine years before as a highly promising 14-year-old long jumper and had then become a pentathlon age-group record-holder at 16. She first chose the 100 metres hurdles as her preferred senior event and won this at the Commonwealth Games of 1986. The next year she had a tentative try at the 400 hurdles, as recommended by her astute coach, Bruce Longden (who had also guided Daley

Thompson), and progressed so rapidly that she placed fifth at the Seoul Olympics. At the 1991 World Championships she had lost very narrowly to another Soviet athlete, Tatyana Ledyevskaya, 53.11 to 53.16.

In Barcelona Gunnell, who earned her living not as an athlete but as a solicitor's clerk, put no foot wrong, winning heat, semi-final and then the final, with Ledyevskaya back in fourth place. (PLATE 20) Gunnell was the archetypal British champion athlete: unassuming off the track, totally assertive on it. Her hurdling technique was immaculate; a powerful stride on the flat and then a decisive snap and drive of the leg as each barrier was cleared. Yet even the Olympic final was part of a learning curve as for the first time she achieved her target of running a consistent 15 strides between hurdles to the sixth flight and then 16 strides between each of the next four.

In the final she was drawn in the favoured lane three, with Sandra Farmer-Patrick, of the USA, in four, and later described the finish of the race in these terms: 'I really stretched for the last hurdle. Last year I had a negative thought at that stage, but this time I was so determined and had run it so often in my mind that I was going to get there. I was still running scared, waiting for Sandra to come up, but I was just as determined that she wasn't going to be able to. Technically, it was my best race.' There was further delight to come when a couple of evenings later Gunnell paid a social call to the hotel where the British supporters' travel group was staying, and as the fans realised she was there so a roar of acclamation – 'Sall-ee! Sall-ee! Sall-ee!' – swept upwards from floor to floor. The next year she won the World Title and in the process stamped out the world record held by Styepanova.

The last time Britain had won a cycling gold medal had been 72 years before, and that was in an event which was no longer on the Olympic schedule (rather a shame, as it happens, because the tandem sprint was – and still is when it is occasionally staged in other competitions – one of the most spectacular sights on the track). 'Spectacular' was not the obvious term to describe the bike-rider who ended Britain's losing sequence at the Olympics – 'relentless', 'remorseless' being adjectives which more readily sprung to mind. (PLATE 21) Chris Boardman, from Hoylake, the seaside town on the Wirral peninsula better known for being the location of the Royal Liverpool Golf Club, had won three Commonwealth bronze medals, in 1986 and 1990, and had placed ninth in the world championships individual pursuit in 1991, but that was no pointer to what was to come on the wooden 250-metre track at Val d'Hebron.

The individual pursuit involves two riders starting on opposite sides of the track and racing 4000 metres with each trying to catch the other. The event had been first held at the Olympics in 1964 and Britain had never won a medal. It was obvious to us all at the velodrome, though, after the first round, in which Boardman broke the Games record by over four seconds, and then improved a further three seconds to 4 minutes 24.496 seconds, that things would be different this time. Privileged to be in the press-box watching Boardman's progress in the few days before the athletics began, I hurried back to the BBC Radio studios in the centre of Barcelona that afternoon and buttonholed the programme editor to tell him, 'Boardman's going to win the gold'. Not only did he live

20 Perfect technique: supple, relaxed, and totally concentrated. Sally Gunnell in stylish action in the 400 metres hurdles at the 1992 Games in which she won gold. She had finished fifth as a relative novice in 1988 but took the title in Barcelona by a clear three metres from her familiar American rival, Sandra Farmer-Patrick. At the world championships a year later Gunnell beat Farmer-Patrick again, though by a narrower margin, and set a world record in the process.

BY COURTESY OF MARK SHEARMAN

21 In individual pursuit cycle-racing two riders on opposite sides of the track try to gain time on each other. Only once in 17 Olympic finals for men or women has one rider overtaken the other, and that was in Barcelona in 1992 when Chris Boardman outclassed his German opponent and rendered the stopwatches irrelevant. Boardman turned professional, won Tour de France time-trials, and set a phenomenal one-hour distance record of 56.375 kilometres.

TOPFOTO

22 Three times an Olympic yachting champion – in the Laser class in 2000 and in the Finn in 2004 and 2008 – Ben Ainslie started young, as have so many others in the sport. His first competition was in 1987 at the age of 10, and the International Sailing Federation has named him 'World Sailor of the Year' in 1998, 2002 and 2008. His birthplace, though, is not one immediately associated with sailing – Macclesfield, in Cheshire.

TOPFOTO

23 It had been a long hard road to Olympic fame for Jonathan Edwards. He had been 23rd in the triple jump in 1988, 35th in 1992 and 2nd in 1996 after setting a prodigious world record of 18.29 metres the previous year. In Sydney his best was well short of that, 17.71, but still a handy 24 centimetres ahead of anyone else.

BY COURTESY OF MARK SHEARMAN

24 Speed, strength and stamina: Denise Lewis had managed to reconcile all those differing demands which were made on her training programme, and her shot effort of 15.55 metres was way ahead of all her rivals in Sydney. She was the best long jumper in Britain during 2000, third best at 100 metres hurdles, fifth in the shot, and ninth best in Britain in the high jump and javelin.

BY COURTESY OF MARK SHEARMAN

25 In 2004 Kelly Holmes became the first British middle-distance runner since Albert Hill in 1920 to win both the 800 metres and 1500 metres at the Olympic Games. Previously only two Soviet runners, in 1976 and 1996, had completed the same double in the women's events.

BY COURTESY OF MARK SHEARMAN

26 Britain's first gold medal in the 4 × 100 metres relay for 92 years was won at the 2004 Games by, from left to right, Mark Lewis-Francis, Jason Gardener, Marlon Devonish and Darren Campbell. The USA had been favourites for the title as usual, having won 15 of the 20 previous finals, but they got one of their all-important baton-changes wrong – and Britain didn't.

BY COURTESY OF MARK SHEARMAN

27 A superhuman final effort as Nicole Cooke wins the 2008 women's cycling road race from Emma Johansson of Sweden (*left*), and Tatiana Guderzo of Italy (*right*). Sir Chris Hoy later wrote in his autobiography that this victory helped inspire Cooke's Great Britain cycling team-mates to their profusion of victories in the track events in the Beijing velodrome. Nicole also became in 2008 the first woman to be Olympic and world road-race champion in the same year.
TOPFOTO

28 Britain's cyclists out-pedalled the rest of the world to win seven of the ten track events at the Beijing velodrome in 2008, and Bradley Wiggins (*left*) and Chris Hoy (*right*) were two of the delighted champions. Wiggins took gold in the individual pursuit and the team pursuit, while Hoy took gold in the individual sprint, team sprint and keirin. Hoy was the first British triple gold-medallist in any sport at a single Games since the swimmer, Henry Taylor, 100 years earlier.
TOPFOTO

29 Even among the elite of Olympic gold-medallists Rebecca Romero is unique. Winner of the individual pursuit track cycling gold in 2008, she was already a silver-medallist and a world champion for quadruple-sculls rowing from 2004, and is the only British woman to have competed in two Olympic summer sports. She had switched from rowing to cycling in 2006 because of a back problem and was a world title winner on two wheels within a year.

30 The 4000 metres team pursuit requires perfect co-ordination between the four riders as each takes it in turn to lead, and the British quartet of Ed Clancy, Paul Manning, Geraint Thomas and Bradley Wiggins got it absolutely right at the 2008 Games. After setting the fastest time in the first round, they broke the world record in the semi-finals with 3 minutes 55.202 seconds, and then again, with 3:53.314, in the final, in which they outclassed the hapless Danish quartet.

31 Canoeing was not a sport that had brought Britain any Olympic success for 64 years. No medals had been won since its introduction to the Games in 1936 until Tim Brabants took the bronze for the 1000 metres kayak singles in Sydney in 2000. After placing fifth in 2004 and then completing his medical studies, he returned in 2008 (pictured here) to win the same event ahead of the 2004 champion, Eirik Verås Larsen, of Norway.

TOPFOTO

32 The first British woman to win an Olympic 400 metres title, Christine Ohuruogu judged her season's form and her race tactics to perfection at the 2008 Games, taking the lead in the last 30 metres. Six of the eight runners are shown in the photograph: from left to right, Sanya Richards (USA) 3rd, Shericka Williams (Jamaica) 2nd, Yulia Gushchina (Russia) 4th, Ohuruogu, Tatyana Firova (Russia) 6th, Rosemarie Whyte (Jamaica) 7th.

BY COURTESY OF MARK SHEARMAN

33 Paul Goodison was one of Britain's highly successful yachting team at the 2008 Games, triumphant in the Laser class. A key part of his apprenticeship had been to serve as training partner to Ben Ainslie in Sydney in the year 2000. The Laser is a small dinghy, sailed single-handed at the Olympics, and there are now some 250,000 of this craft in use throughout the world.

TOPFOTO

34 At the 2008 Games James DeGale won Britain's fifth middleweight boxing title. His predecessors had been Johnny Douglas (1908), Harry Mallin (1920 and 1924) and Chris Finnegan (1968). DeGale followed the customary route for British Olympic champions of more recent years in the ring by turning professional before the end of the year and in 2010 gained his first title at WBA super-middleweight.

TOPFOTO

35 In 2008 Rebecca Adlington became Britain's first Olympic swimming champion for twenty years and the first for a century to win more than one gold medal at a Games. She won the 800 metres freestyle in world-record time; the previous record had stood for 19 years, all but four days, and had been set when Rebecca was six months old. Here she proudly displays another medal awarded to her – the OBE.
TOPFOTO

36 Amy Williams gave up 400 metres running on the track in 2002 to try the skeleton sled event on a practice facility at the University of Bath and eight years later became the first British woman to win an individual event at the Winter Games since the figure-skater, Jeannette Altwegg, 58 years before. It was perhaps a matter of natural progression for Great Britain because Alexandra Coomber had been third when the skeleton event was introduced at the 2002 Winter Games, and Shelley Rudman had been second in 2006.
TOPFOTO

up to our expectations, but he became the first man in Olympic history to overtake his opponent in the final; in this instance, the luckless silver-medallist was Jens Lehmann, of Germany, a talented rider but totally outclassed on the day.

Boardman later improved the record for the event to 4:11.114, and this would last until the year 2011. He took on other challenges, setting a world record for the hour of 52.270 kilometres before joining the professional team sponsored by a French insurance company, Gan, in order to ride in the Tour de France. In 1994 he won the Tour's opening time-trial, wearing the leader's prized yellow jersey for three days, and he was also world champion that year for the individual pursuit and the road time-trial. Boardman's supreme ability was that his talent for solitary endeavour on two wheels extended from four kilometres to more than 50, and he even managed to complete the three weeks of the Tour de France, through the mountain ranges of the Alps and Pyrenees, on two occasions. His favoured leisure-time pursuit these days as a respite from his successful business activities is conducted in a very different medium – that of deep-sea diving.

It was an anomaly of Olympic competition that cycle-racing at the Games in 1992 was still amateur, while other sports such as rowing and athletics had gone 'open'. Not that the change had immediately brought untold fortune as well as fame even to gold-medallists such as Steve Redgrave and Linford Christie. Redgrave, now married and

Sir Steve Redgrave (*right*) is the most successful British competitor in Olympic Games history, with five rowing gold medals in successive Olympics, from 1984 to 2000. His coxless pairs partner on three occasions was Sir Matthew Pinsent (*left*), who went on to add a fourth gold to his collection in 2004. Only swimmer Henry Taylor and Sir Chris Hoy have matched Pinsent's total medal haul.
TOPFOTO

with a one-year-old daughter, seriously contemplated retirement after Barcelona. In his autobiography he explains, 'I didn't want to be in a situation I'd known for many years when I didn't know where the next cheque was coming from and whether I could pay my mortgage off that month'. To the rescue came the assurance company, ManuLife, later Canada Life, whose sponsorship provided him and his fellow oarsman, Matthew Pinsent, with £25,000 a year each. Even so, says Redgrave, 'It was not until 1996 that I was able to bring a smile to my bank manager's face – by not being in debt'.

Christie renewed his sprint rivalry with Carl Lewis the next year and won the world title at 100 metres in 1993 in even faster time, 9.87 seconds, with Lewis back in fourth place, but remained coy about his earning power. Of another confrontation with Lewis that year he wrote, 'There was a lot of talk about money at the time of the race against Carl Lewis in Gateshead. The figure of £100,000 kept surfacing, but at no stage did I confirm or deny it. There were complaints that £100,000 was far too much money. Assuming the figure is correct, £100,000 is next to nothing when compared to Nigel Mansell's eight-figure annual income in recent years or the sums earned by heavyweight boxers.'

Whether or not Christie *did* get paid £10,000 a second for his Gateshead track appearance, the fact is that cash was not exactly awash on the athletics track, as compared with the motor-racing circuit, tennis court or golf course, for instance. The Grand Prix series of 16 meetings organised throughout the world during 1993 by the ruling body of athletics provided a modest $30,000 for the winner of each event and $100,000 for the two overall champions, who were the pre-eminent pole-vaulter from the Ukraine, Sergey Bubka, and Sally Gunnell's hurdles rival, Sandra Farmer-Patrick.

Still, however much money there was to support them, it was enough for Redgrave, Christie and Boardman to all turn out again the next time the Olympics came round, in Atlanta in 1996. Of this trio, only Redgrave won. In fact, had it not been for Redgrave and Pinsent, Britain would have had no gold medals at all … and that would have been unprecedented in Olympic history. Christie got to his third Olympic 100 metres final at the age of 36 but was ignominiously disqualified for false starting. Boardman was third in the 52-kilometre individual road time-trial which was introduced that year but did achieve an astounding 56.375 kilometres in the hour on the boards of the Manchester velodrome a month or so later. No one will ever know if this is the ultimate because the sport's ruling body, the Union Cycliste Internationale, promptly decided to ban as unsafe Boardman's 'superman' style whereby his arms were stretched out full length in front of him.

By the time that the coxless pairs final began at just after ten o'clock on the morning of Saturday 27 July 1996 at the Lake Lanier rowing venue, 55 miles from Atlanta, Britain's only medallist in the 80 finals which had been decided across ten sports – athletics, cycling, equestrianism, fencing, gymnastics, judo, shooting, swimming, weight-lifting and wrestling – was the Scots-born swimmer, Graeme Smith, who had placed third in the 1500 metres freestyle. 'The further you get in your career, the worse the pressure becomes, especially when you've had a highly successful one like mine,' Redgrave was later to reflect. But his description as he and Pinsent led in the closing stages of the race in which he achieved his fourth gold medal spoke legion for the vast experience which they had accumulated:

> Now, 250 metres is 30–35 strokes from winning an Olympic gold; it's your final spurt. And we were still at our cruising speed. What happened was that the principal danger, the Australians, were increasing their rate and coming back at us. Only at that moment did we actually pick it up again, because they were coming back so quickly at us from about 350 metres. But never, at any stage, did I think, 'I'm knackered here. I'm never going to be able to keep this up.' It was totally controlled. It was covering tactics.

Redgrave had convinced himself some weeks before that this would be the last race of his career. He was soon to be dissuaded.

As we have seen, even Olympic champions as eminent as Redgrave had struggled financially, despite moves towards professionalism in most sports. Yet the overall cost of Olympic participation was rising inexorably. Simple arithmetic has it that Britain's sole gold medal in 1996 cost many millions. The British Olympic Association had persuaded 25 major companies to lend their support to the Games preparations, including such household names as Adidas, Barclaycard, Cadbury's, Coca-Cola, Kellogg's, Kodak, Midland Bank, Panasonic, Rank Xerox, Royal Mail and Visa. A nationwide appeal, with 166 voluntary fund-raising groups, had been set up to raise a further £4 million. Baron de Coubertin did not, perhaps, turn in his grave, but must at least have stirred restlessly. In future years the trend of increasing cost would only continue.

THIRTEEN

The Games of 2000

Four men in a boat: Redgrave's fifth gold, Pinsent's third, Foster and Cracknell's first

B Y the start of the twenty-first century, 104 years after Jack Boland and Launceston Elliot had so casually won the very first of Britain's titles, every Olympic medal now had its price, for lottery money was radically changing the face of Olympic sport in Britain. The three golds won on the open sea were worth a £2.5 million boost to their sport's funding, while nothing better than a fifth place in the calmer waters of the swimming pool was to be penalised by a shortfall of £500,000. Winners prosper; losers suffer.

The National Lottery had begun in 1994 and three years later UK Sport was set up to administer the funds being made available to Olympic aspirants. While previous government bodies in Britain had had as their principal aim increasing participation at the grass-roots level, this new body was initially tasked with identifying, supporting and funding elite athletes in order to succeed at the highest levels, including the Olympics. The funding of certain sports was transformed. In contrast to the hand-to-mouth existence of even the likes of Steve Redgrave in earlier years, the benefactors were dealing in riches beyond the dreams of avarice. For the Sydney Games of the year 2000, UK Sport distributed £58.9 million, of which athletics received £10.6 million, rowing £9.6 million, swimming £6.9 million, and cycling, gymnastics and yachting more than £5 million apiece. But in return each sport had to deliver, and that meant nothing less than places on the victory-ceremony rostrum.

Of Britain's 11 gold medals in Sydney, sailing contributed three, athletics and rowing two each, and boxing, cycling, modern pentathlon and shooting the rest. Of the 28 medals in total, athletics had six, sailing five, cycling four and rowing three. Canoeing, modern pentathlon and shooting had two each; badminton, boxing, equestrianism and judo one each. By way of reward, these sports would all receive substantially more from the kitty in the years leading up to the 2004 Games, although, because of their particular administrative set-up, the boxers were financed separately. Not that Britain's first Olympic super-heavyweight champion, Audley Harrison, was too concerned where the money came from as he turned professional in 2001 to cash in on his new-found fame. The swimmers and the gymnasts had no medals to show for their endeavours and by way of retribution from those who held the purse-strings would be given less money in future – 30 per cent less in the latter's case.

In point of fact, the profiles of many of the British gold-medallists in Sydney – of which there were 22 in all, allowing for the numbers which formed the crews in the rowing events – proved that it takes rather longer than four years to make an Olympic champion, although the lottery's largesse could no doubt provide the finishing touches which make all the difference. Steve Redgrave was at his fifth Olympics and Matthew Pinsent his third. One of their coxless four crew-mates, Tim Foster, had a bronze medal from 1996; the other, James Cracknell, had missed the 1992 Games through injury and then gone down with tonsillitis in Atlanta. Jonathan Edwards (triple jump) was at his fourth Olympics and had been the silver-medallist in Atlanta, while Denise Lewis (heptathlon) had won bronze there. Ben Ainslie (yachting), though still only 23, had been another silver-medallist that year. Shirley Robertson (also yachting), aged 32, had competed at the 1992 and 1996 Games. Another 23-year-old, Richard Faulds (shooting), had been fifth in 1996.

More obviously among the later arrivals in Britain's elite class, and therefore one could say products of the 'Lottery Generation', were Jason Queally (cycling), Iain Percy (yachting) and Stephanie Cook (modern pentathlon).

Queally was 30 years old and a graduate in biological science from Lancaster University. He had only taken up track cycle racing five years earlier, having previously represented British Universities at water-polo and then tried the triathlon. In Sydney in 2000 he was the thirteenth of the 16 riders to set off in the one kilometre individual time-trial. Even among his keenest supporters, Queally began his effort with no great hope of gold, because still to come were the two men who between them had won every World Championship since 1995: Shane Kelly, of Australia, and Arnaud Tournant, of France. Yet Queally beat his previous best time to cover the distance in 1 minute 1.609 seconds, an average of 58.433 kilometres per hour from a standing start. Maybe daunted by such an unexpected challenge, neither Kelly nor Tournant could match this, and Queally was champion by 0.878 of a second (or about 15 metres). Queally was never to win another time-trial gold medal at Olympic, World or Commonwealth level but deserves immense credit as the pace-setter for what would soon become a dominant British hierarchy in cycle velodromes around the world.

Percy, 24, came from the sailing stronghold of Southampton, and was competing in his first major championships, although like so many other yachtsmen and yachtswomen he had been introduced to the pastime by his family very early in life – in his case aged six. His win in the Finn class ahead of Luca Devoti, of Italy, 35 points to 46, was the first Olympic success for Britain in that class of single-handed dinghy. The Finn had been designed in 1949 not by a Finn, as might be supposed, but by a Swede, Richard Sarby, and had featured at every Olympics since 1952. At those first Games Sarby himself was third and a Briton, Charles Currey, was second, but there had been no other British medallist since. Yet the wind of change was beginning to blow at Sydney; by 2008 Britain would have won the event three times in succession.

In an era of spreading professionalism, the Scots-born Stephanie Cook was something of a throwback to an almost forgotten era, of the dedicated amateur with aims in life other than that of being a full-time athlete. Aged 28, she was a former rower who had discovered the modern pentathlon as an undergraduate reading clinical medicine at Lincoln College, Oxford. Having somehow combined her sporting activities with the demanding duties of a junior doctor, she decided to put her medical career on hold in 1999 to pursue her Olympic ambition, and after winning the gold in Sydney and then the world title the next year she retired, saying, 'I am so thankful that I was able to do it, but I'm happy to be back in medicine'.

The modern pentathlon had featured in the Games since 1912, but for men only; the event comprised, in sequence, shooting, fencing, swimming, show-jumping and cross-country running. The women's version was introduced in Sydney in 2000, with all the events held within a single day, starting at 6.45 a.m., and to a formula designed to ensure a dramatic finish. Each performance was awarded points and the competitors then started the last event at timed intervals based on those points scores, with the overall leader going off first. In this 'catch-me-if-you-can' situation, Cook was eighth when she began the 3000 metres run, 49 seconds down, and overtook the last of the seven in front of her with only 300 metres remaining. Her team-mate, Kate Allenby, was third, and in recognition of this dual success the discipline's income from UK Sport for the next four-year cycle was boosted by almost 100 per cent to £2 million. Team golds had been awarded for the modern pentathlon at the Olympics in the past – Great Britain's men having won in 1976 – but this practice had been discontinued after 1992.

In the immediate wake of his fourth gold in Atlanta, Steve Redgrave had famously declared to the nation that he would never get in a boat again. He was to retract that decision when, the next year, he and Matthew Pinsent were persuaded by the head coach, Jurgen Grobler, to form a coxless four in preparation for Sydney together with Tim Foster and James Cracknell. 'It was the right time to try a new challenge,' Redgrave was to recall, and his sense of well-being was bolstered by the fact that at last his financial situation had stabilised. The bankers, Lombard, had agreed a £1 million sponsorship deal for him and Pinsent over the next four years, and so the Olympic champions had no need of any Lottery backing. Lombard's investment was rewarded as, in a desperately close Sydney final, the Great Britain foursome got home by just 0.38 seconds from Italy. It was Redgrave's fifth gold and Pinsent's third. Foster, who had missed gold by less than a second four years before, later summed up his feelings thus:

> I realised it wasn't just our gold; it was one that thousands of others shared with us. There was so much more to it than just the national anthem. In order of magnitude this was a hundred times greater than I'd ever imagined. I'd dreamed of this moment for 16 years, pushed through hard times and injury. When it

finally happened it was worth it ten times over. Still is. Nothing had prepared me for the way it felt and the way it continues to feel.

Foster, at 6 feet 3 inches (1.91 metres) and 13½ stone (86kg), was the smallest man in the boat. In his autobiography, written in 2004, he cheerfully re-told in detail Jurgen Grobler's eccentric eve-of-race 'pep' talk. 'James,' Grobler had said to Cracknell, 'you are the most powerful bow man in the world. You are so strong no one can beat you.' Turning to Redgrave and Pinsent, Grobler had enthused, 'Steve, Matthew, you are Olympic champions and world-beaters. No one will beat you when you put on the pressure.' Then it was Foster's turn. Grobler searched for words and when they eventually came to mind they weren't exactly inspirational: 'Tim ... Tim. You row very well.'

There was also gold for Britain in the eights final – the first at Olympic level since 1912. The crew had been brought together in 1997 mostly from the ranks of former junior or under-23 internationals and had thus benefited throughout from Lottery funding. At the 1999 World Championships they had lost narrowly to the USA but won in Sydney by 0.80 of a second from Australia, with Croatia a close third. One of the British crew, Luka Grubor, born in Zagreb, had himself previously competed for Yugoslavia and then Croatia. There were also two Oxbridge products, Andrew Lindsay (Oxford) and Kieran West (Cambridge), in the boat, and among those alongside them was a convert from another sport, in the mould of Jason Queally and Stephanie Cook, as Louis Attrill had been a British junior kick-boxing champion. Two gold medals and a silver from the 14 men's and women's rowing events in Sydney would be more than acceptable when it came to debating Lottery money allocations for the next Olympic challenge.

The traditional term 'yachting' had largely been superseded by 'sailing', which was a more accurate description of the sport now that the multi-ton vessels had been scrapped from the schedule. The tally of medals by Britains sailors in Sydney was even better than that of rowing – three golds and a silver – and in addition to the newcomer, Iain Percy, there was a win for an 'old hand', all of 23 years of age, in another class of dinghy usually sailed single-handed, the Laser. Various types of dinghy had figured at the Games since 1920, but the only British medals prior to 2000 had been Charles Currey's Finn silver in 1952 and a bronze won by Peter Scott, a future naturalist of world renown, in 1936 in what was called the International Olympia class. The Laser was of much more recent vintage, originating in Canada in 1970, and had made its Games debut in 1996 when Robert Scheidt, of Brazil, won from Britain's teenage Ben Ainslie.

Ainslie, world champion in 1998 and 1999, and Scheidt, his predecessor since 1995, met again in Sydney, and frequently during the series of races the 'meetings' came close to being collisions. In their account of the Games the International Sailing Federation colourfully said of the protagonists that 'these Laser sailors were at it like alley cats', and for once the intenseness of Olympic sailing competition, otherwise so often remotely conducted nearer the horizon than the shoreline, was superbly caught by the Australian television cameramen. Anslie was shown tacking repeatedly back and forth alongside Scheidt to deny him the benefit of the prevailing wind, and all that the pair of them seemed to lack was a cutlass apiece to fight it out in true pirate style! Scheidt won 5 of the 11 races and Ainslie only 2, with the other 40 other competitors mostly occupied as onlookers, but Ainslie consistently tacked to the gold with two points to spare. Coincidentally, Ainslie and Iain Percy had attended the same school in the 1990s – the Peter Symonds College in Winchester, in Hampshire, named after its original sixteenth-century merchant benefactor – but their sailing careers had already developed separately by then. (PLATE 22)

It was by the same two-point margin that the third of Britain's sailing champions, Shirley Robertson, beat Margriet Matthijsse, of Holland, who had also been second in 1996, and 25 other women for the title in the Europe class – single-handed dinghies ideal for sailors weighing between 50 and 75 kilogrammes. Robertson led the overall standings from the second race onwards, save for a fleeting intrusion by an Argentinian, Serena Amato, on day eight. Born in Dundee, the first British woman to win Olympic sailing gold since 1920 was now 32 years of age and another of those early starters on the water. From the age of seven she sailed a Mirror Miracle dinghy built from a kit by her father in the garage of their home in Clackmannanshire and sailed it on Loch Ard.

The six athletics medals would also provide a solid bargaining factor for future financial support. As it happens, though, all the Britons in addition to Jonathan Edwards and Denise Lewis who found a place on the rostrum had been very well-established athletes years before such funding had become available. Darren Campbell (200 metres) and Steve Backley (javelin) won silver and Katharine Merry (400 metres) and Kelly Holmes (800 metres) bronze. Backley had three European titles and two Commonwealth titles to his credit since 1990. Campbell and Merry had both been European junior champions, as had Backley before them. Holmes had been a world championships semi-finalist in 1993 and European silver-medallist the next year.

Since Mary Peters' win in 1972, the pentathlon competition for women had been extended to become a heptathlon, and the addition of an 800 metres event placed extra demands of stamina on the athletes, but Denise Lewis, here celebrating her 2000 gold, was still capable of a highly respectable time for the distance in addition to her speed and agility in the other events.

BY COURTESY OF MARK SHEARMAN

Edwards, with Olympic experience almost as extensive as Redgrave's, was English schools' triple-jump champion back in 1984 and had graduated from Durham University with a degree in physics. Under the coaching guidance of Carlton Johnson, he developed a technique that was so superior to anyone else's that at the time of writing his world record of 18.29 metres, set at the world championships of 1995, still stands. It was actually a fellow-Briton, Larry Achike, who led after the first round in Sydney, with exactly a metre less than Edwards' record, but Edwards settled things in round three with a relatively modest (for him) 17.71.

At 34, Edwards was the oldest ever Olympic champion in the event. Achike was fourth and another Briton, Phillips Idowu, sixth. Idowu would be silver-medallist in 2008, with Edwards by now a distinguished-looking BBC TV commentator with a touch of silver in his hair and no doubt beginning to wonder if he'd ever get the chance to describe his world record being beaten. Edwards' competitive forte was that he was very fast on the runway – he could run 100 metres in 10.48 seconds – but was able to control this pace so well that when he touched ground at the end of the hop phase and then the step phase his body remained firmly upright, thus avoiding the 'braking' effect that would have occurred had he been leaning even slightly backwards or forwards. (PLATE 23)

Denise Lewis gained her first English schools' title in the long jump at the age of 13 in 1986 and three years later won the first heptathlon she contested. This event had replaced the pentathlon in which Mary Peters had taken Olympic gold in 1972 and consisted of 100 metres hurdles, high jump, shot and 200 metres on the first day, with long jump, javelin and 800 metres on the second. Like the decathlon, this was no last resort for athletes who could not make the top grade in individual events but a real test of speed, strength and stamina across a range of disciplines. During Olympic year the wonderfully graceful Miss Lewis – later to become a successful television ballroom-dancer – ran 100 metres hurdles in 13.13 seconds (equal second best in Britain for the year), high jumped 1.84 metres (ninth) and long jumped 6.69 metres (first). Despite her lack of muscular bulk, she was also capable of 15.55 metres in the shot (fifth in Britain that year). (PLATE 24)

In Sydney she was not quite at her best, but then nor were her main rivals, and the woman who had beaten her in the previous year's world championships, Eunice Barber, of France, pulled out injured in the long jump. After the sixth event – the javelin – Lewis led Natalya Sazanovich of Belarus by 63 points. There was a Russian, Yelena Prokhorova, within striking distance who two months before had run an exceptional 2 minutes 4.27 seconds for the closing 800 metres, compared to Lewis's best of 2:12.20. Prokhorova scored almost 100 points more over those two laps, but was six seconds slower than her best and Lewis valiantly stayed close enough to take the gold by 53 points. The new champion revealed afterwards that, like Barber, she had sustained an injury in the long jump and paid warm tribute to the unsung members of the 'back-room' staff: 'The physios did everything possible to get me through. If it wasn't for them I wouldn't have made it.' Lewis had been born on 27 August 1972: Britain's previous Olympic women's multi-event champion, Dame Mary Peters, had won her gold seven days later.

In the same year of 1987 that one of the British athletics medallists in Sydney, Steve Backley, had had his first major success as European junior javelin champion, Richard Faulds' father, owner of a 300-acre farm at Longparish, in Hampshire, bought his son shooting lessons for his tenth birthday; the lad promptly hit 17 of his first 25 clay targets. Such precocious promise was soon confirmed. At 13 he competed internationally; at 16 he was world junior champion. After his fifth place at the 1996 Olympics, he won a European title the next year and took up shooting full-time. In Sydney the double trap event was being held for only the second occasion at the Games, and when the title-holder, Russell Mark, of Australia, led in the qualifying round by two points with an Olympic-record score the vociferous home crowd was understandably ecstatic.

But Faulds tied the scores in the final, and in the closing seconds of the shoot-off it was Mark who was wide of the mark, and Faulds won the gold. In the organisers' official report there was just a hint of the 'whingeing', of which the Aussies are wont to accuse the 'Poms' when such a loss occurs: 'Rapturous applause and intense support can be dysfunctional in precision events such as shooting and archery,' they pointed out. 'They can be distracting and even precipitate a sense of over-arousal. During the final the collective expectation and desire for gold poured out of the steep scaffold stands and perhaps that worked against the Australian.' Perhaps. But what about Faulds? He didn't allow himself to be distracted, it seems. Nor was there any evidence of 'over-arousal' on the part of another Australian shooter, aptly named Michael Diamond, who won gold in the single trap competition ahead of the Briton, Ian Peel.

At the Sydney 2000 Games Audley Harrison became the thirteenth British boxer to win an Olympic title, but the first in 32 years. His success was achieved in the super-heavyweight division (over 91 kilogrammes) that had been introduced in 1984. He was awarded an MBE in the Honours List and then turned professional, forming his own company, A-Force Promotions, and signing a deal with BBC Sport.

TOPFOTO

Nine different countries took gold in the ten shooting events and 11 others had silver or bronze. So Britain's two medals were particularly good value. In all, Richard Faulds and Ian Peel hit 329 out of 350 clay targets between them in winning gold and silver, and this was sufficient to bring £1.4 million into the sport from the exchequer and the National Lottery over the next four years.

Audley Harrison's boxing success was achieved in the grand manner, convincingly beating in turn a Russian, a Ukrainian and an Italian before coming up against the splendidly named Mukhtarkhan Koblanbekovich Dildekov in the final. Dildekov was from Kazakhstan, the former republic of the USSR which had won three gold medals, including light-heavyweight boxing, at its first independent Summer Olympics appearance in 1996. But he fared no better than Harrison's other hapless opponents and lost on points 30–16. Harrison's was thus the thirteenth boxing gold won by Britons since 1908 and the first since Chris Finnegan in 1968, but he was not actually the first Londoner to win the super-heavyweight division introduced in 1984. The champion at the 1988 Games had been Lennox Lewis, who represented Canada, having emigrated there at the age of nine, but who would gain greater renown for Britain as a professional, becoming world heavyweight champion in 1992.

In the overall medals table at Sydney the USA led Russia by 40 golds to 32, and with 97 medals to 88. China was third, with 28 gold and 59 medals overall. Great Britain placed ninth, with its 11 golds and 28 medals. Still ahead were four countries with which comparisons could more readily be made: Australia (16/58), Germany (13/56), France (13/38) and Italy (13/34). Cuba, with a population only one-tenth the size of Britain's, proved that state-aid still worked very effectively in a Communist régime by winning the same number of gold medals as Britain and one more medal in total.

A study by Cambridge University's Centre for Mathematics which is building up towards the 2012 Olympics provides further food for thought. In terms of medals per head of the population at those 2000 Games, Australia (one for every 324,000 or so) was the fourth most successful country behind the Bahamas, Barbados and Iceland, and therefore roughly six times more efficient than Great Britain. The British return was one medal per 2,099,614 people.

It had been a joy to be witness to those Sydney Olympics. No people in the world embraced sport in all its aspects as passionately as did the Australians, and the victory in the 400 metres of Cathy Freeman, of aboriginal background, had brought the 112,000 capacity crowd in the Olympic Stadium to a fever pitch of excitement. There is nothing like a 'home' win – and especially one with such sociological and emotional overtones – to set the tone and to seal the success of a Games. Sydney had been expensive to stage, but it had been a gloriously cosmopolitan spectacle, with 199 nations taking part, 80 of which came away with medals. It was all on a somewhat larger scale than when the whole business had started in ancient Athens 2,776 years before. The Sydney organisers certainly recognised their debt to history – the road in which the magnificent main stadium was built had been named 'Edwin Flack Avenue' in honour of the country's pioneering 800 metres and 1500 metres champion at those first modern Games of 1896.

FOURTEEN

The Games of 2002 and 2004

Again one medal for every two million people, and so Britain loses to the Bahamas

B ETWEEN 2001 and 2004 UK Sport had £70 million to distribute to elite Olympic sports, which was an increase of almost 20 per cent on the funds available for the 2000 Games. The chief recipients were athletics with £11.4 million, rowing £10.6 million, cycling £8.6 million, sailing £7.6 million and swimming £6.4 million. As there would be 46 events in athletics at the Athens Games, 14 in rowing, 18 in cycling, 11 in sailing and 32 in swimming, the head count of potential competitors – bearing in mind that 32 crew places would need to be filled for five of the rowing races – showed that it was actually the sailors who proportionally benefited most.

More countries than ever before claimed gold in the Athens Games of 2004, 56 in all, and Britain's nine wins were actually two fewer than four years earlier, although the total of medals was up slightly, from 28 to 30. The medals table had a familiar look about it, with the USA leading in terms of titles from China and Russia (respectively 36, 32 and 27 golds). Australia again came a distant fourth (17 golds), followed by Japan (16), Germany (13), France (11) and Italy (10). Britain's score of nine was equalled by Cuba, again, and by the Republic of Korea (more commonly known as South Korea) and Ukraine.

The highest overall medal totals were 103 for the USA, 92 for Russia and 63 for China, with Great Britain again equal ninth. A preferably accurate guide to national achievements, though, would have been to calculate once more the number of medals won per head of the population, but only the academics concerned themselves with that. This was a pity, because a different and much more interesting story emerges, very similar to four years before: the Bahamas first with one medal per 150,000 or so population, followed by Australia (406,000), Cuba (419,000), Estonia (447,000) and Slovenia (503,000). By this reckoning Great Britain finished thirty-third, with one medal for every 2,009,000 of its population.

Of course, statistics such as these were irrelevant to the British gold-medallists themselves. At the Summer Games in Athens in 2004 there were 16 of them in all, 9 of whom had already stood on an Olympic rostrum in previous years. Oarsman Matthew Pinsent won his fourth gold medal, and crew-mate James Cracknell and sailors Ben Ainslie and Shirley Robertson their second apiece. There had been silver medals four years earlier for sprinter Darren Campbell, time-trial track cyclist Chris Hoy and three-day-event horseman Leslie Law. Middle-distance runner Kelly Holmes and pursuit cyclist Bradley Wiggins had both won bronze at those Games.

The precise share-out of British gold was three for athletics, two each for cycling and sailing, and one each for equestrianism and rowing. There were 29 sports on the schedule, and Britain also had medals in archery, badminton, boxing, canoeing, modern pentathlon, swimming and diving. Sports which had provided gold in the past but not this time were fencing (a best placing of eighth), hockey (ninth) and shooting (seventh).

Yet again, the 'national game' of football had no chance to figure in the British medal-count. The Olympic tournament had been opened to professionals in 1984 and from 1992 onwards had been largely restricted to players aged under 23 (three over-23s were allowed in each squad). Yet no Great Britain team had taken part in the Games tournament since 1960, when the results had been actually quite respectable – losing 4–3 to Brazil, drawing 2–2 with Italy, beating China 3–2 – but not good enough to survive the qualifying group. The over-riding and really rather ridiculous reason for the continuing British absence in more recent years was that the four separate home unions simply could not agree a common selection policy.

At the Winter Games of 2002 there *was* a British team sport which had no problems deciding who to send to a Games: Scotland provided all of the five women who had gone to Salt Lake City for the Winter Olympics curling. To the surprise of many, they won gold. It seemed highly unlikely that they would do so after they had lost four of their nine group matches, but they then beat Germany and Sweden in play-offs and Canada 6–5 in the semi-finals and Switzerland 4–3 in the final. Thus a British tradition of picking up gold from time to time on the ice had been revived. It had happened on eight previous occasions since 1908, five of them in figure-skating or ice-dancing, but not at all since the Winter Olympics had been re-scheduled from 1994 onwards to take place halfway between each Summer Games. The curling gold in 2002 had also been achieved against all odds – at the time Canada had 1,100 ice rinks, Scotland 30. *The Scotsman* newspaper described the winners, with every good intention but perhaps with unconscious chauvinism, as 'ordinary women with families and jobs'. Within a couple of years Olympic history would be re-vamped and it would be revealed that this wasn't the first time Scots had won Olympic curling gold: a team of Scotsmen had done so back in 1924, but as we shall see in a later chapter, they would not receive proper recognition for doing so for more than 80 years.

In the 2004 Summer Games in Athens Kelly Holmes became the first Briton to win two gold medals at the same Games since the horseman, Richard Meade, in 1972, and the only British middle-distance runner since 1920 – Coe included – to have done so.

(PLATE 25) It had been a long and winding trail to get there. Her first major success had been at the age of 13 in the junior 1500 metres at the 1983 English Schools' Championships, where Sally Gunnell won the senior 100 metres hurdles but Jonathan Edwards was only ninth in the senior triple jump. In 1987 Holmes was senior champion at the same meeting, but then went into the army. It was not until 1993, as a corporal physical training instructor that she began running seriously again. Within a year she was European silver-medallist and Commonwealth champion at 1500 metres. Yet she had to wait another eight years for her next gold medal, again in the Commonwealth 1500.

Frequent injuries disrupted Holmes's career, but by the time she travelled at the age of 34 to Athens she had the vast experience, sometimes chastening, of four previous Olympic finals: in 1996 she had been fourth at 800 metres, eleventh at 1500; in 2000 third at 800 and seventh at 1500. After she won the Athens 1500, her recollections of the finishing straight are curiously matter-of-fact: 'There is no one close to me with a better kick than mine, and with 90 metres left I make my move. But not 100 per cent. Then I put in a second kick with 50 metres to go. I open up and the feeling when I cross the line is indescribable.' This, though, was day ten of the Olympics and grasping gold was no longer a novelty for Kelly Holmes. Five days before she had won the 800, having not even decided to run it until after she had arrived in Athens. One of her less likely accomplishments is that she holds a heavy goods vehicle driving licence (ability at manoeuvring in tight corners also comes in useful in 800-metre and 1500-metre running).

Her Athens diary, written with the help of a perceptive *Sunday Times* journalist, Richard Lewis, and published later in 2004, provides an exhilarating insight into what it is like to have become an Olympic champion; particularly those feelings and reactions in the rare interludes away from the track, the crowds, the photographers, the TV interviews, the press conferences. The opening remarks for day six read as follows:

> It is morning. I wake up still in disbelief. I have the medal on the pillow next
> to me and I am staring at it. Gold from the 800 metres. Just a few days ago I
> was undecided about even running the distance, and now I am the Olympic
> champion. But it is time to focus on what is going to be another long day. I
> could lie here all day, I suppose, just thinking back to last night. Did it happen?
> Did it really happen?

The way it had happened, was that in the 800 metres she had overtaken the defending champion, Maria Mutola, of Mozambique, in the last few metres, having astutely followed in her friend's and rival's footsteps throughout the second lap. Then at 1500 metres, and in her sixth race of the Games, Holmes moved from eighth place as the bell sounded for the last lap to take the lead 60 metres from the end. She thus became Britain's seventh woman Olympic champion in athletics (after Mesdames Packer, Rand, Peters, Sanderson, Gunnell and Lewis). Any comparison is of little real significance, but it is mildly interesting that her British-record 1500 metres time of 3 minutes 57.90 seconds was almost four seconds faster than the only other Briton to have completed the Olympic 800/1500 double, Albert Hill, 84 years before.

Britain's other athletics gold came in the men's 4×100 metres relay. (PLATE 26) Sprint relays are always tense and highly technical affairs: pure running speed is crucial, obviously, but so is the ability to transfer the baton safely, cleanly and quickly. In Athens Britain's men did just that and the obvious favourites, the USA, did not. For pure speed the Americans held a huge advantage: they had the winners of both the 100 and 200 metres in their team, plus the world-record holder for 100 metres, Maurice Greene, whereas none of the four Britons had got to either individual final. However, this mattered not at all, for one fumbled exchange by the Americans gave the British a two-metre lead on the anchor stage, and Mark Lewis-Francis held on for a startling victory by just one-hundredth of a second.

It was the only medal of any kind for Britain's male athletes in Athens, and no one was more delighted than Darren Campbell. Campbell, in particular, was deserving of an Olympic gold, as he had also been second to the Greek, Kostás Kentéris, in the Sydney Olympic 200 metres, and Kentéris had subsequently been banned for drug abuse. Campbell then suffered further fall-out from a drugs issue when his team-mate, Dwain Chambers, was suspended for the same reason, and relay gold medals from the 2002 European Championships and silver from the next year's world championships were forfeited in retrospect. The Athens success came 92 years after Britain's only previous Olympic 4×100 metres victory. In 1912 Britain had lost to the USA in the semi-finals by 0.4 seconds. In 2004 Britain lost in the qualifying heats to the USA by 0.51 seconds. The USA had won 15 of the 20 finals in that event over the years.

Campbell, Lewis-Francis and the lead-off runner, Jason Gardener, had all been outstanding youthful talents. In the biennial world junior championships Campbell and Gardener had both been second at 100 metres and Lewis-Francis had then won the title in the year 2000. The other man to complete the quartet in Athens, Marlon Devonish, was something of a late developer, ranking only twelfth fastest in Britain as an under-20, but he would be still among the best in the country 18 years later as the 2012 Games drew near. He would suffer his own relay misfortune in the heats at the 2008 Games when the British quartet was disqualified, as again were the USA.

Cycling's two winners were Chris Hoy in the one kilometre time-trial and Bradley Wiggins in the four kilometres individual pursuit. Although there had been two rudimentary time-trials at the inaugural 1896 Games (contrastingly, at one lap of the track and 300 laps), the distance had not been standardised until 1928, and Hoy succeeded the only other British title-winner, Jason Queally, who had won gold in 2000. As Hoy came in for Queally in 2004, many of the other protagonists from other nations were they same as they had been in Sydney: Stefen Nimke (Germany) had been second in 2000, Shane Kelly (Australia) third and Arnaud Tournant (France) fourth. Dramatically, as each of them took to the track Queally's Olympic record was broken first by Kelly, then by Niemke, and then by Tournant. Chris Hoy came on last, was ahead on time all of the way, but only just held on to win from Tournant, 1 minute 00.711 seconds to 1:00.986. Increasing specialisation, improved training, huge time gains from modern equipment, and faster velodromes, had all contributed to a dramatic reduction in times since 1928, the first occasion the kilometre time-trial had been held at the Olympics. Then the winning time had been 1:14.4 – equivalent to virtually a complete lap of the track slower than Hoy in 2004.

Unforgettably there had also been a single previous British success in the individual pursuit event on the velodrome since the event had been introduced in 1964, and which remains one of my fondest Olympic memories – Chris Boardman's triumph of 1992. Bradley Wiggins did not quite emulate Boardman by catching his opponent, Bradley McGee of Australia, but he did win by the decisive margin of more than four seconds. Like most of Britain's cyclists Wiggins went on to further Olympic success four years later. He also switched disciplines, to compete successfully in the Tour de France, where he was fourth overall in 2009, and in the Vuelta a Espana (Tour of Spain), where he finished third overall in 2011. Cycling's income from the National Lottery funds had increased by almost 60 per cent for the years 2001 to 2004, and the Athens wins were only a foretaste of what was to come. More, much more, will be said about that in later chapters.

Experienced sailors were also using their funding to good effect. Ben Ainslie's success this time came in the Finn class after having won the Laser in 2000; Shirley Robertson's gold as a member of the crew of three in the women's Yngling class followed her single-handed victory in the Europe class four years before. The Yngling (pronounced 'Ing-ling' and designed by a Norwegian, Jan Linge, although the title he devised is actually the word for 'youngster' in his language, as he built the original for his son) has been described as 'the ideal women's racing boat' because it is light-weight and relatively easy to handle. In Athens there were four sailing events for men, four for women, and three open, and Britain again won more medals (two gold, two silver, one bronze) than any other country. Shirley Robertson was a week ahead of Kelly Holmes in becoming the first British woman in 92 years to win two golds, also equalling the score of fellow Scots sailor Rodney Pattisson. Holmes's wins came on 23 and 28 August; Robertson's series of seven races finished on 21 August. The only other women to be double gold-medallists for Britain had accomplished that feat in a very different age. They were the tennis players, Chattie Cooper (1900) and Edith Hannam (1912).

Ainslie, at his third Olympics, and now having switched boats from Laser to Finn, made by no means the ideal of starts and was nineteenth overall after two races. Fortunately, rather better was to come with four first places and never lower than fourth in the next eight races. So on the closing day he could afford to follow unobtrusively in the wake of his nearest rival, Rafael Trujillo, of Spain; they placed thirteenth and fourteenth, with Ainslie thus the gold-medallist, 38 points to 51. The International Sailing Federation waxed lyrical about his nautical skills: 'His starts were courageous and inch perfect. He was in synch with the shifts and picked off competitors at will.' Ainslie's old rival from Brazil, Robert Scheidt, regained the Laser title instead.

Shirley Robertson, was partnered in the Yngling craft by Sarah Ayton and Sarah Webb, and their victory earned them the breezy media tag of 'three blondes in a boat', which they accepted with good grace. Both the Sarahs had been born in Ashford, in Surrey, though three years apart. Sarah Ayton had been introduced to sailing by her parents, seeking a leisure-time outlet for her at the age of six and for her ten-year-old brother. The Queen Mary's Sailing Club at Staines provided hire of a boat for 50 pence an hour, and, as she was to recall later, she thrilled to the joys of 'getting wet, capsizing, playing around in the water'. The role model, though, was provided by another sport entirely, at the age of 12 watching on television Sally Gunnell win the 1992 Olympic 400 metres hurdles. 'That was my inspiration to get to the Olympics,' Sarah Ayton has said, and she overcame suffering from meningitis and septicaemia two years later to realise her ambition.

The other Sarah later related a charming tale of how she occupied herself on the final day of racing when the British did not need to start because the gold was already assured ahead of Ukraine and Denmark. 'It was the final of the men's four rowing,' she said, 'so I decided I would go and watch that. Driving past the marina where all our competitors were getting ready to go on the water, I felt really odd, as if I would get a phone call asking where on earth I was as we needed to sail. Turning up at the rowing, there were so many British supporters, and even though we hadn't had our medal ceremony everyone knew I had won. The atmosphere was electric, and then watching the men's four also win gold was really special.'

Leslie Law's individual win in the equestrian three-day event, riding his distinctive Irish grey mount, Shear L'Eau, was backed up by Pippa Funnell in third place; the team placed second overall, thus maintaining a proud tradition in that competition. Between 1968 and 1988 individual British horsemen and horsewomen had won one gold, two silvers and two bronzes, plus, as teams, two golds and two silvers and silver again in 2000. Law, who had also been in the team at the 2000 Olympics, but riding the brother of Shear L'Eau, had been a front-rank competitor for 15 years, but his gold medal award came about in contentious circumstances. The original winner, Bettina Hoy, of Germany, was disqualified after accidentally crossing the starting-line twice, was reinstated, and was then disqualified again on further appeal by the British and French management. Shear L'Eau was eventually retired at the age of 15 in 2007, by which time both he and his owner had emigrated to the USA.

For the first time in 20 years there was no Redgrave in the British rowing squad, but his long-time partner, Matthew Pinsent, successfully bid for a fourth gold. It was Britain's sixth win at coxless fours, in 1908, then 1924/28/32, and now 2000 and 2004. In 1924 the margin over Canada had been a comfortable one, close to ten seconds; 80 years later in Athens Canada were again second but this time by almost as small a measure as one could imagine, 0.08 of a second: the lead appeared to change with every stroke in the last few hundred metres. Pinsent could trace his family tree back to William the Conqueror, so perhaps he could thank the blood of warriors that coursed through his veins. Redgrave and Pinsent had achieved a remarkable sequence of Olympic victories, but even they would have to salute the most decorated Olympic rower of all time, the Romanian Elisabeta Lipă, who by 2004 had won a total of eight medals in every Games since 1984, including five gold (in 1984, 1992, 1996, 2000 and 2004).

In Athens 74 of the 201 competing countries collected medals, 56 of them winning gold, and that was justification in itself for returning the Games to their ancestral home.

Yet it is a sobering thought as to what might have happened had Athens been awarded, instead, the 2012 or 2016 Games and therefore been faced with all the massive planning and construction costs involved while simultaneously trying to deal with the severe economic crisis into which the country has been plunged. On the positive side, the worrying delays in completing the facilities in time for the 2004 Games left no mark on the competitions themselves, and the city itself has benefited from the new international airport, rail and tram systems, and the pedestrian walks linking tourist attractions.

Three years earlier China had become the 22nd nation to be awarded a Summer or Winter Games (technically, though, it is cities, rather than countries, that apply to be hosts), and so the next Summer Games would be held for the third time in Asia, after Tokyo in 1964 and Seoul in 1988. The Communist rulers of the People's Republic of China, with its 1,300 million population, could be relied upon to ensure that their Games would be bigger than any previously. Whether they would be better was another matter.

FIFTEEN

The Games of 2008 and 2010

Cycling sets the pace with 'a philosophy to search for perfection in every domain'

IN BRITAIN, Beijing 2008 will probably be remembered most clearly for the performance of its cyclists. Their dominance was extraordinary, winning golds in three of the four track pursuit events, in three of the four sprint events, plus the men's keirin and the women's road race. British cyclists, indeed, won one more gold than French competitors did across all Olympic events. As we have seen, Britain's track cyclists had already collected several notable Olympic medals at previous Games, but by 2008 it was the widespread nature of success at the elite level that was so remarkable.

By this date, too, British road cycling success was becoming more evident and more frequent: on the roads in Beijing Emma Pooley took silver in the time-trial, while Nicole Cooke did one better in dramatically winning the women's road race. Mark Cavendish has become one of the most successful road-racing cyclists in the world, and could well become the best road-race sprinter the world has ever known, with an astonishing burst of speed. By the age of just 26 he had already won thirty Grand Tour stages, including twenty in the Tour de France, and in 2011 became only the second ever British road-race world champion (after Tom Simpson in 1965). It is remarkable, then, that at the 2008 Games in Beijing Cavendish was the only one among the 14 British track competitors who did not win a medal. The only Olympic event he took part in was the Madison – best described as a two-man relay – in which he partnered Bradley Wiggins. But they could only finish ninth, partly because as reigning world champions and one of the favourite pairings they were closely marked by the competition, and partly because Wiggins must have been feeling the effects of his other exploits in the velodrome: he had already successfully defended his individual pursuit title and, just two days later, was also in the quartet that won the team pursuit, during which they set new world records in both the semi-final and the final.

At the 2008 Beijing Games opening ceremony Mark Foster became only the second swimmer after Anita Lonsbrough 44 years before to have carried the British flag. Foster, then 38 years of age, was nominated by his team leaders and selected from a short-list drawn up by the British Olympic Association. When the first Olympic march-past had been held at the Games of 1906 the flag-bearer had been Lord Desborough, a future chairman of the Association, whose sporting achievements had included twice swimming across the waters at the foot of the Niagara Falls.

BY COURTESY OF MARK SHEARMAN

Yet even Wiggins's two Olympic golds in Beijing did not represent the best that any British bike rider could do: Chris Hoy became the first Briton to win three golds at the same Olympic Games since the swimmer, Henry Taylor, exactly 100 years earlier. It requires further reference to the London results of a century previous to find the last occasion on which as many gold, silver and bronze medals were won by Britain in any single sport as the 14 that were accumulated by the cyclists in individual and team events in Beijing. In that Edwardian era, when competition was so much less severe, 21 medals had been won in shooting, 17 in athletics and 14 in boxing. Not even the most ardent of Olympic traditionalists could possibly claim that the achievements of 1908 matched those of 2008. Of the ten events in the Beijing cycling velodrome Britain won seven and Argentina, Holland and Spain one each. In the share-out of the 30 medals, the countries which ranked after Britain's 14 were Spain, with three, and Australia and France with two each.

It was a measure of how dramatically Britain's Olympic expectations had changed in just over a decade that it was no longer the number of medals won that counted but whether they were as many as the planners had hoped for. Two months prior to the 2008 Games, UK Sport had finalised Britain's Olympic 'target' as being 35 medals, including

10 to 12 gold, and this score was massively exceeded – 47 medals in all, of which 19 were gold. Overall Britain placed fourth in the 2008 medals table behind only the USA (110), China (100) and Russia (73), and again fourth as regards gold medals – China 51, USA 36, Russia 23. Against Australia, the sporting arch-rival, Britain finished ahead – 19 golds to 14, 47 medals to 46 – for the first time in 20 years.

Such was the proliferation of British victories in 2008, 12 of them by men, 7 by women, that it is worth listing them here, in chronological order:

10 August – Nicole Cooke. *Cycling,* Road race.
11 August – Rebecca Adlington. *Swimming,* 400 metres freestyle.
15 August – Chris Hoy, Jason Kenny, Jamie Staff. *Cycling,* Team sprint.
16 August – Rebecca Adlington. *Swimming,* 800 metres freestyle.
16 August – Tom James, Andy Triggs-Hodge, Peter Reed, Steve Williams. *Rowing,* Coxless fours.
16 August – Bradley Wiggins. *Cycling,* Individual pursuit.
16 August – Chris Hoy. *Cycling,* Keirin.
17 August – Mark Hunter, Zac Purchase. *Rowing,* Lightweight double sculls.
17 August – Sarah Ayton, Sarah Webb, Philippa Wilson. *Sailing,* Yngling class.
17 August – Ben Ainslie. *Sailing,* Finn class.
17 August – Rebecca Romero. *Cycling,* Individual pursuit.
18 August – Ed Clancy, Paul Manning, Geraint Thomas, Bradley Wiggins. *Cycling,* Team pursuit
19 August – Paul Goodison. *Sailing,* Laser class.
19 August – Victoria Pendleton. *Cycling,* Sprint.
19 August – Chris Hoy, *Cycling,* Sprint.
19 August – Christine Ohuruogu. *Athletics,* 400 metres.
21 August – Iain Percy, Andrew Simpson. *Sailing,* Star class.
22 August – Tim Brabants. *Canoeing,* Kayak singles 1000 metres.
23 August – James DeGale. *Boxing,* Middleweight.

Thus gold medals were earned in seven sports – eight for cycling; four for sailing; two each for rowing and swimming; one each for athletics, boxing and canoeing. The tally of fourteen medals for cycling was followed by rowing, swimming and sailing (six each), athletics (four), boxing and canoeing (three each), equestrianism (two), gymnastics, modern pentathlon and taekwondo (one each). One Australian wit pointed out that, with so many medals in cycling, yachting and rowing, the British seemed to be the best in the world … at sitting down, or going backwards.

No medals were won in 11 other sports – archery, badminton, diving, fencing, hockey, judo, shooting, synchronised swimming, tennis, triathlon and weight-lifting. More importantly, of the 17 sports in which medals had been targeted the six which exceeded expectations were all of those in which gold had been won, with the notable exception of athletics, where the rewards of four medals fell one short of the number targeted. Three other sports hit their targets exactly: gymnastics, modern pentathlon, taekwondo. Seven more which failed to achieve the targets set for them were archery, badminton, diving, equestrianism, judo, shooting and triathlon. For the sake of a single medal, one prominent fall-guy was the UK Athletics performance director, Dave Collins, who resigned after the Games. The margin of error was infinitesimal. The British men's 4×400 metres relay team missed bronze by 0.75 seconds; Goldie Sayers missed women's javelin bronze by 38 centimetres. These days the Olympic Games is a ruthless business for the managers as well as the competitors.

The cyclists, of course, had had a lot of money spent on them – £22,151,000 over four years. One could see where the money had gone, in the quality of the kit, the advanced skinsuits (destroyed after the Games so that their technical composition could be kept secret), the rigorous training and the intense attention to detail. Indeed, cycling received almost ten per cent of the total budget handled by UK Sport, the responsibilities of which had now been vastly extended to cover the development of sporting talent at every level. The velodrome that had been built as the National Cycling Centre in Manchester in 1994, and which had been the venue for the world championships of 1996 and 2000 and the Commonwealth Games events of 2002, provided unrivalled facilities for training. Inevitably, there were mutterings from vanquished overseas rivals about lavish buying of success, but it was the way that the money was being spent, not necessarily the amount, that was bringing dividends. One of Britain's most knowledgeable cycling writers, William Fotheringham, has described the approach of the sport's British administrators as being that of 'a philosophy to search for perfection in every domain' and explained: 'They have the finest and most innovative bikes and clothing, but the kit is there for anyone who has the drive, the imagination and the finance. The coaches and technicians are the best, but that expertise is available on the open market.' Team manager Dave Brailsford described the process as an aggregation of tiny improvements which cumulatively had made the difference.

The first of the cycling golds for Britain went to Nicole Cooke, who won the women's road-race cycling title on the third day of the Games and became the first Welsh Olympic champion since horseman Richard Meade 36 years before and only the second Welsh female champion after relay swimmer Irene Steer 96 years earlier. (PLATE 27) Of most immediate import, the effect on the rest of the cycling team in Beijing was inestimable. Chris Hoy, preparing for his triple gold bid, later wrote of Cooke's achievement as 'a dream start … it was a fantastic performance, the mood in the camp was already positive, and that lifted it even higher.'

Born in Swansea into a cycling-friendly family, Nicole Cooke had been taken on tandem touring holidays from a very young age and she had her first competition at 11. A multiple junior world champion as a road racer, time-trialist and mountain biker, she had enterprisingly gone off to live and race professionally in Italy after taking her A-levels at the age of 18 and was fifth in the 2004 Olympic road event. In Beijing she seemed to have misjudged matters as she was contending the lead with a Swedish and an Italian rider, with the finish only 200 metres away, but her finishing speed was irresistible. It was the first British medal in any of the seven women's road races held at the Games since 1984.

The prolific cycling medallists, Chris Hoy and Bradley Wiggins, were both also seasoned Olympic veterans, having won gold at the 2004 Games, and between the two of them they now had 11 Olympic medals. Wiggins's collection included bronze in 2000 from the team pursuit, plus silver in that event and bronze in the Madison in 2004, when he was the first British triple medallist at the Games for 40 years. Hoy also had a silver from the team sprint in 2000. (PLATE 28)

Even Wiggins, with his six medals and a share in two world records in the team pursuit, had to give precedence to Hoy, who in the Laoshan Velodrome in Beijing won gold in the individual sprint (Jason Kenny taking silver), the team sprint (with Jamie Staff and Jason Kenny), and keirin (with Ross Edgar taking silver for Britain). The last and least known of these events had been devised in Japan in 1948 but not accepted for Olympic competition until 2000. Raced over a distance of 2,000 metres, it involves six riders following, in pre-arranged single file, a light motor-cycle (or 'derny', named after its French inventor), the pace of which is gradually increased to 50 kilometres per hour some 600–700 metres from the finish. The derny then swings aside, leaving the competitors to sprint it out the rest of the way. In the Beijing final two British cyclists lined up against each other. After the derny pulled out Hoy remained watchful in second position for a time before using his legendary power (reportedly around 2,300 watts) to surge around the outside to take the front with a lap and a half to go. In the end he crossed the line with a totally commanding lead of around 20 metres, while Ross Edgar moved through to take the silver.

In addition to Hoy's sprint victory over Jason Kenny, there was another all-British final in which Rebecca Romero took gold over Wendy Houvenaghel in the women's individual pursuit. (PLATE 29) Romero, whose father was Spanish, already had a silver medal from 2004 and a world title from 2005 but in a different sport, rowing, having switched from quadruple sculls to track cycling because of a back problem. Incidentally, the only other Britons to have figured in medal successes in two sports were Rob Derbyshire, Jack Jarvis and Paul Radmilovic in the associated disciplines of swimming and water-polo in the early years of the twentieth century. Even then, Jarvis had played only in a water-polo qualifying round in 1900 and not in the final. A rather more meaningful and impressive comparison with Romero's achievement is that the one other woman from any country to have won medals in two Summer Olympic sports is Roswitha Krause, of East Germany, with relay swimming silver in 1968 and handball silver and bronze in 1976 and 1980.

In his autobiography, published the next year (and for which a respected cycling writer, Richard Moore, is credited for his help), Hoy naturally dwells on the intense excitement of those five days of racing. But his most interesting observations concern the reaction of some of those who had been swept aside by the British avalanche of success. 'Something special had happened – and was happening – in the Laoshan Velodrome,' he wrote before describing the third of his gold-medal successes in the sprint final against Jason Kenny, with whom he and Jamie Staff had shared the team sprint title four evenings before:

But some, inevitably, didn't see it like that. We became aware of veiled remarks from one or two other nations that our success was 'suspicious'. There were no outright accusations, but the implication was clear, and it had been made in the past – that there was some sinister explanation for our success. For me, in a period when there is increased drugs testing, especially at and around the major events, it is more suspicious to be slower at the Olympics than at a World Cup or Grand Prix meeting nine months earlier.

I find it odd that people can go to the biggest race of their lives and go slower than they have gone at other times of the year. You go there fresh, motivated, tapered, and with the best equipment. The explanation for our success was very simple: we paid incredible attention to detail and we got everything spot on. We raised our game when it counted and the others didn't. Many nations even under-performed. Sour grapes are perhaps inevitable. But I have always given my rivals the benefit of the doubt when they produce amazing performances. Call me naïve, but I like to think that if I can win clean, then they can, too.

Born in Edinburgh, Hoy had been successful in a variety of sports by the age of 18, including representing Scotland at rowing, before concentrating on track cycling and reaching the British sprint final in 1994 and then winning the title the next year. These, though, were still the pre-Lottery years, with no significant sponsorship for promising youngsters like him, and he recalled, 'For me the most potent motivational fuel was not ambition, I think, but curiosity. I wanted to see how far I could go.' By Olympic year, 2000, a world class performance programme was in place, backed by unprecedented funding, and Hoy was one of the trio which took the team sprint silver behind the French.

Wiggins was born in Belgium of an Australian father, who was himself a professional racing cyclist specialising in indoor six-day events, and an English mother, but the marriage ended in 1982 when the youngster was only two years of age. Encouraged instead by his grandfather, he started racing as a 12-year-old at the Herne Hill velodrome near his home in south London and developed rapidly into a junior world champion. Wiggins beat a New Zealander, Hayden Roulston, in the individual pursuit final in Beijing in a time some five seconds slower than Chris Boardman had achieved in 1992, but in the team pursuit, in which Wiggins was joined by Ed Clancy, Paul Manning and Geraint Thomas, the world record was broken in the semi-finals and again in the final, with a time of 3 minutes 53.314 seconds for the 4000 metres, which equates to an average speed in excess of 65 kilometres per hour from a standing start. The Danish quartet took silver, almost seven seconds behind. (PLATE 30)

Wiggins's views on the support he had received over the years are enthusiastically expressed. 'I rode my first World Championships as an 18-year-old in 1998, just after the formation of the World Class Performance plan by Peter Keen, and it's great to be part of it, watching it all grow,' he has said. 'It's also great to be on the inside, watching Australia and the other nations looking at us and wondering how we do it … it's the way people feel about all successful set-ups from Manchester United to the All-Blacks, and it says a lot about where we've got to.' Peter Keen had been appointed Britain's chief cycling coach at the age of 25 and had guided Chris Boardman to Britain's first Olympic cycling gold for 72 years, in 1992. Having headed British Cycling's performance programme, he had joined UK Sport and became performance director in 2004.

An indication of the demands being made on the racing cyclists in the months and years before the Olympics was given by Victoria Pendleton, who had beaten Anna Meares, of Australia, decisively 2–0 in the best-of-three individual sprint final. Towards the end of 2008 Pendleton reflected, 'After I won the gold, I didn't have much time to think about it. The whole experience was like a high-speed roller-coaster, and I was straight into training for the World Cup. It sounds boring, but it's true.' Pendleton had started racing at the age of nine and had already won six world titles before the 2008 Games, but hers was the first medal of any kind for Britain in the women's sprint since the discipline had been introduced in 1988.

Winners in athletics and canoeing for Britain in Beijing also established 'firsts' of historic significance. Having earned a kayak canoeing bronze in 2000, and then placing fifth in 2004, Tim Brabants was the first ever British gold-medallist in 180 finals since the sport had been introduced at the Games of 1936. (PLATE 31) Despite the demands of his doctor's practice, Brabants had reached gold-medal calibre by fitting in some 4½ hours of training a day, on the water and running track, and in the gymnasium, and his world record of 3 minutes 24.412 seconds for 1,000 metres set in the 2004 Games heats represents a speed of just over 18 kilometres an hour.

Christine Ohuruogu, Britain's sole athletics champion in 2008, was the first to win the women's 400 metres after the close second places by Ann Packer in 1964 and Lillian Board in 1968. (PLATE 32) Ohuruogu, whose parents were from Nigeria, was already Commonwealth champion from 2006 and world champion from 2007, but the latter title had been won under something of a cloud. Earlier in the same month she had completed a one-year suspension sentence for missing three out-of-competition drug tests, and that transgression, as it stood, would keep her out of the Olympics. The British Olympic Association had decided as a matter of policy not to endorse the selection in any sport of competitors who had served such bans. Fortunately for Ohuruogu, though, the authorities relented at the end of 2007 and declared her eligible again.

During Olympic year she had not shown the form to suggest she would complete the hat-trick of titles (alongside her Commonwealth and world titles), but in the Beijing final she took the lead where it counted most, 30 metres from the finish, and won by less than one-tenth of a second from Shericka Williams, of Jamaica. Such fine judgement was no chance affair. 'My coach, Lloyd Cowan, has always said to me, "You don't train for the Grand Prix races. You don't train for the trials. You train for the three Championship days",' Ohuruogu explained. Her time of 49.62 seconds was commendable enough, although it was the slowest to win at the Olympics since 1972, and the world record, set in 1985 by an East German, Marita Koch, at 47.60, seemed far out of reach, as did other women's records of the 1980s.

The lightweight division of rowing was a relatively recent innovation, dating from 1996, and the pairing of Mark Hunter and Zachary Purchase were Britain's first medallists in the event. The qualifications for their double sculls event were limits of 70 kilogrammes average body weight and 72.5 kilogrammes individually. The British pair had only come together a year before the Olympics, but they won by less than a second from Greece. Hunter had started rowing at 14 with the Poplar, Blackwall & District club on the Isle of Dogs. As a member of the Company of Watermen and Lightermen, established in 1555, he is steeped in Thames history and tradition. Each year the company, which traditionally controlled passenger transport and the carriage of goods on the river, holds a race of 4 miles 1100 yards (7.4 kilometres) which passes under eleven Thames bridges and for which the prize is 'Doggett's Coat and Badge', named after its original donor, Thomas Doggett. First held in 1715, this is the oldest rowing competition in the world, and in the year 2000 Mark Hunter had shared in a Millennium celebration double sculls win over the course. Zac Purchase, an under-23 world champion in 2005, had learned his rowing at King's School, Worcester, which has the inestimable advantage of possessing within its own grounds a boat-house bordering on to the river Severn.

The coxless four in the 'no weights barred' rowing provided Britain with a third successive win, entailing a second gold for Steve Williams. The margin over Australia, champions in 1992 and 1996, was little more than a second, and this was an event which Britain had now won on seven occasions at the Games. Williams was the only member of the gold-medal four from 2004 to have continued competing and was in the world championship winning crew of 2005 and 2006 with fellow Beijing gold-medallists, Peter Reed and Andy Triggs-Hodge, though they slipped to fourth in 2007. Tom James came into the crew in 2008, having taken part in four Boat Races for Cambridge since 2003 and been a member of the Olympic eight in 2004. He was the first Welsh-born rowing gold-medallist for 100 years, and it was a curious fact that winning British oarsmen born in the USA were much more common: Jack Wilson in 1948, Rowley Douglas in 2000, and now Peter Reed in 2008.

Sailing had been the second highest beneficiary from the 2005–08 funding programme, receiving £22,292,000 (athletics was top of the list at £26,513,000), and the rewards for Britain were twice as many medals as any other country (four gold, a silver and a bronze). Ben Ainslie acquired his third gold and Iain Percy, Sarah Ayton and Sarah Webb their second. Ainslie won four of his races and had three second places to take the Finn title convincingly from Zachary Railey, of the USA, 23 points to 45. Only one other sailor in Olympic history now had a more successful record than Ainslie, and that was the legendary Dane, Paul Elvström, who had won four successive golds from 1948 to 1960 and had competed in his eighth Games in 1988.

At the age of 31 Ainslie's sailing experience extended for most of his lifetime. Born in Macclesfield, in Cheshire, the son of a round-the-world yachtsman, he started learning to sail at the age of four, first raced at eight, and made his international competitive debut at twelve. Now said by one of his rivals to be 'a gentleman but a brutal competitor', Ainslie has expressed his motivation in a way which every weekend sailor happily messing about in boats could readily understand: 'I just love the motion of the water and getting away from all those issues that you have on land.' One of the foremost sailing websites warily but affectionately describes the type of craft which he sailed as 'absolutely unforgiving

Andrew Simpson (*left*) and Iain Percy won the 2008 Star class in sailing to repeat a British success in this event of 20 years before, and the pair of them followed up with the world title in 2010. Theirs was the fourth gold medal at those 2008 Games by British sailors, and Percy was already an Olympic champion, having won the Finn class in 2000.

on the race course, with the slightest misjudgement costing boat lengths almost instantly, which is exactly why Finn sailors love them'.

A further yardstick of Ainslie's success was that he had become only the fifth Briton to win a gold medal at three successive Olympics. Interestingly, all of the others had also been achieved in or on water, by the water-polo players, Charlie Smith and George Wilkinson, and the rowers, Steve Redgrave and Matthew Pinsent.

Iain Percy, having been Ainslie's predecessor as Finn champion in 2000, joined forces with Andrew Simpson to win the double-handed Star class this time, and who should be one half of the second-placed crew but Ainslie's ex-rival from Brazil, Robert Scheidt. Percy and Simpson had had plenty of time to get to know each other's sailing skills, having first met up when they were six-year-olds at the picturesque Datchet Water inland reservoir near Slough, with its panoramic views towards Windsor Castle, but they did not form a team until after the 2004 Games, in which Percy and his previous partner, Steve Mitchell, had placed sixth.

Emerging from Ainslie's shadow, having been his training partner at the 2000 Games, was Paul Goodison, who won the Laser class of single-handed dinghy. (PLATE 33) He had placed fourth in 2004, and that frustrating finishing position, so close and yet so far from a medal, had given him no true satisfaction, as he later was to admit, 'I just remember thinking that I never wanted to feel like that again'. This time he won from Vasilij Žbogar, of Slovenia, who had been the bronze-medallist in 2004. Goodison was born in the village of Brinsworth, near Rotherham in Yorkshire, while the winner of the inaugural women's Laser Radial (slightly smaller than the Radial) class was Anna Tunnicliffe, whose birthplace five years later in 1982 was half an hour away along the A630 in Doncaster. Both had learned to sail locally as children, but allegiances were by now strictly divided because the latter had emigrated with her family to the USA in 1994 at the age of 12.

Sailing events specifically for women had been brought into the Games in 1988, though Mrs Frances Rivett-Carnac had been the first British woman gold-medallist 80 years before as a crew-member on her husband's 7-metre class yacht, 'Heroine'. The first modern British success had been by Shirley Robertson in 2000, and she had won a second gold four years later. Now it was the turn of her crew-mates then, Sarah Ayton and Sarah Webb, to share gold with Pippa Wilson in the Yngling class. Ayton and Webb had both been born in Ashford, in Surrey, and after the 2004 Games had split from Robertson, eventually recruiting Wilson, from Southampton. The Ayton-Webb-Wilson combination had then beaten Robertson and her crew to gain Olympic selection in somewhat fractious circumstances.

The contest for Yngling gold in Beijing was intense, and Britain by sheer persistence led Holland by only one point, 22 to 23, with three races left, though the Dutch had won three times and Britain not at all. Then, agonisingly, the next two races were cancelled because of hopelessly difficult weather conditions, but in the deciding 'medal race', in which only the ten leading crews took part and points counted double, Britain won, Holland was fourth: Britain took the gold, 24 points to 31. After the 2008 Olympics, Sarah Ayton married Nick Dempsey, who had been wind-surfing bronze-medallist in 2004 and fourth in 2008.

Olympic boxing had been the cause of regular controversies over the years, and had even been excluded from the 1912 Games in Sweden because the sport was banned in that country. Yet it survives on the schedule, and rightly so; its appeal particularly to Third World countries remaining undiminished. Accordingly, Britain's gold medal in the middleweight division (69 to 75 kilogrammes) was won against as cosmopolitan an opposition as anyone could wish for. There were 28 fighters involved: nine from Europe (Armenia, France, Germany, Great Britain, Greece, Ireland, Sweden, Russia, Ukraine), six each from Asia (China, India, Kazakhstan, South Korea, Thailand, Uzbekistan), the Americas (Argentina, Cuba, Dominica, Ecuador, USA, Venezuela), and Africa (Algeria, Congo, Egypt, Gambia, Ghana, Morocco), plus Australia.

Beijing gold-medallist James DeGale had started boxing at the age of ten at a club near his north-west London home in Harlesden, and his only previous championship medal was a Commonwealth bronze in 2006, but he beat the Egyptian and US representatives in the first two rounds with decisive points scores of 13–4 and 11–5 respectively. He then defeated the 2004 Olympic welterweight champion, Bakhtiyar Artayev, of Kazakhstan, 8–3 in the quarter-finals. His semi-final opponent was an Irishman, Darren Sutherland, who had won four of their five previous encounters, but DeGale got the decision convincingly, 10–3. The final, by contrast, was a disappointingly disjointed affair which DeGale won 16–14 against Emilio Correa, of Cuba, whose two-point deficit was due to his having unwisely bitten DeGale on the shoulder in the first round. The British champion turned professional the following December for a contract reported to be worth £1.5 million and by 2011 was repaying the investment as European super-middleweight champion. (PLATE 34)

One of the most remarkable of British successes in Beijing came in the swimming pool, as Rebecca Adlington took gold in both the 400 and the 800 metres freestyle. (PLATE 35) The previous British freestyle swimming champion had been the prolific Henry Taylor a century earlier. In London 1908 Taylor had taken 5 minutes 36.8 seconds to complete his 400 metres event; Miss Adlington won hers in 4:03.22, a full minute and a half quicker. Taylor had also set the first recognised world record for 880 yards at 11 minutes 25.4 seconds; she won her Olympic 800 metres (874.8 yards) in 8:14.10, breaking a world record that had lasted for 19 years, having been set when she was six months old. Taylor could only afford to train in the local baths on 'dirty water' days, when admission was cheaper, whereas Adlington had the luxury of being able to swim some 55 kilometres a week in her home-town pool at Mansfield, in Nottinghamshire.

Adlington won the 400 metres freestyle by the tiniest of margins, 0.07 seconds ahead of Katie Hoff, of the USA, but the 800 metres final five days later was much clearer-cut, with more than six seconds to spare over Alessia Filippi, of Italy. Whatever the manner of them, such Olympic successes have not apparently transformed Becky Adlington's life. Interviewed by *The Guardian* newspaper a couple of years later, she said, 'Everyone seems to think I'm some millionaire now who is completely different. But I'm in exactly the same swimming squad, have exactly the same friends, and have the same daily routine. The only thing that's changed is that a few people ask me for an autograph these days.' One other tangible alteration to her lifestyle is that every time she goes to her local Sherwood Baths she's confronted by an emblazoned sign across the fascia of the building pronouncing that it is now the 'Rebecca Adlington Swimming Centre'. Mansfield Council spent £5 million on refurbishment in her honour.

The revival of British swimming in Beijing amounted to six medals won – five of them by women – against a target of three and had been helped no end by UK Sport's funding of £20,659,001. Ironic then that in 2010 the British government should withdraw £25 million promised for repairs to 44 ageing swimming pools. Britain's best known swimmer, rallying to the support of opposition organised by the sport's national authorities and its chief sponsors, British Gas, expressed her concern: 'Swimming is not only fun but a great way for the family to exercise. More and more pools around the country seem to be closing down and we have to fight it before it's too late.' Greater irony still that one of those many doomed pools was in the Lancashire mill town of Chadderton, where Henry Taylor had once been a member of the local swimming club.

The most recent of Britain's Olympic gold-medallists is Amy Williams, who in Canada in 2010 became the first British woman to win individual gold at the Winter Games since

Jeannette Altwegg in 1952, and like some of those Great Britain champions in Beijing two years before she set a precedent in the process. She was the first British winner in the skeleton event, a form of tobogganing for which the nearest available racing facility for Britons is in France. Williams had discovered the sport at the age of 19 while studying at the University of Bath, where there is a concrete practice track, and promptly decided to abandon what had been a promising athletics career as a 200 metres and 400 metres runner to hurl herself head first down mountain-sides on what might be described as a glorified tin tray with no steering or braking devices. 'Exhilarating and terrifying' was how she understandably described her initial reaction.

The name 'skeleton' derives from the shape of an early design of the small steel sled which is used, and like so many sports the origins are British. In 1884 Major William H. Bulpett had built the first 'Cresta Run' track at St Moritz, in Switzerland, financed by an astute local hotelier with an eye to drumming up winter trade in a town then known to its numerous British visitors only as a summer mineral-springs spa resort. St Moritz having successfully exploited its new role, the event was included when the Winter Olympic Games were held there in 1928 and 1948. British men won the bronze medal on both occasions, and the first of these was the 11th Earl of Northesk, David Ludovic George Hopetoun Carnegie, one of whose ancestors had been third-in-command at the Battle of Trafalgar. Twenty years later John Crammond emulated the Earl at the age of 41, and after a successful career as a stockbroker he was to spend 25 years in retirement enviably sailing his yacht around the Mediterranean.

Even so, Amy Williams would perhaps have found more of a kindred spirit in the person of the 'Lady Tobogganer' who contributed an anonymous chapter to a book entitled *Tobogganing on Crooked Runs* written in St Moritz in 1894 by the Honourable Harry Gibson, though her method of progression was rather more seemly, as befitted the Victorian age. 'For tobogganing as a sport for ladies there need be no apology for it adopts itself to them,' the intrepid authoress wrote. 'We may admit at once that the view of them speeding feet foremost down an ice run is neither an extremely graceful or an elevating sight. Yet it is at least a perfectly decent and an exhilarating exercise.'

Despite this glorious example, it took more than another century for the skeleton event to be introduced for women at the Winter Games. When it was at last recognised, in 2002, there were immediate British rewards for Alexandra Coomber, third that year, and Shelley Rudman, second in 2006, both of whom had also trained in Bath. The track for the 2010 competition at Whistler, near Vancouver, was 1,450 metres in length, with 14 curves and an average gradient of 10.5 per cent, and Amy Williams set a record of 53.68 seconds, reaching a top speed of around 145 kilometres per hour. Had she persevered with her 400 metres running as a member of Wessex & Bath Athletic Club, that same time of 53.68 seconds would have ranked her a respectable 13th in Britain that year and about 300th in the world. (At an average speed about 5½ times faster, though, perhaps the skeleton had the edge for excitement and exhilaration?) (PLATE 36)

We have already seen how UK Sport funding was instrumental in promoting Olympic success. In the case of the skeleton, it had amounted to £2.1 million since 2006. Following the success at Beijing more money is being spent than ever. The fund-providers at UK Sport have put up £264,036,053 in total from 2009 onwards. Rowing is receiving £27,240,700, cycling £26,390,000, swimming £25,096,600, athletics £25,073,000, and sailing £22,926,600.

By the beginning of the twenty-first century, the amount of money involved in the Olympic Games had increased dramatically since the early years. Recall, for instance, the 30 guineas (£31.50) that George Stuart Robertson had spent – out of his own pocket – to travel with the Thomas Cook party to Athens in 1896 and win his Olympic laurels. A comprehensive Cambridge University mathematical study leading up to the London Games of 2012 suggests that on past evidence Britain's competitors, aided by 'playing at home', could possibly win as many as 30 gold medals. If that proves to be so, the cost will work out at about £8.8 million each from UK Sport's coffers. Money might be regarded as the root of all evil, in sport as in so many other aspects of modern life, but there is no point in harking back nostalgically to some supposed heyday of amateurism, which in any case had largely been an indulgence reserved only for those who could afford it. These days the Olympic Games are an unashamedly professional enterprise and therefore completely unrecognisable – and probably repugnant – to Baron de Coubertin and his fellow idealists of the 1890s.

In other respects, though, the Baron would certainly be consoled by the knowledge that the Olympic movement he espoused so fervently has survived, expanded and prospered. At times such an outcome was not at all certain, particularly when threatening issues surrounded the shaky ventures of the formative years, or when a terrorist outrage might have undermined the whole movement. In Berlin in 1936, and during several boycotts of later Games, it also seemed quite possible that international politics might compromise or destroy the whole notion that the Olympics would be the supreme sporting forum for every nation. De Coubertin's vision did not wither on the vine.

Not only that, the Baron would assuredly take delight in the fact that in virtually every sport on the programme an Olympic gold is, to this day, prized more highly by the competitors, the media and the public than any other award, world titles included. The IAAF, ruling body of the focal Olympic sport, athletics, enviously introduced its world championships in 1983 as a rival to the Olympics, and from 1991 onwards these have been held every two years, but the effect has been, if anything, merely to devalue the worth of a world title. The Olympics, too, take place every two years, but only because the Games hierarchy astutely switched their winter version to intervening dates. Perhaps the IOC will one day even give thought to incorporating the indoor sports – basketball, boxing, gymnastics, judo and the rest – into the winter programme and thus reduce the burden of cost of the Summer Games, affordable now by so few cities.

Having attended the Games for the first time as a youthful fan, and then in later years as a privileged member of the press corps, broadcasting for BBC Radio, I remain totally committed to the Olympic principles and to the idea of the pre-eminence of the Games as a sporting spectacle. In concluding a book specifically about *British* achievements at the Olympic Games I happily admit to being at heart an 'internationalist' rather than a 'nationalist'. I cite the fact that as much an abiding memory of my first Games, in 1960, as Don Thompson winning the walk for Britain, is that of a previously unknown Ethiopian, Abebe Bikila, winning the marathon. One Olympic opening ceremony or closing ceremony is much like another after you have attended a profusion of them, but the spirit is still irresistibly stirred as the joyous teams enter the thronged arena, the trumpets resound, and the flags wave bravely. In the end, for all their materialism, the Olympics remain the supreme contest of athlete against athlete, in which their physical and mental attributes are put to the severest test.

In Beijing 2008, there was a grand total of 11,028 competitors, each hoping to climb the top step of the podium in his or her chosen sport or discipline. For the 10,395 who did not come away with a gold medal, it was truly, as Baron de Coubertin would affirm, a case of not so much the winning as the taking part, not the triumph but the struggle.

Great Britain's Olympic gold medals and gold-medallists, 1896–2010

T HIS is the most complete listing of Great Britain's Olympic gold-medallists yet compiled. In total Great Britain has won 234 Olympic titles, and there have been around 482 different recognised gold-medallists, allowing for team events and team sports and for multiple winners. Yet this figure of 482 cannot be regarded as precise because only the owner of a winning British yacht at the 1900 Games has so far been identified and none of the names of his crew-members (of whom there may have been as many as 25) is known. But then one of the delights of Olympic research is that not all questions can be answered, and history might be the duller if they could be.

The total number of both gold medals and gold-medallists is given below for each Games, Summer and Winter, because for medals table purposes each event in all sports, whether contested by individuals or teams, is designated as having been awarded a single gold medal. In team sports (cricket, curling, football, hockey, ice-hockey, polo, water-polo) there is obviously more than one gold-medallist per event, as is also the case in relay races (athletics, swimming) and those events in other sports which involve more than one competitor (bobsleigh, equestrianism, lawn tennis, modern pentathlon, motor-boating, racquets, rowing, shooting, skating, yachting). In addition to all individual, team and relay gold-medallists, reserve members in team and relay events are noted where known, whether or not they competed in qualifying rounds, and whether or not they received gold medals.

Abbreviations and explanatory note: b date of birth, d date of death. Commonly used first names are underlined where they are not the first name listed. Familiar first names or nicknames, where known, are given in brackets after the full Christian names. Where no full details of place or date of birth are known, any relevant information to indicate origins, such as club membership, is referred to. Regarding places of birth, some civic and county boundaries have altered over the years.

1896 (Athens, 6–15 April),
3 gold medals, 2 gold-medallists

Lawn tennis:

Boland, John Mary Pius (Jack). b 16.9.1870 Dublin; d 17.3.1958. Men's Singles, Men's Doubles with Fritz Traun (Germany). *Note*: Friedrich Adolf ('Fritz') Traun. b 29.3.1876, Wandsbek, Hamburg, Germany; d 11.7.1908.

Weight-lifting:

Elliot, Launceston. b 9.6.1874 Bombay (now Mumbai), India; d 8.8.1930. One-handed lift.

1900 (Paris, 20 May–28 October),
25 gold medals, 59 gold-medallists

Athletics:

Bredin, Edgar Chichester. b .3.1866 Gibraltar; d 1939. 400 metres, 800 metres, 1500 metres, Professional.

Tysoe, Alfred Edward. b 21.3.1874 Skerton, Lancs; d 26.10.1901. 800 metres, 5000 metres team.

Bennett, Charles. b 28.12.1870 Shapwick, Dorset; d 18.12.1948. 1500 metres, 5000 metres team.

Rimmer, John Thomas. b 27.4.1878 Ormskirk, Lancs; d 5.6.1962. 4000 metres steeplechase, 5000 metres team.

Robinson, Sidney John. b 1.8.1876 Denton, Northants; d 3.2.1959. 5000 metres team.

Rowley, Stanley Rupert. b 11.9.1876 Young, NSW, Australia; d 1.4.1924. 5000 metres team (non-scoring). *Note*: Australian nationality.

Cricket:

Beachcroft, Charles B.K. b 1871 Rickmansworth, Herts. *Note*: all of the players were members of the Devon and Somerset Wanderers club.

Birkett, Arthur Ernest Barrington. b 25.10.1875 St David, Exeter, Devon; d 1.4.1941.

Bowerman, Alfred James. b 22.11.1873 Broomfield, Bridgwater, Somerset; d 1959.

Buckley, George John. b 1876; d 14.2.1955 (*see Note* above).

Burchell, Francis Romulus. b 25.9.1873 Bristol, Gloucs; d 6.7.1947.

Christian, Frederick William James (Fred). b 1877; d 13.5.1941 (*see Note* above).

Corner, Harry Richard. b 9.7.1874 Taunton, Somerset; d 7.6.1938.

Cuming, Frederick William (Fred). b 27.5.1875 Tiverton, Devon; d 22.3.1942.

Donne, William Stephens. b 2.4.1876 Wincanton, Somerset; d 24.3.1934.

Powlesland, Alfred James. b 1875 Newton Abbot, Devon; d 25.3.1941.

Symes, John OBE. b 11.1.1879 Crediton, Devon; d 21.9.1942.

Toller, Montague Henry. b .2.1871 Barnstaple, Devon; d 5.8.1948.

Note: the matches were played 12-a-side.

Cycling:

Chase, Arthur Adalbert. b 6.6.1873 Blackheath, Kent. 100 kilometres road, Professional.

Football:

Barridge, T.E. (or Burridge, or J.E.). No details known. *Note*: all of the players were members of Upton Park FC, Essex.

Buckenham, Claude Percy. b 16.1.1876 Wandsworth, London; d 23.2.1937.

Chalk, Alfred Ernest. b 27.11.1874 West Ham, Essex; d 1954.

Gosling, William Sullivan. b 19.7.1869 Hassiobury, Bishop's Stortford, Essex; d 2.10.1952.

Haslam, A. (or Haslom). No details known (*see Note* above).

Jones, John H. No details known (*see Note* above).

Nicholas, J. No details known (*see Note* above).

Quash, William Francis Patterson (Bill). b 27.12.1868 Barking, Essex; d 17.5.1938.

Spackman, F.G. possibly d 4.6.1941 (*see Note* above).

Turner, Arthur R. No details known (*see Note* above).

Zealey, James Edward (Jim). b 7.3.1868 Mile End, Middlesex; d 1934.

Lawn tennis:

Doherty, Hugh Laurence (Laurie). b 8.10.1875 Wimbledon, Surrey; d 21.8.1919. Men's Singles, Men's Doubles.

Doherty, Reginald Frank (Reggie). b 14.10.1872 Wimbledon, Surrey; d 29.12.1910. Men's Doubles, Mixed Doubles.

Burke, Thomas Arthur (Tom). b Ireland; d 1921. Men's Singles, Professional; Men's Doubles, Professional.

Kerr, George. b Ireland; d .3.1954. Men's Doubles, Professional. *Note*: Kerr was reported as being aged 75 at the time of his death, but this is clearly wrong by some 15 years because he had already been appointed assistant professional at the Fitzwilliam club, in Dublin, in 1883.

Cooper, Charlotte Reinagle ('Chattie'). b 22.9.1870 Ealing, Middlesex; d 10.10.1966. Women's Singles, Mixed Doubles.

Polo:

Beresford, the Honourable John George. b 10.6.1847 Dover, Kent; d 8.5.1925.

Daly, Denis St George. b 5.9.1862 Athenry, County Galway, Ireland; d 16.4.1942.

Keene, Foxhall Parker. b 18.12.1867 Oakland, California, USA; d 25.9.1941. *Note*: US nationality.

MacKey, Frank Joseph. b 20.3.1852 Gilboa, New York, USA; d 24.2.1927. *Note*: US nationality.

Rawlinson, Alfred ('Toby'), later Sir Alfred Rawlinson Bt. CMG CBE DSO. b 17.1.1867 London; d 1.6.1934.

Note: all of the team were members of the Foxhunters Hurlingham club, in London, which entered the Olympic tournament *from* Great Britain rather than *for* Great Britain. Thus Keene and Mackey could well be considered as much gold-medallists for the USA. Three weeks after the Olympics they both played for the USA in a match against Great Britain!

Swimming:

Jarvis, John Arthur (Jack). b 24.2.1872 Leicester; d 9.5.1933. 1000 metres freestyle, 4000 metres freestyle.

Greasley, Stanley W. b 1871. 4000 metres freestyle, Professional.

Water-polo:

Coe, Thomas (Tom). b 1880. *Note*: all of the team were members of the Manchester Osborne club.

Derbyshire, John Henry ('Rob'). b 29.11.1878 Manchester, Lancs; d 30.7.1938.

Kemp, Peter. b 1878 (*see Note* above).

Lister, William Houghton (Bill). b 1882 (*see Note* above).

Robertson, Arthur G. b 1879 (*see Note* above).

Robinson, Eric. b 1878 (*see Note* above).

Wilkinson, George. b 3.3.1879 Gorton, Manchester, Lancs; d 7.8.1946.

The following played in one match but not in the final:

Crawshaw, Robert Arnold. b 6.3.1869 Bury, Lancs; d 4.9.1952.

Henry, William, later Sir William Henry. b 28.6.1859 St Pancras, London; d 20.3.1928. *Note*: his name at birth was Henry William Nawrocki.

Jarvis, John Arthur – *see* 1900 Games swimming.

Lindberg, Viktor (or Victor). *Note*: an Australian national swimming champion, he arrived in England only one month before the Games.

Stapleton, F. (or S.). b 1880.

Yachting:

Currie, Lorne Campbell. b 25.4.1871 le Havre, France; d 21.6.1926. Open Class, 0.5 Ton–1 Ton Class.

Gretton, John MP, later Lord Gretton of Stapleford PC CBE DL JP MP. b 1.9.1867 Newton Sotney, Derbyshire: d 2.6.1947. Open Class, 0.5 Ton–1 Ton Class.

Maudslay, Algernon CBE. b 10.1.1873 Tetbury, Gloucs; d 2.3.1948. Open Class, 0.5 Ton–1 Ton Class.

Exshaw, William Edgard. b 15.2.1866 Arcachon, France; d 16.3.1927. 2 Tons–3 Tons Class.

le Lavasseur, Jacques. b France. 2 Tons–3 Tons Class. *Note*: French nationality, member of the Société Nautique de Marseille.

Blanchy, Gaston Frédéric. b 1868 Bordeaux, France; d . .1944. 2 Tons–3 Tons Class. *Note*: French nationality.

Hore, Edward. b 17.11.1849 Knightsbridge, London. 3 Tons–10 Tons Class.

Jefferson, H.N. No details known. 3 Tons–10 Tons Class.

Taylor, John Howard. No details known. 3 Tons–10 Tons Class.

Quentin, Cecil. b 1852 Waterford, Co. Waterford, Ireland; d 29.10.1926. Over 20 Tons Class.

Note: there clearly must have been other crew-members in the Over 20 Tons Class which was sailed in the Channel off Le Havre as the winning yacht was a 96-ton yawl, measuring 114ft (34.74m) in length, but mention is made only of Cecil Quentin, who was the owner, in all reports of the Games. According to an expert in 2011, David Orton, secretary of the British Classic Yacht Club, Quentin's yawl would have required a crew of 20 to 25, depending on the rigging. A Belgian Olympic researcher, Herman de Wael, states that there were 14 un-named British crew-members at the yachting events in 1900. Whatever the figure, there remains a rather large number of unknown British gold-medallists! Quentin was a member of the Royal Portsmouth Corinthian Yacht Club, and his crew may have been drawn from there.

1904 (St Louis, 1 July–23 November), 1 gold medal, 1 gold-medallist

Athletics:

Kiely, Thomas Francis (Tom). b 25.8.1869 Ballyneale, County Tipperary, Ireland; d 6.11.1951. All-Around Competition.

1906 (Athens, 22 April–2 May), 8 gold medals, 9 gold-medallists

Athletics:

Hawtrey, Henry Courtney. b 29.6.1882 Southampton, Hants; d 16.11.1961. 5 Miles.

Leahy, Cornelius (Con). b 27.4.1876 Cregane, Charleville, County Cork, Ireland; d 1921. High jump.

O'Connor, Peter. b 18.10.1874 Ashtown, County Wicklow, Ireland; d 9.11.1957. Hop Step and Jump (now Triple Jump).

Cycling:

Pett, William James (Billy). b 25.8.1873 St Peter, Derbyshire; d 27.12.1954. 20 kilometres track.

Matthews, Thomas John (Johnnie). b 16.8.1884 Kensington, London; d 20.10.1969. Tandem, 20 kilometres track.

Rushen, Arthur. Probably b London. No details known. Tandem, 20 kilometres track. *Note*: he was a member of the Putney Cycling Club in London.

Note: In addition to winning the tandem event, Matthews and Rushen also acted as pacemakers for Pett in the 20 kilometres track race, for which they have never previously been credited as gold-medallists.

Shooting:

Merlin, Gerald Eustace. b 3.8.1884 Piraeus, Greece; d 1945. Clay Pigeon, Single Shot.

Merlin, Sidney Louis Walter. b 26.4.1856 Piraeus, Greece; d 1952. Clay Pigeon, Double Shot.

Note: Sidney Merlin was the uncle of Gerald Merlin.

Swimming:

Taylor, Henry. b 17.3.1885 Oldham, Lancs; d 28.2.1951. 1 mile freestyle.

1908 (London, 27 April–31 October), 56 gold medals, 137 gold-medallists

Archery:

Dod, William (Willie). b 18.7.1867 Lower Bebington, Cheshire; d 8.10.1954. York Round.

Archery, women:

Newall, Sybil Fenton ('Queenie'). b 17.10.1854 Calderbrook, Lancs; d 24.6.1929. York Round.

Athletics:

Halswelle, Wyndham. b 30.5.1882 Mayfair, London; d 31.3.1915. 400 metres.

Voigt, Emil Robert. b .12.1882 Manchester, Lancs; d 16.10.1973. 5 miles.

Coales, William (Bill). b 8.1.1886 Aldwinckle, Thrapston, Northants; d 19.1.1960. 3 miles, Team.

Deakin, Joseph Edmund (Joe). b 6.2.1879 Shelton, Stoke-on-Trent, Staffs; d 30.6.1972. 3 miles, Team.

Hallows, Norman Frederick. b 29.12.1886 Doncaster, Yorks; d 16.10.1968. 3 miles, Team (non-scoring).

Robertson, Arthur James. b 19.4.1879 Sheffield, Yorks; d 18.4.1957. 3 miles, Team.

Wilson, Harold Allan. b 22.1.1885 Horncastle, Lincs; d 1916. 3 miles, Team.

Russell, Arthur. b 13.3.1886 Walsall, Staffs; d 23.8.1972. 3200 metres steeplechase.

Ahearne, Timothy (Tim). b 18.8.1885 Athea, County Limerick, Ireland; d .11.1968. Hop Step and Jump (now Triple Jump).

Larner, George Edward. b 7.3.1875 Langley, Bucks; d 4.3.1949. 3500 metres walk, 10 miles walk.

Barrett, Edward Edmond. b 3.11.1880 Ballyduff, County Kerry, Ireland. Tug-of-War.

Goodfellow, Frederick William (Fred). b 7.3.1874 Walsall, Staffs; d 22.11.1960. Tug-of-War.

Hirons, William (Bill). b 5.6.1871 Wolston, Warwickshire; d 5.1.1958. Tug-of-War.

Humphreys, Frederick Harkness (Fred). b 28.1.1878 Marylebone, London; d 10.8.1954. Tug-of-War.

Ireton, Albert. b 15.5.1879 Baldock, Herts; d 4.1.1947. Tug-of-War.

Merriman, Frederick Goodfellow (Fred). b 18.5.1873 Chipping Campden, Gloucs; d 27.6.1940. Tug-of-War.

Mills, Edwin Archer. b 17.5.1878 Stretton Baskerville, Warwickshire; d 12.11.1946. Tug-of-War.

Shepherd, John James. b 2.6.1884 Bicknor, Gloucs; d 9.7.1954. Tug-of-War.

Boxing:

Thomas, Albert Henry (Harry). b 1.7.1888 Birmingham, Warwickshire; d 13.1.1963. Bantamweight.

Gunn, Richard Kenneth (Dick). b 16.2.1871 Charing Cross, London; d 23.6.1961. Featherweight.

Grace, Frederick (Fred). b 29.2.1884 Edmonton, Middlesex; d 23.7.1964. Lightweight.

Douglas, John William Henry Taylor (Johnny). b 3.9.1882 Clapton, Middlesex; d 19.12.1930. Middleweight.

Oldman, Albert Leonard. b 18.11.1883 Mile End, Middlesex; d 15.1.1961. Heavyweight.

Cycling:

Johnson, Victor Louis (Vic). b 10.5.1883 Aston, Birmingham, Warwickshire; d 29.6.1951. 660 yards.

Jones, Benjamin (Ben). b 1882 Wigan, Lancs. 5000 metres; 1980 yards Team Pursuit.

Kingsbury, Clarence Brickwood (Clarrie) b 3.11.1882 Portsea Island, Hants; d 4.3.1949. 20 kilometres, Track; 1980 yards Team Pursuit.

Meredith, Lewis Leon. b 2.2.1882 St Pancras, London; d 27.1.1930. 1980 yards Team Pursuit.

Payne, Ernest (Ernie). b 23.12.1884 Worcester; d 10.9.1961. 1980 yards Team Pursuit.

Bartlett, Charles Henry. b 6.2.1885 Southwark, London; d 30.11.1968. 100 kilometres, Track.

Figure-skating, women:

Syers, Florence Madeline ('Madge'). b 16.9.1881 Kensington, London; d 9.9.1917.

Football:

Bailey, Horace Peter. b 3.7.1881 Derby; d 1.8.1960.

Berry, Arthur. b 3.1.1888 Liverpool, Lancs; d 15.3.1953.

Chapman, Frederick William. b 10.5.1883 Nottingham; d 7.9.1951.

Corbett, Walter Samuel ('Watty'). b 26.11.1880 Wellington, Shropshire; d 23.11.1960.

Hardman, Harold Payne. b 4.4.1882 Kirkmanshulme, Lancs; d 9.6.1965.

Hawkes, Robert Murray (Bob). b 18.10.1880 Breachwood Green, Herts; d 12.9.1945.

Hunt, the Reverend Kenneth Reginald Gunnery. b 24.2.1884 Oxford; d 28.4.1949.

Purnell, Clyde Honeysett. b 14.5.1877 Ryde, Isle of Wight; d 14.8.1934.

Smith, Herbert. b 22.11.1879 Witney, Oxfordshire; d 6.1.1951.

Stapley, Henry (Harry). b 29.4.1883 Tunbridge Wells, Kent; d 29.4.1937.

Woodward, Vivian John. b 3.6.1879 Kennington, Surrey; d 31.1.1954.

Note: the following were also selected for the tournament but did not play in any of the three matches:

Barlow, George H. No details known. *Note*: Wigan Grammar School Old Boys.

Bell, Albert Eduard. No details known. *Note*: Woking FC.

Brebner, Ronald Gilchrist (Ron). b 23.9.1881 Darlington, County Durham; d 11.11.1914.

Crabtree, W. No details known. *Note*: Blackburn Crosshill FC.

Daffern, Walter. No details known. *Note*: Depot Battalion Royal Engineers AFC.

Porter, Thomas C. No details known. *Note*: Stockport County FC.

Scothern, Albert E. No details known. *Note*: Oxford City FC.

There were 32 players originally nominated, and the following were also listed in the official report as having been entered: J.J. Bayley, A.A. Bell (Burnley FC), J. Charnley, P. Hayden, W.C. Jordan (Oxford University), L.A. Louch (Portsmouth FC), E. Mansfield (Preston Winchley FC), C.H. Pierce, J.A. Prest, J. Prosser, E.B. Proud, J.E. Raine (Newcastle United FC), Harold J. Uren, Edward Gordon Dundas Wright (b 3.10.1884 Earlsfield Green, Surrey; d 5.6.1947).

Hockey:

Baillon, Louis Charles. b 5.8.1881 Fox Bay, Falkland Islands; d 2.9.1965.

Freeman, Harry Scott. b 7.2.1876 Staines, Middlesex; d 5.10.1968.

Green, Eric Hubert. b 28.8.1878 Epsom, Surrey; d 23.12.1972.

Logan, Gerald. b 29.12.1879 Copse Hill, Wimbledon, Surrey.

Noble, Alan Henry. b 1885 Loughborough, Leics; d 1952.

Page, Edgar Wells MC. b 31.12.1884 Wolverhampton, Staffordshire; d 12.5.1956.

Pridmore, Reginald George (Reggie). b 29.4.1886 Birmingham, Warwickshire; d 13.3.1918.

Rees, Percy Montague. b 27.9.1883 Camberwell, London; d 12.6.1970.

Robinson, John Yate. b 6.8.1885 Burton-on-Trent, Staffs; d 23.8.1916.

Shoveller, Stanley Howard MC. b 2.9.1881 Kingston Hill, Surrey; d 24.2.1959.

Wood, Harvey Jesse. b 10.4.1885 Beverley, Yorks; d pre-1945.

Note: there were 36 players nominated in total, but the only ones who played were the 11 named above. The following were also listed in the official report as having been entered – H.F. Baker (Midlands), E.T. Bell (Durham), A.D. Bond (Yorkshire), S.R. Brazier (Wiltshire), J.N. Burns (Staffordshire), S. Butterworth (Cheshire), R.M.B.I. Cromie (Dorset), A.I. Draper (Cheshire), Arthur Rolls Edgell (b Teddington, Middlesex), Reverend E.F. Edge-Partington MC (Cambridge University), H.J. Goodwin (Cambridge University), G. Hardy (Cheshire), C.P. Hare (Yorkshire), B. Hatch (Somerset), H.R. Jordan (b 1882 Anerley, Surrey), Arthur Francis Leighton MC (Cambridge University, b 1889), Charles William Marshall (Cheshire, b 1882; d 3.3.1928), F.B. Peel (Cheshire), Laurence Milner Robinson (b 6.8.1885 Burton-on-Trent, Staffs), A.L.F. Smith (Northumberland, b probably Oxford), T.S. Stafford (Warwickshire), Andrew Deays Stocks CB OBE (Warwickshire, b 2.12.1884 probably Leicester), J.L. Stocks (Kent), Francis William Twigg (Staffordshire), Walter Hanbury Twigg (b 6.5.1883 Stafford; d 5.2.1963).

Note: John Robinson and Laurence Robinson were twin brothers; A.D Stocks and J.L. Stocks were brothers; Francis and Walter Twigg were very probably brothers.

Lawn tennis:

Ritchie, Major Josiah George. b 18.10.1870 Westminster, Middlesex; d 28.2.1955. Men's Singles.
  Note: Major was a Christian name, not an army rank.
Gore, Arthur William Charles ('Wentworth'). b 2.1.1868 Lyndhurst, Hampshire; d 1.12.1928. Men's Singles, Indoors; Men's Doubles, Indoors.
Doherty, Reginald Frank (Reggie) – *see also* 1900 Games. Men's Doubles.
Hillyard, George Whiteside. b 6.2.1864 Hanwell, Middlesex; d 24.3.1943. Men's Doubles.
Barrett, Herbert Roper. b 24.11.873 Upton, Essex; d 27.7.1943. Men's Doubles, Indoors.

Lawn tennis, women:

Lambert Chambers, Dorothea Katharine ('Dolly'). b 3.9.1878 Ealing, Middlesex; d 7.1.1960. Women's Singles.
Eastlake-Smith, Gladys Shirley (Gwen). b 14.8.1883 Lewisham, London; d 18.9.1941. Women's Singles, Indoors.

Motor-boating:

Field-Richards, John Charles OBE. b 10.5.1878 Penzance, Cornwall; d 18.4.1959. 60 Foot Class, 6.5 Metre–8 Metre Class.
Redwood, Bernard Boverton. b 21.11.1874 Finchley, London; d 28.9.1911. 60 Foot Class, 6.5 Metre–8 Metre Class.
Thornycroft, Isaac Thomas (Tom). b 22.11.1881 Chiswick, Middlesex; d 6.6.1955. 60 Foot Class, 6.5 Metre–8 Metre Class.

Polo:

Miller, Charles Darley. b 23.10.1868 Marylebone, London; d 22.12.1951.
Miller, George Arthur. b 6.12.1867 Kensington, London; d 21.2.1935.
Nickalls, Patteson Wormersley DSO. b 23.1.1876 Widdington, Essex; d 10.9.1946.
Wilson, Herbert Haydon DSO. b 14.2.1875 London; d 11.4.1917.

Note: Charles and George Miller were brothers.

Racquets:

Noel, Evan Baillie. b 23.1.1879 Stanmore, Middlesex; d 22.12.1928. Singles.
Astor, John Jacob, later Lord Astor. b 20.5.1886 New York; d 19.7.1971. Doubles.
Pennell, Vane Hungerford. b 16.8.1876 Kensington, London; d 17.6.1938. Doubles.

Rowing:

Blackstaffe, Henry Thomas (Harry). b 28.7.1868 Islington, London; d 22.8.1951. Single Sculls.
Fenning, John Reginald Keith. b 23.6.1885 Fulham, London; d 3.1.1955. Coxless Pairs.

Thomson, Gordon Lindsay DSC DFC. b 27.3.1884 Wandsworth, London; d 8.7.1953. Coxless Pairs.

Cudmore, Robert Collier, later the Honourable Sir R.C. Cudmore. b 13.6.1885 Wentworth, NSW, Australia; d 16.5.1971.. Coxless Fours. *Note*: Australian nationality.

Gillan, James Angus, later Sir J.A. Gillan KBE CMG. b 11.10.1885, Aberdeen, Scotland; d 23.4.1981. Coxless Fours.

Mackinnon, Duncan. b 29.9.1887 Paddington, London; d 9.10.1917. Coxless Fours.

Somers-Smith, John Robert MC. b 15.12.1887 Walton-on-Thames, Surrey; d 1.7.1916. Coxless Fours.

Bucknall, Henry Cresswell. b 4.7.1885 Lisbon, Portugal; d 1.1.1962. Eights

Burnell, Charles Desborough DSO OBE. b 13.1.1876 Beckenham, Kent; d 3.10.1969. Eights.

Etherington-Smith, Raymond Broadley ('Ethel'). b 11.4.1877 Putney, London; d 19.4.1913. Eights.

Gladstone, Albert Charles, later Sir A.C. Gladstone Bt MBE. b 25.10.1886 Hawarden Castle, Flintshire, Wales; d 2.3.1967. Eights.

Johnstone, Banner Carruthers ('Bush') OBE. b 11.11.1882 Bebington, Cheshire; d 20.6.1964. Eights.

Kelly, Frederick Septimus DSC. b 29.5.1881, Sydney, NSW, Australia; d 13.11.1916. Eights.

Maclagen, Gilchrist Stanley. b 5.10.1879 Chelsea, London; d 25.4.1915. Eights.

Nickalls, Guy ('Gully'). b 13.11.1866 Sutton, Surrey; d 8.7.1935. Eights.

Sanderson, Ronald Harcourt. b 11.12.1876 Uckfield, Sussex; d 17.4.1918. Eights.

Note: despite the unusual surname, there is no evidence that Guy Nickalls is directly related to Patteson Nickalls, who won a gold medal for polo.

Shooting:

Carnell, Arthur Ashton. b 21.3.1862 Somers Town, London; d 11.9.1940. Small-Bore Rifle, Prone.

Millner, Joshua Kearney ('Jerry'). b 5.7.1847 Dublin, Ireland; d 16.11.1931. Free Rifle.

Fleming, John Francis. b 26.8.1881 Keswick, Cumberland; d 9.1.1965. Small Bore Rifle, Moving Target.

Styles, William Kensett. b 11.10.1874 Kensington, London; d 8.4.1940. Small Bore Rifle, Disappearing Target.

Amoore, Edward John ('Peepo'). b 20.3.1877; d 11.7.1955. Small Bore Rifle, Team.

Humby, Harry Robinson. b 8.4.1879 St Pancras, London; d 23.2.1923. Small Bore Rifle, Team.

Matthews, Maurice Kershaw. b 21.6.1889 St Pancras, London; d 20.6.1937. Small Bore Rifle, Team.

Pimm, William Edwin. b 10.12.1864 Bow, London; d 1952. Small Bore Rifle, Team.

Easte, Philip (or Peter). No details known. Clay Pigeon, Team.

Maunder, Alexander (Alex). b 3.2.1861 Loxbear, Devon; d 2.2.1932. Clay Pigeon, Team.

Moore, Frank W. No details known. Clay Pigeon, Team.

Palmer, Charles. b 18.8.1869 Old Warden, Bedfordshire. Clay Pigeon, Team.

Pike, James F. No details known. Clay Pigeon, Team.

Postans, John Musgrove. b 1869 Samford, Suffolk; d 1934. Clay Pigeon, Team.

Note: The Small-Bore Rifle Prone competition was actually won for Great Britain by Philip Edward V.G. Plater (b 6.6.1866 Kensington, London; d 1943) with a world-record score, but it was discovered a few days later that he had been the 13th British competitor to shoot and the rules limited each country's representation to 12. Plater was thus disqualified but was later presented with a special medal and record certificate by the British Olympic Council.

Swimming:

Taylor, Henry – *see also* 1906 Games. 400 metres freestyle, 1500 metres freestyle, 4 x 200 metres freestyle.

Holman, Frederick (Fred). b .3.1885 Dawlish, Devon; d 23.1.1913. 200 metres breaststroke.

Derbyshire, John Henry – *see also* 1900 Games Water-polo. 4 × 200 metres freestyle relay.

Foster, William (Willie). b 10.7.1890 Bacup, Lancs; d 17.12.1963. 4 × 200 metres freestyle relay.

Radmilovic, Paolo Francesco (Paul, 'Raddy'). b 5.3.1886 Cardiff; d 29.9.1968. 4 × 200 metres freestyle relay.

Water-polo:

Cornet, George Thomson. b 15.7.1877 Inverness, Scotland; d 22.11.1952.

Forsyth, Charles Eric (Charlie). b 10.1.1885 Manchester, Lancs; d 24.2.1951.

Nevinson, George Wilfrid. b 3.10.1882 Wigan, Lancs; d 13.3.1963.

Radmilovic, Paolo Francesco – *see also* 1908 Games Swimming.

Smith, Charles Sydney (Charlie). b 26.1.1879 Pemberton, Lancs; d 6.4.1951.

Thould, Thomas Henry (Tommy). b 11.1.1866 Weston-super-Mare, Somerset; d 15.6.1971.

Wilkinson, George – *see also* 1900 Games.

Wrestling:

de Relwyskow, George Frederick William. b 18.6.1887 Kensington, London; d 9.11.1942. Freestyle, Lightweight.

Bacon, Stanley Vivian. b 13.8.1885 Camberwell, London; d 13.10.1952. Freestyle, Middleweight.

O'Kelly, George Cornelius (Con). b 29.10.1886 Gloun, County Cork, Ireland; d 3.11.1947. Freestyle, Heavyweight.

Yachting:

Crichton, Charles William Harry. DSO. b 7.7.1872 Colchester, Essex; d 8.11.1958. 6 Metre Class.

Laws, Gilbert Umfreville. b 6.1.1870 Tynemouth, Northumberland; d 3.12.1918; 6 Metre Class.

McMeekin, Thomas Doodputlee (Tom). b 1866 Cachar, Assam, India; d 1952. 6 Metre Class.

Bingley, Frederick Sparkes Norman. b 17.9.1863 Hanover Square, London; d 16.1.1940. 7 Metre Class.

Dixon, Richard Travers. b 20.11.1865 Sydney, NSW, Australia; d 14.11.1949. 7 Metre Class.

Rivett-Carnac, Charles James. b 18.2.1853 Brahmapur, India; d 9.9.1935. 7 Metre Class.

Rivett-Carnac, Frances Clytie. b 1875; d 1.1.1962. 7 Metre Class.

Campbell, Charles Ralph, later Sir C.R. Campbell Bt. b 14.12.1881 Newton Abbot, Devon; d 19.4.1948. 8 Metre Class.

Cochrane, Blair Onslow OBE. b 11.9.1853 Darlington, County Durham; d 7.12.1928. 8 Metre Class.

Rhodes, John Edward. b 13.2.1870 Twyford, Berks; d 6.2.1947. 8 Metre Class.

Sutton, Henry Cecil. b 26.9.1868 Skeffington Hall, Leics; d 24.5.1936. 8 Metre Class.

Wood, Arthur Nicholas Lindsay, later Sir A.N.L. Wood Bt. b 29.3.1875 Chester-le-Street, County Durham; d 1.6.1939. 8 Metre Class.

Aspin, Robert Bain. b 21.3.1872 Glasgow; d 19.2.1960. 12 Metre Class.

Buchanan, John. b 1.1.1884 Rhu, Scotland; d 17.11.1943. 12 Metre Class.

Bunten, James Clark. b 28.3.1875 Glasgow; d 3.6.1935. 12 Metre Class.

Downes, Arthur Drummond. b 23.2.1883 Kelvinside, Scotland; d 12.9.1956. 12 Metre Class.

Downes, John Henry. b 18.10.1870 Glasgow; d 1.1.1943. 12 Metre Class.

Dunlop, David. probably b Scotland. 12 Metre Class. *Note*: like the other members of the crew he was a member of the Royal Clyde Yacht Club.

Glen-Coats, Thomas Coats Glen (Tom), later Sir T.C.G. Glen-Coats Bt. b 5.5. 1878 Paisley, Scotland; d 7.3.1954. 12 Metre Class.

Mackenzie, John. b 21.9.1886 Greenock, Scotland; d 9.12.1949. 12 Metre Class.

Martin, Albert. Probably b Scotland. 12 Metre Class (*see Note* above).

Tait, Thomas Gerald. b 7.11.1866 Campbeltown, Scotland; d 19.12.1938. 12 Metre Class.

Note: Charles and Frances Rivett-Carnac were husband and wife; Arthur and Henry Downes were brothers. The owner of the 8 Metre Class winning yacht was the Duchess of Westminster (née Constance Edwina Cornwallis-West. b 1876; d 1971) and she was aboard during the Olympic regatta but most probably only as a spectator and therefore cannot be considered as a gold-medallist, though conversely one report in 1909 described her as the 'pilot'. The 12-metre Class yachting was held on the River Clyde; not at Cowes, where the other yachting events took place.

1912 (Stockholm, 5 May–22 July), 10 gold medals, 44 gold-medallists

Athletics:

Jackson, Arnold Strode Nugent, later Strode-Jackson DSO CBE. b 5.4.1891 Addlestone, Surrey; d 13.11.1972. 1500 metres.

Applegarth, William Reuben (Willie). b 11.5.1890 Guisborough, Yorks; d 5.2.1958. 4 × 100 metres relay.

D'Arcy, Victor Henry Augustus (Vic). b 30.6.1887 Rotherhithe, London; d 12.3.1961. 4 x 100 metres relay.

Jacobs, David Henry. b 30.4.1888 Cardiff; d 5.6.1976. 4 × 100 metres relay.

Macintosh, Henry Maitland. b 10.6.1892 Kelso, Scotland; d 26.7.1918. 4 × 100 metres relay.

Football:

Berry, Arthur – *see also* 1908 Games.

Brebner, Ronald Gilchrist – *see also* 1908 Games.

Burn, Thomas Christopher (Tom). b 29.11.1888 Spittal, Berwick-upon-Tweed, Northumberland.

Dines, Joseph (Joe). b 12.4.1886 King's Lynn, Norfolk; d 27.9.1918.

Hoare, Gordon Rahere. b 18.4.1884 Blackheath, Kent; d 27.10.1973.

Knight, Arthur Egerton. b 7.9.1887 Godalming, Surrey; d 10.3.1956.

Littlewort, Henry Charles. b 7.7.1882 Ipswich, Suffolk; d 21.11.1934.

McWhirter, Douglas S. b 13.8.1886 Erith, Kent; d 14.10.1966.

Sharpe, Ivan Gordon. b 15.6.1889 St Albans, Herts; d 9.2.1968.

Walden, Harold Adrian (Harry). b 10.10.1889 Manchester, Lancs; d 2.12.1955.

Woodward, Vivian John – *see also* 1908 Games.

Note: the following also played in the tournament but not in the final –

Hanney, Edward Terrance (Ted). b 19.1.1889 Reading, Berks; d 30.11.1964.

Stamper, Harold Jack. b 6.10.1889 Stockton-on-Tees, County Durham, d .1.1939.

Wright, Edward Gordon Dundas – *see also* 1908 Games.

Four other players were selected but did not play in any of the matches –

Bailey, Horace Peter – *see also* 1908 Games.

Bailey, W.G. No details known. *Note*: Reading FC.

Martin, W.W. No details known. *Note*: Ilford FC.

Sanders, S.C. No details known. *Note*: Nunhead FC.

Lawn tennis:

Dixon, Charles Perry. b 7.2.1873 Grantham, Lincs; d 29.4.1939. Mixed doubles, Indoors.

Hannam, Edith Margaret. b 28.11.1878 Bristol, Gloucs; d 16.1.1951. Women's singles, Indoors; Mixed doubles, Indoors.

Rowing:

Kinnear, William Duthie (Wally). b 3.12.1880 Laurencekirk, Scotland; d 5.3.1974. Single sculls.

Burgess, Edgar Richard. b 23.9.1891 Kensington, London; d 23.4.1952. Eights.

Fleming, Philip. b 15.8.1889 Newport-on-Tay, Scotland; d 13.10.1971. Eights.

Garton, Arthur Stanley. b 31.3.1889 Epsom, Surrey; d 20.10.1960. Eights.

Gillan, James Angus – *see also* 1908 Games. Eights.

Horsfall, Ewart Douglas MC DFC. b 24.5.1892 Liverpool, Lancs; d 1.2.1974. Eights.
Kirby, Alister Graham. b 14.4.1886 Brompton, London; d 29.3.1917. Eights.
Swann, Sidney Ernest. b 24.6.1890 Sulby, Isle of Man; d 19.9.1975. Eights.
Wells, Henry Bensley MBE. b 12.1.1891 Kensington, London; d 4.7.1967. Eights.
Wormald, Leslie Graham MC. b 19.8.1890 Maidenhead, Berks; d 10.7.1965. Eights.

Shooting:
Lessimore, Edward John. b 20.1.1881 Clifton, Gloucs; d 7.3.1960. Small Bore Rifle 50 metres, Team.
Murray, Robert Cook (Bob). b 18.2.1870 Edinburgh; d 28.4.1948. Small Bore Rifle 50 metres, Team.
Pepé, Giuseppe Pietro (Joseph). b 5.3.1881 Manchester, Lancs; d 1970. Small Bore Rifle 50 metres, Team.
Pimm, William Edwin – *see also* 1908 Games. Small Bore Rifle 50 metres, Team.

Swimming, women:
Fletcher, Jennie. b 19.3.1890 Leicester; d 17.1.1968. 4 × 100 metres freestyle relay.
Moore, Isabella Mary (Belle). b 23.10.1894 Tynemouth, Northumberland; d 7.3.1975. 4 x 100 metres freestyle relay.
Speirs, Annie Coupe. b 14.7.1889 Liverpool, Lancs; d 9.10.1926. 4 × 100 metres freestyle relay.
Steer, Irene. b 10.8.1889 Cardiff; d 18.4.1947. 4 × 100 metres freestyle relay.

Water-polo:
Bentham, Isaac. b 26.10.1886 Wigan, Lancs; d 5.5.1917.
Bugbee, Charles G (Charlie). b 29.8.1887 Stratford, London; d 18.10.59.
Cornet, George Thomson – *see also* 1908 Games.
Hill, Arthur Edwin. b 9.1.1888 Birmingham, Warwickshire.
Radmilovic, Paolo Francesco – *see also* 1908 Games Water-polo and Swimming.
Smith, Charles Sydney (Charlie) – *see also* 1908 Games.
Thould, Thomas Henry (Tommy) – *see also* 1908 Games.
Wilkinson, George – *see also* 1900 and 1908 Games.

1920 (Antwerp, 20 April–12 September), 14 gold medals, 51 gold-medallists

Athletics:
Hill, Albert George. b 24.3.1889 Tooting, London; d 8.1.1969. 800 metres, 1500 metres. *Note*: Hill later claimed to be aged 35, not 31 at the time of the Games.
Hodge, Percy. b 26.12.1890 St Sampson, Guernsey, Channel Islands; d 27.12.1967. 3000 metres Steeplechase.
Ainsworth-Davis, John Creyghton (Jack). b 23.4.1895 Aberystwyth, Cardiganshire, Wales; d 3.1.1976. 4 × 400 metres relay.
Butler, Guy Montagu. b 25.8.1899 Harrow, Middlesex; d 22.2.1981. 4 × 400 metres relay.
Griffiths, Cecil Richmond. b 20.1.1901 Worcester; d 29.7.1973. 4 × 400 metres relay.
Lindsay, Robert Alexander. b 18.4.1890 Wandsworth, London; d 21.10.1958. 4 × 400 metres relay.
Canning, George Walter. b 23.8.1889. Tug-of-War.
Holmes, Frederick William (Fred). b 9.8.1886 Cosford, Shropshire; d 9.9.1944. Tug-of-War.
Humphreys, Frederick Harkness (Fred) – *see also* 1908 Games. Tug-of-War.
Mills, Edwin Archer – *see also* 1908 Games. Tug-of-War.
Sewell, John. b 23.4.1882 Halfmorton, Scotland; d 18.7.1947. Tug-of-War.
Shepherd, John James – *see also* 1908 Games. Tug-of-War.
Stiff, Harry Joseph. b 23.10.1881 Sudbury, Suffolk; d 17.4.1939. Tug-of-War.
Thorne, Ernest Arthur (Ernie). b 7.6.1887 Wandsworth, London; d 18.11.1968. Tug-of-War.

Note: the rules then in force did not allow substitutions between the heats and final of the 4 × 400 metres relay, and the following were reserves and did not take part in the heats – Bullough, Dennis R. (Denny). b 29.11.1895 Allerton Bywater, Castleford, Yorks; d 3.4.1975. Worthington-Eyre, Hedges Eyre. b 8.9.1899 Kingstown (now Dun Laoghaire), Ireland; d 22.10.1979.

Boxing:
Mallin, Henry William (Harry). b 1.6.1892 Shoreditch, London; d 8.11.1969. Middleweight.
Rawson, Ronald Rawson MC. b 17.6.1882 Kensington, London; d 30.3.1952. Heavyweight.

Cycling:
Lance, Thomas Glasson (Tommy). b 14.6.1891 Paddington, London; d 29.2.1976. Tandem.
Ryan, Harry Edgar. b 21.11.183 St Pancras, London; d 14.4.1961. Tandem.

Hockey:
Atkin, Charles Sydney. b 26.2.1889 Sheffield, Yorks; d 9.5.1958.
Bennett, John Hadfield (Jack). b 11.8.1885 Chorlton, Lancs; d 27.5.1973.
Cassels, Harold Kennedy. b 4.11.1898 Paoling, China; d 23.1.1975.
Cooke, Harold Douglas R. b. c.1898 Birmingham, Warwickshire.
Crockford, Eric Bertram. b 13.10.1888 Wylde Green, Warwickshire; d 17.1.1958.
Crummack, Reginald William (Rex). b 16.2.1887 Salford, Lancs; d 25.10.1966.
Haslam, Harry Eustace OBE. b 7.2.1883 Aston, Worcs; d 7.2.1955.
Leighton, Arthur Francis MC. b 6.3.1889 Esk, Queensland, Australia; d 15.6.1939.
McBryan, John Crawford William (Jack). b 22.7.1892 Box, Wilts; d 14.7.1983.
McGrath, George F. No details known. *Note*: he lived in Wimbledon and played for the Wimbledon club and Surrey.
Marcon, Charles Sholto Wyndham. b 31.3.1890 Headington, Oxfordshire; d 17.11.1959.
Shoveller, Stanley Howard MC – *see also* 1908 Games.
Smith, William Faulder. b 14.11.1886 Carlisle, Cumberland; d 3.3.1937.
Wilkinson, Cyril Theodore Anstruther. b 4.10.1884 Durham; d 16.12.1870.

Note: the only known photograph of the team shows these 14 dressed in their playing kit, thus suggesting that all played in one or more of the three matches, though only 11, of course, did so in the final. A fifteenth player, Colin H. Campbell, is also listed as a member of the team but does not appear to have travelled to Antwerp.

Lawn tennis:
Turnbull, Oswald Graham Noel MC. b 23.12.1890 Highgate, London; d 17.12.1970. Men's Doubles.
Woosnam, Maxwell (Max). b 6.9.1892 Liverpool, Lancs; d 14.7.1965. Men's Doubles.

Lawn tennis, women:
McKane, Kathleen (Kitty). b 7.5.1896 Bayswater, London; d 19.6.1992. Women's Doubles.
McNair, Winifred Margaret. b 9.8.1877 Donnington, Berks; d 28.3.1954. Women's Doubles.

Polo:
Barrett, Frederick Whitfield ('Rattle'). b 20.6.1875 Cork City, County Cork, Ireland; d 7.11.1949.
Lockett, Vivian Noverre. b 18.7.1880 New Brighton, Cheshire; d 30.5.1962.
Melvill, Teignmouth Philip ('Tim'). b 13.2.1877 Cape Town, South Africa; d 12.12.1951.
Wodehouse, Lord John MC (Jack), later the Earl of Kimberly CBE MC. b 11.11.1883 Witton Park, Norfolk; d 16.4.1941.

Water-polo:
Bugbee, Charles – *see also* 1912 Games.
Dean, William Henry (Billy). b 6.2.1887 Manchester, Lancs; d 2.5.1949.

Jones, Christopher (Chris). b 23.6.1886 Pontypridd, Glamorgan, Wales; d 18.12.1937.
Peacock, William (Bill). b 6.12.1891 Poplar, London; d 14.12.1948.
Purcell, Noel Mary. b 14.11.1891 Dublin; d 31.1.1962.
Radmilovic, Paolo Francesco – *see also* 1908 and 1912 Games.
Smith, Charles Sydney – *see also* 1908 and 1912 Games.

Yachting:
Coleman, Robert Henry Schofield. b 1888 Ballarat, Victoria, Australia; d 1.1.1960. 7 Metre
    Class.
Maddison, William J. No details known. 7 Metre Class. *Note*: a member of the Royal Burnham
    Yacht Club, Essex, as were the other three crew-members.
Wright, Cyril Macey. b 17.9.1885 Hampstead, London; d 27.6.1960. 7 Metre Class.
Wright, Dorothy Winifred. b 19.8.1889 Leytonstone, Essex. 7 Metre Class.

Note: Cyril and Dorothy Wright were husband and wife; also listed as British gold-medallists
in some sources, including the archives of the International Olympic Committee, are Thomas
Hedberg and Francis Augustus Richards, 18ft Dinghy Class, but they were the only entrants
and did not complete the course in the one race that was held!

Winter Games, 1924 (Chamonix/Mont Blanc, 25 January–4 February), 1 gold medal, 4 gold-medallists

Curling:
Jackson, Lawrence. b 16.1.1900 Carnwath, South Lanarkshire, Scotland ; d 27.7.1984.
Jackson, William Kilgour (Willie). b .3.1871 Lamington, South Lanarkshire, Scotland;
    d 26.1.1955.
Murray, Thomas B. (Tom). b 3.10.1877 Biggar, South Lanarkshire, Scotland; d 3.6.1944.
Welsh, Robin. b 20.10.1869 Edinburgh; d 21.10.1934.

Note: These are the four who are believed to have played in the final, but there remains a great
deal of confusion concerning the composition of the team. Willie and Lawrence Jackson were
father and son, and the four players listed above are named in the caption to a photograph
of what is said to be the winning team. They are also recorded as the finalists by the British
Olympic Association and the International Society of Olympic Historians, while the following
have been noted as 'alternates':

    Astley, Major D.G. possibly b Ireland.
    Brown, William. b Scotland.
    Cousin, R. b Scotland.
    McLeod, John. b Scotland.
    Robertson-Aikman, Colonel John Thomas S. b Scotland.

However, the official report of the Games – which on balance does not seem to be entirely
reliable – has Astley, Brown, McLeod, Murray, Robertson-Aikman and Welsh listed as
competitors, and Cousin and William Jackson as non-competitors. The name of Lawrence
Jackson does not appear in the official report, either in the text or in the separate list of
competitors in all sports.

1924 (Paris, 4 May–27 July), 9 gold medals, 15 gold-medallists

Athletics:
Abrahams, Harold Maurice CBE. b 15.12.1899 Bedford; d 14.1.1978. 100 metres.
Liddell, Eric Henry. b 16.1.1902 Tsientsin (now Tianjin), China; d 21.2.1945. 400 metres.
Lowe, Douglas Gordon Arthur. b 7.8.1902 Manchester, Lancs; d 30.3.1981. 800 metres.

Boxing:
Mallin, Henry William (Harry) – *see also* 1920 Games. Middleweight.
Mitchell, Harold James (Harry). b 5.1.1898 Tiverton, Devon; d 8.2.1983. Light-heavyweight.

Rowing:
Beresford, Jack CBE. b 1.1.1899 Chiswick, Middlesex; d 3.12.1977. Single Sculls. *Note*: his
surname at birth was Wiszniewski.
Eley, Charles Ryves Maxwell. b 16.9.1902 Samford, Suffolk; d 15.1.1983. Coxless Fours.
Macnabb, James Alexander OBE. b 26.12.1901 Keighley, Yorks; d 6.4.1990. Coxless Fours.
Morrison, Robert Erskine. b 26.3.1902 Richmond, Surrey; d 19.2.1980. Coxless Fours.
Sanders, Terence Robert Beaumont CB. b 2.6.1901 Charleville, County Cork, Ireland;
d 6.4.1985. Coxless Fours.

Shooting:
Mackworth-Praed, Cyril Winthrop OBE. b 21.9.1891 Mickleham, Surrey; d 30.6.1974. Running
Deer Double Shot, Team.
Neame, Philip VC DSO, later Lieutenant-General Sir P. Neame VC KBE DSO, DL.
b 12.12.1888 Faversham, Kent; d 28.4.1978. Running Deer Double Shot, Team.
Perry, Herbert Spencer. b 23.1.1894 Bridport, Dorset; d 20.7.1966. Running Deer Double Shot,
Team.
Whitty, Allen DSO. b 5.5.1867 Martley Hillside, Worcs; d 22.7.1949. Running Deer Double
Shot, Team.

Swimming, women:
Morton, Lucy. b 23.2.1898 Blackpool, Lancs; d 26.8.1980. 200 metres breaststroke.

1928 (Amsterdam, 17 May–12 August),
3 gold medals, 6 gold-medallists

Athletics:
Lowe, Douglas Gordon Arthur – *see also* 1924 Games. 800 metres.
Burghley, Lord David George Brownlow Cecil, later the Marquess of Exeter KCMG. b 9.2.1905
Stamford, Lincs; d 22.10.1981. 400 metres hurdles.

Rowing:
Beesly, Richard. b 27.7.1907 Barnt Green, Worcs; d 28.3.1965. Coxless Fours.
Bevan, Edward Vaughan. b 3.11.1907 Chesterton, Cambridgeshire; d 23.2.1988. Coxless Fours.
Lander, John Gerard Heath. b 7.9.1907 Liverpool, Lancs; d .12.1941. Coxless Fours.
Warriner, Michael Henry MBE. b 3.12.1908 Chipping Norton, Oxfordshire; d 7.4.1986. Coxless
Fours.

Note: J.A.F. Beale, who like the four gold-medallists was an undergraduate at Trinity College,
Cambridge, is listed in the official report of the Games as reserve for the Coxless Fours.

1932 (Los Angeles, 30 July–14 August),
4 gold medals, 7 gold-medallists

Athletics:
Hampson, Thomas (Tommy). b 28.10.1907 Clapham, London; d 4.9.1965. 800 metres.
Green, Thomas William (Tommy). b 30.3.1894 Fareham, Hants; d 29.3.1975. 50 kilometres
walk.

Rowing:
Clive, Lewis. b 8.9.1910 Tooting, London; d 2.8.1938. Coxless Pairs.
Edwards, Hugh Robert Arthur ('Jumbo') AFC DFC. b 17.11.1906 Woodstock, Oxfordshire;
d 21.12.1972. Coxless Pairs, Coxless Fours.

Badcock, John Charles ('Felix'). b 17.1.1903 West Ham, Essex; d 29.5.1976. Coxless Fours.

Beresford, Jack – *see also* 1924 Games. Coxless Fours.

George, Roland David DSO OBE. b 15.1.1905 Bath, Somerset; d 9.9.1997. Coxless Fours.

Winter Games, 1936 (Garmisch-Partenkirchen, 6–16 February), 1 gold medal, 12 gold-medallists

Ice-hockey:

Archer, Alexander (Sandy). b 1.5.1911 West Ham, Essex; d 29.7.1997.

Borland, James Andrew (Jimmy). b 25.3.1911 Manchester, Lancs.

Brenchley, Edgar ('Chip'). b 10.2.1912 Sittingbourne, Kent; d 13.3.1975.

Chappell, James (Jimmy). b 25.3.1914 Huddersfield, Yorks; d 3.4.1973.

Coward, John (Johnny 'Red'). b 28.8.1907 Ambleside, Cumberland; d 8.2.1989.

Dailley, Gordon Debenham (Don). b 24.7.1911 Winnipeg, Manitoba, Canada; d 3.5.1989.

Davey, John Gerald (Gerry). b 5.9.1914 Port Arthur, Ontario, Canada; d 12.2.1977.

Erhardt, Carl Alfred. b 15.2.1897 Beckenham, Kent; d 3.5.1988.

Foster, James (Jimmy). b 13.9.1905 Glasgow; d 4.1.1969.

Kilpatrick, John (Jack). b 7.7.1917 Bootle, Lancs; d 18.12.1989.

Stinchcombe, Archibald (Archie). b 17.11.1912 Cudworth, Yorks; d 3.11.1994.

Wyman, James Robert (Bob). b 24.4.1909 West Ham, Essex; d 1978.

Note: also selected but did not play in the tournament:

Child, Arthur John (Art). b 15.9.1916; d c.1996.

1936 (Berlin, 1–16 August), 4 gold medals, 12 gold-medallists

Athletics:

Brown, Arthur Godfrey Kilner. b 21.2.1915 Bankura, India; d 4.2.1995. 4 × 400 metres relay.

Rampling, Godfrey Lionel. b 14.5.1909 Greenwich, London; d 20.6.2009. 4 × 400 metres relay.

Roberts, William (Bill). b 5.4.1912 Salford, Lancs; d 5.12.2001. 4 × 400 metres relay.

Wolff, Frederick Ferdinand (Freddie). b 13.10.1910 Hong Kong; d 26.1.1988. 4 x 400 metres relay.

Whitlock, Hector Harold MBE. b 16.12.1903 Hendon, Middlesex; d 27.12.1985. 50 kilometres walk.

Note: the following were reserves for the 4 × 400 metres relay, for which the rules then in force did not allow substitutions between the heats and final –

Handley, Francis Richard (Frank). b 31.10.1910 Salford, Lancs; d 31.10.1985.

MacCabe, Brian Farmer. b 9.1.1914 Willesden, Middlesex; d 31.10.1992.

Pennington, Alan. b 4.4.1916 Wallasey, Cheshire; d 2.6.1961.

Powell, John Vincent (Jack). b 2.11.1910 Hendon, Middlesex; d 17.7.1982.

Rowing:

Beresford, Jack – *see also* 1924 and 1932 Games. Double Sculls.

Southwood, Leslie Frank ('Dick'). b 18.1.1906 Fulham, London; d 7.2.1986. Double Sculls.

Yachting:

Bellville, Miles Aubrey MC MBE. b 28.4.1909 Leicester; d 27.10.1980. 6 Metre Class.

Boardman, Christopher Alan (Chris). b 11.6.1903 Norwich, Norfolk; d 29.9.1987. 6 Metre Class.

Harmer, Russell Thomas. b 5.11.1896 Cambridge; d 31.10.1940. 6 Metre Class.

Leaf, Charles Symonds. b 13.11.1895 Marylebone, London; d 19.2.1947. 6 Metre Class.

Martin, Leonard Jack. b 24.11.1901 Wandsworth, London; d 1968. 6 Metre Class.

Note: the following were selected as reserves for the 6 Metre Class but did not take part in the regatta – N.A. Bacon, M.C. Becher, Frederick Gilbert ('Tiny') Mitchell (b 20.1.1884; d 8.10.1962), L.F.W. Morley.

1948 (London, 29 July–14 August), 3 gold medals, 6 gold-medallists

Rowing:
Burnell, Richard Desborough (Dickie). b 26.7.1917 Henley-on-Thames. Double Sculls.
Bushnell, Bertie Thomas. b 7.5.1909 Woking, Surrey; d 10.1.2010. Double Sculls.
Laurie, William George Ranald Mundell (Ran). b 4.5.1915 Grantchester, Cambridgeshire; d 19.9.1998. Coxless Pairs.
Wilson, John Hyrne Tucker (Jack). b 17.9.1914 Bristol, R.I., USA; d 16.2.1997. Coxless Pairs.

Yachting:
Bond, David John Ware. b 27.3.1922 Falmouth, Cornwall. Swallow Class.
Morris, Stewart Harold OBE. b 25.5.1909 Bromley, Kent; d 24.2.1991. Swallow Class.

Winter Games, 1952 (Oslo, 14–25 February), 1 gold medal, 1 gold-medallist

Figure-skating, women:
Altwegg, Jeannette Eleanor CBE. b 8.9.1930 Bombay (now Mumbai), India.

1952 (Helsinki, 19 July–3 August), 1 gold medal, 3 gold-medallists

Equestrianism:
Llewellyn, Henry Morton OBE (Harry), later Sir H.M. Llewellyn Bt CBE. b 18.7.1911 Aberdare, Glamorgan, Wales; d 15.11.1999. Riding 'Foxhunter'. Prix des Nations, Team.
Stewart, Douglas Norman (Duggie) MC DSO. b 24.6.1913 Doonholm, Ayrhsire, Scotland; d .7.1992. Riding 'Aherlow'. Prix des Nations, Team.
White, Wilfred Harry OBE (Wilf). b 30.3.1904 Nantwich, Cheshire; d 21.11.1995. Riding 'Nizefella'. Prix des Nations, Team.

1956 (Melbourne, 22 November–8 December), 6 gold medals, 8 gold-medallists

Note: because of Australian quarantine regulations, the equestrian events were held in Stockholm, 11–17 June.

Athletics:
Brasher, Christopher William CBE (Chris). b 21.8.1928 Georgetown, British Guiana (now Guyana); d 28.2.2003. 3000 metres steeplechase.

Boxing:
McTaggart, Richard MBE (Dick). b 15.10.1935 Dundee, Scotland. Lightweight.
Spinks, Terence George MBE (Terry). b 28.2.1938 West Ham, Essex. Flyweight.

Equestrianism:
Hill, Albert Edwin (Bertie). b 7.2.1927 Barnstaple, Devon; d 5.8.2005. Riding 'Countryman III'. Three-Day Event, Team.
Rook, Arthur Laurence MC. b 26.5.1921 Bingham, Notts; d 30.9.1989. Riding 'Wild Venture'. Three-Day Event, Team.
Weldon, Francis William Charles MVO MBE MC (Frank). b 2.8.1913 Bombay (now Mumbai), India; d 21.9.1993. Riding 'Kilbarry'. Three-Day Event, Team.

Fencing, women:
Sheen, Gillian Mary. b 21.8.1928 Willesden, London. Individual Foil.

Swimming, women:
Grinham, Judith Brenda (Judy). b 5.3.1939 Neasden, London. 100 metres backstroke.

1960 (Rome, 25 August–11 September),
2 gold medals, 2 gold-medallists

Athletics:
Thompson, Donald James MBE (Don). b 20.1.1933 Hillingdon, Middlesex; d 4.10.2006. 50
   kilometres walk.

Swimming, women:
Lonsbrough, Anita MBE. b 10.8.1941 York. 200 metres breaststroke.

Winter Games, 1964 (Innsbruck, 29 January–9 February),
1 gold medal, 2 gold-medallists

Bobsleigh:
Dixon, the Honourable Thomas Robin Valerian, later Lord Glentoran CBE. b 21.4.1935
   London.
Nash, Anthony James Dillon (Tony). b 18.3.1936 Amersham, Bucks.

1964 (Tokyo, 10–24 October),
4 gold medals, 4 gold-medallists

Athletics:
Davies, Lynn MBE. b 20.5.1942 Nant-y-Moel, Glamorgan, Wales. Long jump.
Matthews, Kenneth Joseph MBE (Ken). b 21.6.1934 Birmingham, Warwickshire. 20 kilometres
   walk.

Athletics, women:
Packer, Ann Elizabeth MBE. b 8.3.1942 Moulsford, Berks. 800 metres.
Rand, Mary Denise MBE. b 10.2.1940 Wells, Somerset. Long jump.

1968 (Mexico City, 12–27 October),
5 gold medals, 9 gold-medallists

Athletics:
Hemery, David Peter CBE. b 18.7.1944 Cirencester, Gloucs. 400 metres hurdles.

Boxing:
Finnegan, Christopher Martin MBE (Chris). b 5.6.1944 Uxbridge, Middlesex; d 2.3.2009.
   Middleweight.

Equestrianism:
Allhusen, Derek Swithen CVO. b 9.1.1914 Chelsea, London; d 24.4.2000. Riding 'Lochinvar'.
   Three-Day Event, Team.
Bullen, Jane Mary Elizabeth. b 7.1.1948 Bridport, Dorset. Riding 'Our Nobby'. Three-Day
   Event, Team.
Jones, Reuben Samuel (Ben). b 19.10.1932 Newport, Shropshire; d 3.1.1990. Riding 'The
   Poacher'. Three-Day Event, Team.
Meade, Richard John Hannay MBE. b 4.12.1938 Chepstow, Monmouthshire, Wales. Riding
   'Cornishman V'. Three-Day Event, Team.

Shooting:
Braithwaite, John Robert MBE (Bob). b 28.9.1925 Arnside, Cumberland. Clay Pigeon.

Yachting:
Macdonald-Smith, Iain Somerled MBE. b 3.7.1945 Oxford. Flying Dutchman.
Pattisson, Rodney Stuart MBE. b 5.8.1943 Campbelltown, Scotland. Flying Dutchman.

1972 (Munich, 26 August–10 September), 4 gold medals, 7 gold-medallists

Athletics, women:
Peters, Mary Elizabeth DBE DL, later Dame Mary Peters. b 6.7.1939 Halewood, Lancs. Pentathlon.

Equestrianism:
Gordon-Watson, Mary Diana. b 3.4.1948 Blandford, Dorset. Riding 'Cornishman V'. Three-Day Event, Team.
Meade, Richard John Hannay – *see also* 1968 Games. Riding 'Laurieston'. Three-Day Event, Individual; Three-Day Event, Team.
Parker, Bridget M. b 5.1.1939 Northumberland. Riding 'Cornish Gold'. Three-Day Event, Team.
Phillips, Mark Anthony Peter CVO. b 22.9.1948 Cirencester, Gloucs. Riding 'Great Ovation'. Three-Day Event, Team.

Yachting:
Davies, Christopher MBE (Chris). b 29.6.1946. Flying Dutchman.
Pattisson, Rodney Stuart MBE – *see also* 1968 Games.

Winter Games 1976 (Innsbruck, 4–15 February), 1 gold medal, 1 gold-medallist

Figure-skating:
Curry, John Anthony. b 9.9.1949 Birmingham, Warwickshire; d 15.4.1994.

1976 (Montreal, 17 July–1 August), 3 gold medals, 6 gold-medallists

Modern pentathlon:
Fox, Jeremy Robert (Jim) OBE MBE. b 19.9.1941 Pewsey, Wilts. Team.
Nightingale, Robert Daniel (Danny). b 21.5.1954 Redruth, Cornwall. Team.
Parker, Adrian Philip. b 2.3.1951 Croydon, Surrey. Team.

Note: The reserve, Andrew Archibald (Andy). b 9.7.1951, did not compete.

Swimming:
Wilkie, David Andrew MBE. b 8.3.1954 Colombo, Ceylon (now Sri Lanka). 200 metres breaststroke.

Yachting:
Osborn, John MBE. b 8.9.1945. Tornado Class
White, Reginald James MBE (Reg). b 28.10.35 Brightlingsea, Essex; d 27.5.2010. Tornado Class.

Note: John Osborn and Reg White were brothers-in-law.

Winter Games 1980 (Lake Placid, 13–24 February), 1 gold medal, 1 gold-medallist

Figure-skating:
Cousins, Robin John. b 17.8.1957 Bristol, Gloucs.

1980 (Moscow, 19 July–1 August), 5 gold medals, 5 gold-medallists

Athletics:
Wells, Allan Wipper MBE. b 3.5.1952 Edinburgh. 100 metres.
Ovett, Stephen Michael James OBE (Steve). b 9.10.1955 Brighton, Sussex. 800 metres.
Coe, Sebastian Newbold, later Lord Coe of Ranmore KBE. b 29.9.1956 Chiswick, London. 1500 metres.
Thompson, Francis Morgan CBE. b 30.7.1958 Notting Hill, London. Decathlon.

Swimming:
Goodhew, Duncan Alexander MBE. b 27.5.1957 Marylebone, London. 100 metres breaststroke.

Winter Games 1984 (Sarajevo, 8 – 19 February), 1 gold medal, 2 gold-medallists

Ice-dancing:
Dean, Christopher Colin OBE. b 27.7.1958 Nottingham.
Torvill, Jayne OBE. b 7.10.1957 Nottingham.

1984 (Los Angeles, 28 July–12 August), 5 gold medals, 9 gold-medallists

Athletics:
Coe, Sebastian Newbold – *see also* 1980 Games. 1500 metres.
Thompson, Francis Morgan ('Daley') – *see also* 1980 Games. Decathlon.

Athletics, women:
Sanderson, Theresa Ione CBE (Tessa). b 14.3.1956 St Elizabeth, Jamaica. Javelin.

Rowing:
Budgett, Richard Gordon McBride OBE. b 20.3.1959 Glasgow. Coxed Fours.
Cross, Martin Patrick. b 21.7.1957 London. Coxed Fours.
Ellison, Adrian Charles. b 11.9.1956 Solihull, Warwickshire. Coxed Fours.
Holmes, Andrew John MBE (Andy). b 15.10.1959 Uxbridge, Middlesex; d 24.10.2010. Coxed Fours.
Redgrave, Steven Geoffrey (Steve), later Sir S.G. Redgrave CBE. b 23.3.1962 Marlow, Bucks. Coxed Fours.

Shooting:
Cooper, Malcolm Douglas MBE. b 20.12.1947 Camberley, Surrey; d 9.6.2001. Small Bore Rifle, Three Positions.

1988 (Seoul, 178 September–2 October), 5 gold medals, 22 gold-medallists

Hockey:
Barber, Paul Jason. b 21.5.1955 Peterborough, Cambridgeshire.
Batchelor, Stephen James. b 22.6.1961 Beare Green, Dorking, Surrey.
Bhaura, Kulbir Singh. b 15.10.1955 Jullundur, India.

Clift, Robert John. b 1.8.1962 Newport, Monmouthshire, Wales.
Dodds, Richard David Allan OBE. b 23.2.1959 York.
Faulkner, David Andrew Vincent. b 10.9.1963 Portsmouth, Hants.
Garcia, Russell Simon. b 20.6.1970 Portsmouth, Hants.
Grimley, Martyn Andrew. b 24.1.1963 Halifax, Yorks.
Kerly, Sean Robin. b 29.1.1960 Whitstable, Kent.
Kirkwood, James William (Jimmy). b 12.2.1962 Lisburn, Northern Ireland.
Leman, Richard Alexander. b 13.7.1959 East Grinstead, Sussex.
Martin, Stephen A. b 13.4.1959 Bangor, County Down, Northern Ireland.
Pappin, Veryan Guy Henry. b 19.5.1958 Henley-on-Thames, Oxfordshire.
Potter, Jonathan Nicholas Mark (Jon). b 19.11.1963 Paddington, London.
Sherwani, Imran Ahmed Khan. b 9.4.1962 Stoke-on-Trent, Staffs.
Taylor, Ian Charles Boucher. b 24.9.1954 Bromsgrove, Worcs.

Rowing:
Holmes, Andrew John (Andy) – *see also* 1984 Games. Coxless Pairs.
Redgrave, Stephen Geoffrey (Steve) – *see also* 1984 Games. Coxless Pairs.

Shooting:
Cooper, Malcolm Douglas – *see also* 1984 Games. Small Bore Rifle, Three Positions.

Swimming:
Moorhouse, Adrian David MBE. b 24.5.1964 Bradford, Yorks. 100 metres breaststroke.

Yachting:
McIntyre, Michael (Mike). b 29.6.1956 Glasgow. Star Class.
Vaile, Philip Bryn. b 16.8.1956 Enfield, Middlesex. Star Class.

1992 (Barcelona, 25 July–9 August),
5 gold medals, 8 gold-medallists

Athletics:
Christie, Linford OBE. b 2.4.1960 St Andrews, Jamaica. 100 metres.

Athletics, women:
Gunnell, Sally Jane Janet OBE. b 29.7.1966 Chigwell, Essex. 400 metres hurdles.

Cycling:
Boardman, Christopher MBE (Chris). b 26.8.1968 Hoylake, Cheshire. 4000 metres individual pursuit. *Note*: Chris Boardman is not related to the 1936 yachting gold-medallist of the same name.

Rowing:
Pinsent, Matthew Clive CBE, later Sir M.C. Pinsent. b 10.10.1970 Holt, Norfolk. Coxless Pairs.
Redgrave, Steven Geoffrey – *see also* 1984 and 1988 Games. Coxless Pairs.
Herbert, Garry Gerard Paul MBE. b 3.10.1969 London. Coxed Pairs.
Searle, Gregory Mark Pascoe MBE (Greg). b 20.3.1972 Ashford, Kent. Coxed Pairs.
Searle, Jonathon William C. MBE (Jonny). b 8.5.1969 Walton-on-Thames, Surrey. Coxed Pairs.

Note: Greg and Jonny Searle are brothers.

1996 (Atlanta, 19 July–4 August),
1 gold medal, 2 gold-medallists.

Rowing:
Pinsent, Matthew Clive – *see also* 1992 Games. Coxless Pairs.
Redgrave, Stephen Geoffrey – *see also* 1984, 1988 and 1992 Games. Coxless Pairs.

2000 (Sydney, 15 September–1 October), 11 gold medals, 22 gold-medallists

Athletics:
Edwards, Jonathan David CBE. b 10.5.1966 London. Triple jump.

Athletics, women:
Lewis, Denise OBE. b 27.8.1972 West Bromwich, Warwickshire. Heptathlon.

Boxing:
Harrison, Hugh Audley MBE ('A-Force'). b 26.10.1971 Park Royal, London.
  Super-Heavyweight.

Cycling:
Queally, Jason Paul MBE. b 11.5.1970 Great Heywood, Staffs. 1 kilometre time-trial.

Modern pentathlon, women:
Cook, Stephanie MBE. b 7.2.1972 Irvine, Scotland.

Rowing:
Cracknell, James OBE. b 5.5.1972 Sutton, Surrey. Coxless Fours.
Foster, Timothy James Carrington (Tim) MBE. b 19.1.1970 Hillingdon, Middlesex. Coxless
  Fours.
Pinsent, Matthew Clive – *see also* 1992 and 1996 Games. Coxless Fours.
Redgrave, Stephen Geoffrey – *see also* 1984, 1988, 1992 and 1996 Games. Coxless Fours.
Attrill, Louis MBE. b 5.3.1975 Newport, Isle of Wight. Eights.
Dennis, Simon MBE. b 24.8.1976 Henley-on-Thames, Oxfordshire. Eights.
Douglas, Rowley MBE. b 27.1.1977 Washington DC, USA. Eights.
Grubor, Luka MBE. b 27.12.1973 Zagreb, Croatia. Eights.
Hunt-Davis, Benedict (Ben) MBE. b 15.3.1972 Tidworth, Wilts. Eights.
Lindsay, Andrew James MBE. b 25.3.1977 Portree, Isle of Skye, Scotland. Eights.
Scarlett, Fred MBE. b 29.4.1975 Ashford, Kent. Eights.
Trapmore, Stephen Patrick MBE (Steve). b 18.3.1975 Hammersmith, London. Eights.
West, Kieran Martin MBE. b 18.9.1977 Kingston-upon-Thames, Surrey. Eights.

Shooting:
Faulds, Richard Bruce MBE. b 15.5.1977 Guildford, Surrey. Double Trap.

Yachting:
Ainslie, Charles Benedict (Ben) CBE. b 5.2.1977 Macclesfield, Cheshire. Laser Class.
Percy, Iain OBE. b 21.3.1976 Winchester, Hants. Finn Class.

Yachting, women:
Robertson, Shirley Ann OBE. b 15.7.1968 Dundee, Scotland. Europe Class.

Winter Games, 2002 (Salt Lake City, 9–24 February), 1 gold medal, 5 gold-medallists

Curling, women:
Knox, Deborah MBE (Debbie). b 26.9.1968 Dunfermline, Scotland.
MacDonald, Fiona MBE. b 9.12.1974 Paisley, Scotland.
Martin, Rhona MBE. b 12.10.1966 Ayr, Scotland.
Morton, Margaret MBE. b 29.1.1968 Ayrshire, Scotland.
Rankin, Janice MBE. b 8.2.1972 Inverness, Scotland.

2004 (Athens, 13–29 August),
9 gold medals, 16 gold-medallists

Athletics, men:

Campbell, Darren Andrew MBE. b 12.9.1973 Manchester, Lancashire. 4 × 100 metres relay.

Devonish, Marlon Ronald MBE. b 1.6.1976 Coventry, Warwickshire. 4 × 100 metres relay.

Gardener, Jason Carl MBE. b 18.9.1975 Bath, Somerset. 4 × 100 metres relay.

Lewis-Francis, Mark Anthony MBE. b 4.9.1982 Darlaston, West Midlands. 4 × 100 metres relay.

Note: the following were reserves for the 4 × 100 metres relay but did not compete:

Grant, Dwayne. b 17.7.1982 Lewisham, London.

Lambert, Christopher Patrick (Chris). b 6.4.1981 Dulwich, London.

Malcolm, Christian Sean. b 3.6.1979 Cardiff.

Smith, Nicholas (Nick). b 6.12.1982 Fife, Scotland.

Athletics, women:

Holmes, Kelly (later Dame). b 19.4.1970 Pembury, Kent. 800 metres, 1500 metres.

Cycling:

Hoy, Christopher Andrew (Chris), later Sir C.A. Hoy MBE. b 23.3.1976 Edinburgh.
1 kilometre time-trial.

Wiggins, Bradley Marc CBE. b 28.4.1980 Ghent, Belgium. 4000 metres individual pursuit.

Equestrianism:

Law, Leslie MBE. b 15.5.65 Hereford. Riding 'Shear L'Eau'. Three-Day Event, Individual.

Rowing:

Coode, Edward MBE (Ed). b 19.6.1976 Bodmin, Cornwall. Coxless Fours.

Cracknell, James – *see also* 2000 Games. Coxless Fours.

Pinsent, Matthew Clive – *see also* 1992, 1996, 2000 Games. Coxless Fours.

Williams, Stephen David OBE (Steve). b 15.4.1976 Leamington Spa, Warwickshire. Coxless
Fours.

Yachting:

Ainslie, Charles Benedict CBE – *see also* 2000 Games. Finn Class.

Yachting, women:

Ayton, Sarah Lianne OBE. b 9.4.1980 Ashford, Surrey. Yngling Class.

Robertson, Shirley Ann – *see also* 2000 Games. Yngling Class.

Webb, Sarah Kathleen OBE. b 13.1.1977 Ashford, Surrey. Yngling Class.

2008 (Beijing, 8–24 August),
19 gold medals, 27 gold-medallists

Athletics, women:

Ohuruogu, Christine Ijeoma MBE. b 17.5.1984 Newham, London. 400 metres.

Boxing:

DeGale, James Frederick MBE ('Chunky'). b 3.2.1986 Harlesden, London. Middleweight.

Canoeing:

Brabants, Tim MBE. b 23.1.1977 Chertsey, Surrey. Kayak Singles 1000 metres.

Cycling:

Hoy, Christopher Andrew – *see also* 2004 Games. 1000 metres Individual Sprint, 750 metres
Team Sprint, Keirin.

Wiggins, Bradley Marc – *see also* 2004 Games. 4000 metres Individual Pursuit, 4000 metres
Team Pursuit.

Kenny, Jason Francis MBE. b 23.3.1988 Bolton, Greater Manchester. 750 metres Team Sprint.

Staff, Jamie Allan MBE. b 30.4.1973 Ashford, Kent. 750 metres Team Sprint.

Clancy, Edward (Ed) MBE. b 12.3.1985 Barnsley, Yorks. 4000 metres Team Pursuit.

Manning, Paul Christian MBE. b 6.11.1974 Sutton Coldfield, West Midlands. 4000 metres Team Pursuit.

Thomas, Geraint Howell MBE ('Gez'). b 25.5.1986 Cardiff. 4000 metres Team Pursuit.

Cycling, women:

Pendleton, Victoria Louise MBE. b 24.9.1980 Stotfold, Bedfordshire. Individual Sprint.

Romero, Rebecca Jayne MBE. b 24.1.1980 Carshalton, Surrey. Individual Pursuit.

Cooke, Nicole MBE. b 13.4.1983 Swansea. Road Race.

Rowing:

James, Thomas MBE (Tom). b 11.3.1984 Cardiff. Coxless Fours.

Reed, Peter MBE (Pete). b 27.7.1981 Seattle, Washington, USA. Coxless Fours.

Triggs-Hodge, Andrew MBE (Andy). b 3.3.1979 Halton, Bucks. Coxless Fours.

Williams, Stephen David – *see also* 2004 Games. Coxless Fours.

Hunter, Mark John MBE. b 1.7.1978 London. Lightweight Double Sculls.

Purchase, Zachary Jake Nicholas MBE (Zac). b 2.5.1986 Cheltenham, Gloucs. Lightweight Double Sculls.

Swimming, women:

Adlington, Rebecca OBE (Becky). b 17.2.1989 Mansfield, Notts. 400 metres freestyle, 800 metres freestyle.

Yachting:

Ainslie, Charles Benedict CBE – *see also* 2000 and 2004 Games. Finn Class.

Goodison, Paul Martin MBE. b 29.11.1977 Rotherham, South Yorks. Laser Class.

Percy, Iain – *see also* 2000 Games. Star Class.

Simpson, Andrew James MBE ('Bart'). b 17.12.1976 Chertsey, Surrey. Star Class.

Yachting, women:

Ayton, Sarah Lianne – *see also* 2004 Games. Yngling Class.

Webb, Sarah Kathleen – *see also* 2004 Games. Yngling Class.

Wilson, Philippa Claire MBE (Pippa). b 7.2.1986 Southampton, Hants. Yngling Class.

Winter Games 2010 (Vancouver, 12–28 February), 1 gold medal, 1 gold-medallist

Skeleton, women:

Williams, Amy Joy MBE. b 29.9.1982 Cambridge.

Gold medals won by sports

Athletics 58, Yachting (now entitled Sailing) 25, Rowing 24, Cycling 21, Lawn Tennis 17, Swimming 17, Boxing 14, Shooting 14, Equestrianism 6, Figure-skating 4, Water-polo 4, Football 3, Hockey 3, Polo 3, Wrestling 3, Archery 2, Curling 2, Modern Pentathlon 2, Motor-boating 2, Rackets 2, Bobsledding 1, Canoeing 1, Cricket 1, Fencing 1, Ice Dancing 1, Ice-hockey 1, Skeleton 1, Weight-lifting 1.

Note: of the 26 sports which will be contested at the 2012 London Olympic Games, Great Britain has never won a gold medal in 11 – Badminton, Basketball, Beach Volleyball, Diving, Gymnastics, Handball, Judo, Table Tennis, Taekwondo, Triathlon and Volleyball.

When no gold medals were won

No gold medals were won at the following Winter Games – 1928 St Moritz, 1932 Lake Placid, 1948 St Moritz, 1956 Cortina d'Ampezzo, 1960 Squaw Valley, 1968 Grenoble, 1972 Sapporo, 1988 Calgary, 1992 Albertville, 1994 Lillehammer, 1998 Nagano, 2006 Turin.

Where the gold-medallists were born

Berkshire 5, Bedfordshire 3, Buckinghamshire 4, Cambridgeshire 5, Cheshire 6, Cornwall 4, County Durham 6, Cumberland 4, Derbyshire 3, Devon 10, Dorset 4, Essex 13, Gloucestershire 10, Greater Manchester 1, Guernsey 1, Hampshire 8, Herefordshire 1, Hertfordshire 4, Ireland (pre-partition) 15, Isle of Man 1, Isle of Wight 2, Kent 15, Lancashire 34, Leicestershire 5, Lincolnshire 3, London 72, Merseyside 1, Middlesex 19, Norfolk 4, Northamptonshire 2, Northern Ireland 2, Northumberland 4, Nottinghamshire 5, Oxfordshire 9, Scotland 38, Shropshire 2, Somerset 7, South Yorkshire 1, Staffordshire 7, Suffolk 4, Surrey 24, Sussex 3, Wales 13, Warwickshire 14, West Midlands 2, Wiltshire 3, Worcestershire 6, Yorkshire 13.

Note: 40 other gold-medallists were born outside Great Britain, as follows – Australia 6, Belgium 1, British Guiana (now Guyana) 1, Canada 2, Ceylon (now Sri Lanka) 1, China 2, Croatia 1, Falkland Islands 1, France 4, Gibraltar 1, Greece 2, Hong Kong 1, India 7, Jamaica 2, Portugal 1, South Africa 1, USA 6.

The earliest-born gold-medallist is the Honourable John Beresford, 10.6.1847.

The most recently born gold-medallist is Rebecca Adlington, 17.2.1989.

Multiple gold-medallists

In all, 60 British competitors, including seven women, have won two or more gold medals, representing the following sports – Athletics 13, Yachting 10, Water-polo 7, Lawn tennis 6, Rowing 6, Swimming 5, Cycling 4, Motor-boating 3, Football 2, Boxing 1, Equestrianism 1, Hockey 1, Shooting 1. *Note*: Two competitors won gold medals in both swimming and water-polo.

5 Sir Steven Redgrave, *Rowing* 1984–1988–1992–1996–2000.

4 Henry Taylor, *Swimming* 1906–1908. Sir Matthew Pinsent, *Rowing* 1992–1996–2000–2004. Sir Chris Hoy, *Cycling* 2004–2008.

3 Edgar Bredin, *Athletics* 1900. Reggie Doherty, *Lawn Tennis* 1900–1908. George Wilkinson, *Water-polo* 1900–1912–1920. Paul Radmilovic, *Swimming* 1908 and *Water-Polo* 1908–1912. Charlie Smith, *Water-polo* 1908–1912–1920. Jack Beresford, *Rowing* 1924–1932–1936. Richard Meade, *Equestrianism* 1968–1972. Ben Ainslie, *Yachting* 2000–2004–2008. Bradley Wiggins, *Cycling* 2004–2008.

2 Jack Boland, *Lawn Tennis* 1896. Charles Bennett, *Athletics* 1900. John Rimmer, *Athletics* 1900. Alfred Tysoe, *Athletics* 1900. Laurie Doherty, *Lawn Tennis* 1900. Chattie Cooper, *Lawn Tennis* 1900. Jack Jarvis, *Swimming* 1900. Rob Derbyshire, *Water-polo* 1900 & *Swimming* 1908. Lorne Currie, *Yachting* 1900. Lord Gretton of Stapleford, *Yachting* 1900. Algernon Maudslay, *Yachting* 1900. Johnnie Matthews, *Cycling* 1906. Arthur Rushen, *Cycling* 1906. George Larner, *Athletics* 1908. Fred Humphreys, *Athletics* (Tug-of-War) 1908–1920. Edwin Mills, *Athletics* (Tug-of-War) 1908–1920. John Shepherd, *Athletics* (Tug-of-War) 1908–1920. Ben Jones, *Cycling* 1908. Clarrie Kingsbury, *Cycling* 1908. Stanley Shoveller, *Hockey* 1908–1920. Wentworth Gore, *Lawn Tennis* 1908. John Field-Richards, *Motor-boating* 1908. Bernard Redwood, *Motor-boating* 1908. Tom Thornycroft, *Motor-boating* 1908. Arthur Berry, *Football* 1908–1912. Vivian Woodward, *Football* 1908–1912. George Cornet, *Water-polo* 1908–1912. Tom Thould, *Water-polo* 1908–1912. Sir Angus Gillan, *Yachting* 1908–1912. Edith Hannam, *Lawn Tennis* 1912. Charles Bugbee, *Water-polo* 1912–1920. Albert Hill, *Athletics* 1920. Harry Mallin, *Boxing* 1920–1924. Douglas

Lowe, *Athletics* 1924–1928. Hugh Edwards, *Rowing* 1932. Rodney Pattisson, *Yachting* 1968–1972. Lord Coe of Ranmore, *Athletics* 1980–1984. Daley Thompson, *Athletics* 1980–1984. Andy Holmes, *Rowing* 1984–1988. Malcolm Cooper, *Shooting* 1984–1988. Iain Percy, *Yachting* 2000–2008. Shirley Robertson, *Yachting* 2000–2004. Dame Kelly Holmes, *Athletics* 2004. Steve Williams, *Rowing* 2004–2008. Sarah Ayton, *Yachting* 2004–2008. Sarah Webb, *Yachting* 2004–2008. Rebecca Adlington, *Swimming* 2008.

Other British-born gold-medallists

There have been a further 56 Olympic gold medals won by competitors who had been born in the British Isles, including Ireland before 1921, but representing other countries:

1896:

Australia. Flack, Edwin Harold (Teddy). Athletics, 800 and 1500 metres. b 5.11.1873 Islington, Middlesex, d 10.1.1936.

1900:

USA. Sweeney, Michael Francis. Athletics, High jump and Long jump, Professional. b 27.10.1872 Ireland.

USA. Flanagan, John Jesus. Athletics, Hammer. b 9.1.1873 Kilbreedy, County Limerick, Ireland, d 3.6.1938.

USA. Carr, William John. Rowing, Eights. b 17.6.1876 Gortnagrace, County Donegal, Ireland; d 25.3.1942.

1904:

USA. Hicks, Thomas John (Tom). Athletics, Marathon. b 7.1.1875 Birmingham, Warwickshire; d 2.12.1963.

USA. Sheridan, Martin John. Athletics, Discus. b 28.3.1881 Bohola, County Mayo, Ireland; d 27.3.1918.

USA. Flanagan, John Jesus. Athletics, Hammer and Tug-of-War – *see also* 1900 Games.

Canada. Hall, Alexander Noble. Football. b 1888 Peterhead, Scotland; d 25.9.1943.

Canada. Linton, Ernest Albert. Football. b 17.2.1880 Scotland; d 6.8.1957.

Canada. Brennaugh (or Brennagh), William Thomas Edmund (Billy). Lacrosse. b 13.8.1877 Brampton, Cumberland; d 23.10.1934.

1906:

USA. Sheridan, Martin John. Athletics, Shot and Discus – *see also* 1904 Games.

1908:

Canada. Kerr, Robert (Bobby). Athletics, 200 metres. b 9.6.1882 Enniskillen, County Fermanagh, Ireland (now Northern Ireland); d 12.5.1963.

USA. Sheridan, Martin John. Athletics, Discus – *see also* 1904 and 1906 Games.

USA. Flanagan, John Jesus. Athletics, Hammer – *see also* 1900 and 1904 Games.

France. Thubron, Emile Blakelock. Motor-Boating, Open Class. b 1861 Boldon, County Durham. *Note*: Emile Thubron is the grandfather of the eminent travel-writer and novelist, Colin Thubron.

1912:

South Africa. McArthur, Kennedy Kane (Ken). Athletics, Marathon. b 10.2.1881 Dervock, County Antrim, Ireland (now Northern Ireland); d 13.6.1960.

USA. McDonald, Patrick Francis (Pat). Athletics, Shot. b 26.7.1881 Killard, County Clare, Ireland; d 16.5.1954.

USA. McGrath, Matthew John (Matt). Athletics, Hammer. b 18.12.1875 Nenagh, County Tipperary, Ireland; d 29.1.1941.

Canada. Goulding, George Henry. Athletics, 10 kilometres walk. b 19.11.1884 Hull, Yorks; d 31.1.1966.

1920:

South Africa. Rudd, Bevil Gordon D'Urban. Athletics, 400 metres. b 6.10.1895 Devon; d 2.2.1948.

USA. Ryan, Patrick James (Pat). Athletics, Hammer. b 4.1.1881 Old Pallas, County Limerick, Ireland; d 13.2.1964.

USA. Fenton, Dennis. Shooting, Free Rifle, Team and Miniature Rifle, Team. b 20.11.1888 Ballincota, County Kerry, Ireland; d 29.3.1954.

USA. Kelly, Michael. Shooting, Military Revolver 30 metres, Team and Military Revolver 50 metres, Team. b 20.3.1872 County Galway, Ireland; d 3.5.1923.

1924 (Winter):

Canada. Munro, Duncan Brown. Ice-hockey. b 19.1.1901 Moray, Scotland, d. 3.1.1958.

1928:

Ireland. O'Callaghan, Patrick (Pat). Athletics, Hammer. b 28.1.1906 Derrygallon, Kanturk, County Cork, Ireland; d 1.12.1991.

New Zealand. Morgan, Edward (Ted). Boxing, Welterweight. b 5.4.1906 East Ham, Essex; d 22.11.1952.

Norway. Crown Prince Olav Alexander Edward Christian Frederik (later King Olav V). Yachting, 6 Metre Class. b 2.7.1903 Sandringham, Norfolk; d 17.1.1991.

1932:

Ireland. O'Callaghan, Patrick (Pat). Athletics, Hammer – *see also* 1928 Games.

1956:

Australia. Rose, Iain Murray. Swimming, 400 metres freestyle, 1500 metres freestyle, 4 x 200 metres freestyle relay. b 6.1.1939 Nairn, Scotland.

New Zealand. Read, Norman Richard. Athletics, 50 kilometres walk. b 13.8.1931 Portsmouth, Hants; d 22.5.1994.

Canada. D'Hondt, Walter Ignace. Rowing, Coxless Fours. b 11.9.1936 Richmond, Surrey.

USA. Williams, Herbert Philip (Herb). Yachting, Star Class. b 24.7.1908 Hove, Sussex; d 10.1.1990.

USA. Wight, David. Rowing, Eights. b 28.7.1934 London.

1960:

Australia. Rose, Iain Murray. Swimming, 400 metres freestyle – *see also* 1956 Games.

1964:

Australia. Northam, Sir William Herbert CBE (Bill). Yachting, 5.5 metre Class. b 28.9.1905 London; d 6.9.1988.

Note: Sir Durward Knowles, who in 1964 won International Star Class sailing gold for the country of his birth, the Bahamas, had competed for Great Britain at the 1948 Games, placing fourth, as the Bahamas was at the time under British rule and had no National Olympic Committee of its own.

1980:

Zimbabwe. Chick, Alexandra (Sandra). Hockey. b 2.6.1947 Burnham Market, Norfolk.

Zimbabwe. Robertson, Sonia. Hockey. b 2.6.1947 Burnham Market, Norfolk. *Note*: Sandra Chick and Sonia Robertson are identical twin sisters.

Australia. Brooks, Neil. Swimming, 4 × 100 metres medley relay. b 27.7.1962 Crewe, Cheshire.

1988:

Canada. Lewis, Lennox. Boxing, Super-Heavyweight. b 2.9.1965 West Ham, London.

1992:

Canada. Nesbitt-Porter, Derek. Rowing, Eights. b 2.11.1967 Belfast.

Canada. Barnes, Jennifer-Kirsten. Rowing, Coxless Fours, Eights. b 26.3.1968 London.

Spain. Zabell Lucas, Theresa. Yachting, International 470 Class. b 22.6.1965 Ipswich, Suffolk.

1996:

Spain. Zabell Lucas, Theresa. Yachting, International 470 Class – *see* 1992 Games.

2002:

Canada. Nolan, Owen Liam. Ice-hockey. b 12.2.1972 Belfast.

Canada. Heaney, Geraldine. Ice-hockey, Women. b 1.1.1967 Lurgan, Northern Ireland.

2006:

Canada. Heaney, Geraldine. Ice-hockey, Women – *see* 2002 Games.

2008:

USA. Tunnicliffe, Anna. Yachting, Laser Radial Class, Women. b 17.10.1982 Doncaster, Yorks.

By countries: USA 22, Canada 14, Australia 8, Ireland 2, New Zealand 2, South Africa 2, Spain 2, Zimbabwe 2, France 1, Norway 1.

Artistic footnote

Arts competitions in various categories were held at the Olympic Games from 1912 to 1948 and there were three winners for Great Britain, as follows:

1928 Graphic Works. William Newzam Prior Nicholson, later Sir William Nicholson. b 5.2.1872 Newark, Notts; d 16.5.1949. *Note*: he was the father of the artist, Ben Nicholson.

1932 Town Planning. John Hughes. b 14.6.1903; d 20.2.1977.

1948 Oils and Water Colours. Alfred Reginald Thomson. b 10.12.1894 Bangalore, India; d 27.10.1979. *Note*: Thomson was deaf and dumb and was the official artist for the RAF during the Second World War.

Bibliography

The principal sources for research, among countless others, have been the following:

Olympic Odyssey, edited by Stan Tomlin (Modern Athlete Publications, 1956)
The Modern Olympic Games, by Dr Ferenc Mezö (Pannonia Press, Budapest, 1956)
Olympic Diary, Rome 1960, by Neil Allen (Nicholas Kaye, 1960)
Meet the Olympians, by Dimiter Mishev (Medicine & Physical Culture Publishing, Sofia, 1964)
Tokyo 1964, by Chris Brasher (Stanley Paul, 1964)
Olympic Diary, Tokyo 1964, by Neil Allen (Nicholas Kaye, 1965)
Munich 1972, by Chris Brasher (Stanley Paul, 1972)
Lexikon der 12,000 Olympioniken, by Erich Kamper (Leykam-Verlag, Graz, 1975)
Olympic Report 1976, by Jim Coote (Kemps, 1976)
The Olympic Games, edited by Lord Killanin and John Rodda (Barrie & Jenkins, 1976)
The Complete Book of the Olympics, by David Wallechinsky (Penguin Books, 1984)
British Olympians, by Ian Buchanan (Guinness, 1991)
Tales of Gold, by Neil Duncanson and Patrick Collins (Queen Anne Press, 1992)
The Modern Olympic Century, 1896–1996, by Ekkehard zur Megede (DGLD, Berlin, 1999)
Les Jeux Olympiques Oubliés, by André Drevon (CNRS Editions, Paris, 2000)
Olympic Almanac 2008, by Stan Greenberg (SportsBooks, 2008)

The official reports of the various Games Organising Committees
The official reports of the British Olympic Association

Index

These page numbers contain references to British gold-medallists or British-born gold-medallists, either in the text or in photograph captions. Colour plate numbers are in bold.